Financial Management

Innovation and Technology Set

coordinated by
Chantal Ammi

Volume 6

Financial Management

USGAAP and IFRS Standards

Aldo Lévy
Faten Ben Bouheni
Chantal Ammi

WILEY

First published 2018 in Great Britain and the United States by ISTE Ltd and John Wiley & Sons, Inc.

Apart from any fair dealing for the purposes of research or private study, or criticism or review, as permitted under the Copyright, Designs and Patents Act 1988, this publication may only be reproduced, stored or transmitted, in any form or by any means, with the prior permission in writing of the publishers, or in the case of reprographic reproduction in accordance with the terms and licenses issued by the CLA. Enquiries concerning reproduction outside these terms should be sent to the publishers at the undermentioned address:

ISTE Ltd
27-37 St George's Road
London SW19 4EU
UK

www.iste.co.uk

John Wiley & Sons, Inc.
111 River Street
Hoboken, NJ 07030
USA

www.wiley.com

© ISTE Ltd 2018
The rights of Aldo Lévy, Faten Ben Bouheni and Chantal Ammi to be identified as the authors of this work have been asserted by them in accordance with the Copyright, Designs and Patents Act 1988.

Library of Congress Control Number: 2018931941

British Library Cataloguing-in-Publication Data
A CIP record for this book is available from the British Library
ISBN 978-1-78630-145-1

Contents

Introduction xi

Chapter 1. Value: IFRS vs. US GAAP 1

1.1. Value and the time. 1
    1.1.1. Cost of money, interest rate (nominal and real) 2
1.2. The time value of money: US GAAP 3
1.3. Future value and present value: capitalization
and discounting in discrete time. 4
    1.3.1. Simple interest 4
    1.3.2. Compound interest 9
1.4. US GAAP: future value and present value
of rules of time travel. 10
    1.4.1. US GAAP: Effective annual rate and
    annual percentage rate 13
    1.4.2. US GAAP: the determinants of interest rates. 16
1.5. Annuities and unearned income: IFRS. 19
    1.5.1. Value of a sum of constant annuities 19
    1.5.2. Current value of a sum of constant annuities 20
    1.5.3. The updating of constant sums over an
    infinite period: the return 21
1.6. Calculating net present value and
future value: US GAAP 22
    1.6.1. Constant annuities of cash flows. 22
    1.6.2. Perpetuity 28
    1.6.3. Growing cash flows. 30
1.7. Market value 35
    1.7.1. Relation required rate: value 36
    1.7.2. Valuation of fixed rate debt 37

1.8. Actuarial rate of return	38
1.9. Value and risk	40
1.9.1. Probabilities and expected returns	40
1.9.2. Uncertain expected rate of return	41
1.9.3. Couple profitability, a risk: representation of expectation/standard deviation	41
1.9.4. Introduction to diversification: the case of two assets	42
1.9.5. Notions of diversification and non-diversifiable risk	43
1.9.6. Modeling randomized profitability with a two-factor model	45
1.10. Value and information	46
1.10.1. Information and uncertainty	46
1.10.2. Information efficiency	50
1.10.3. Exercises	50

Chapter 2. Diagnosis of Financial Statements: IFRS 57

2.1. Economic and financial analysis of business data	57
2.1.1. Principles and levels of study	57
2.1.2. Typology of financial analysis	61
2.1.3. Destination of the financial statement analysis	63
2.2. Financial reading of the balance sheet	66
2.2.1. Principles of financial statement preparation	67
2.2.2. Mechanism	70
2.2.3. Functions: financing, investment, exploitation and distribution	79
2.2.4. Investment study	95
2.2.5. Random analysis	114
2.2.6. Undetermined analysis	125

Chapter 3. Analysis of the Financial Structure: IFRS vs. US GAAP 131

3.1. Major functions of the French Accounting Plan	131
3.1.1. Assets	131
3.1.2. Current liabilities	133
3.1.3. Sustainable resources	135
3.1.4. Fixed assets	141
3.1.5. Calculation of global net revolving fund	142
3.2. The need for working capital requirement (WCR)	144
3.2.1. WCRE (or WCE)	145
3.2.2. WCREE	145
3.2.3. Recommendations on the need for working capital	147
3.2.4. WCR in days of HVAC	149

3.3. Net cash.	154
3.3.1. Cash flow and the result are linked without being correlated.	155
3.3.2. Analysis and recommendations	156
3.3.3. Financial analysis in market value.	160
3.3.4. Presentation of the balance sheet in net asset values	162
3.3.5. Structural risks	164
3.3.6. The risk of imminent failure.	164
3.3.7. Recommendations	164
3.4. Balance sheet analysis: US GAAP.	164
3.4.1. Balance sheet features	165
3.4.2. Balance Sheet Diagnosis.	170

Chapter 4. Analysis of Activity: Analysis of Profit and Loss Account: IFRS vs. US GAAP 179

4.1. Profitability and management performance	179
4.1.1. Intermediate Management Balances.	180
4.1.2. Current exploitation.	183
4.1.3. Non-operating current	191
4.2. Management indicators of the Banque de France.	193
4.2.1. Partial or current indicators	194
4.2.2. Global indicators	198
4.3. Correspondences of FCA indicators – Banque de France	200
4.4. CAF cash flow.	202
4.4.1. Principles	202
4.4.2. FCA approach.	204
4.4.3. Analysis of the Order of Chartered Accountants.	205
4.5. Renewed indicators (IFRS) of management.	205
4.5.1. EBITDA.	206
4.5.2. ROA.	206
4.5.3. ROE	206
4.5.4. NOPAT	206
4.5.5. ROCE	206
4.5.6. COFROI.	206
4.5.7. Free cash flow.	207
4.5.8. EVA MVA	207
4.6. Income statement analysis: US GAAP.	207
4.6.1. Case study 1: Mydeco Corporation	221
4.6.2. Case study 2: Atlas	224

Chapter 5. Analysis of Operational Profitability and Risk: IFRS 227

5.1. Profitability according to the chosen full cost model 228
    5.1.1. Results Achieved in Full Cost by Analysis Centers and Unit Cost of Indirect Costs 228
    5.1.2. Study 232
    5.1.3. Results obtained in full cost by activity (Activity by Costing) 232
5.2. Budget based on normal activity 235
    5.2.1. Activity 236
    5.2.2. Budget for which indirect costs are unbundled in terms of being variable and fixed 236
    5.2.3. Cost-effectiveness 236
    5.2.4. Profitability 246
5.3. The breakeven point 249
    5.3.1. Representation 250
    5.3.2. Indicators of profitability 252
    5.3.3. Decision-making 253
5.4. Operating leverage 262
5.5. Return on equity 270
    5.5.1. Economic profitability 271
    5.5.2. Leverage 272
    5.5.3. Financial Leverage 272

Chapter 6. Analysis by Ratios: IFRS 277

6.1. Composition and evolution ratios 277
    6.1.1. Flow/Level 279
    6.1.2. Level/Level 280
    6.1.3. Levels/Flows 283
    6.1.4. Flux/Flux 285
    6.1.5. Flow/Level 286
    6.1.6. Combination 287
6.2. Database 289
    6.2.1. Activity ratios, profitability, balance, investment, debt, profitability of the Banque de France 290
    6.2.2. Expeditious method of credit managers 300

Chapter 7. Analysis by Flux Tables: IFRS vs. US GAAP 305

7.1. Functional chart of the French Accounting Plan 306
    7.1.1. Table of changes in total net working capital WC 306
    7.1.2. Table of changes in working capital requirement 323

7.1.3. Synoptic diagram of the links between
two-year financial statements 326
7.2. Financing table of the Banque de France 327
  7.2.1. Functional balance 327
  7.2.2. Cash flow statement 330
7.3. Cash flow statement of the French Association
of Chartered Accountants 339
  7.3.1. Net cash flows from operations 339
  7.3.2. Net cash flows from investments 342
  7.3.3. Net cash flows related to financing 342
  7.3.4. Change in balance sheet cash position 343
  7.3.5. Diagnosis of the financing table of the French
  Association of Chartered Accountants 343
7.4. Free cash flow table spanning several years 345
  7.4.1. The method 347
7.5. Summary of the restatements of financing and flow tables 353
  7.5.1. Table 353
  7.5.2. Risk diagnosis 354
7.6. Statement of cash flow analysis: US GAAP 359
  7.6.1. Features of cash flow statement 359
  7.6.2. Cash flow statement diagnosis 362
7.7. Statement of stockholders' equity 364

Conclusion 367

Glossary 369

Bibliography 379

Index 381

Introduction

The International Financial Reporting Standards (IFRS) are standards issued by the IFRS Foundation and the International Accounting Standards Board (IASB)[1] to provide a common global language for company accounts. IFRS are understandable and comparable across international boundaries even in the context of alternative finance [LEV 15]. They are particularly important for companies that have dealings in several countries. They are progressively replacing the different national accounting standards. They represent rules to be followed by accountants to maintain books of accounts which are comparable, understandable, reliable and relevant as per the users, internal or external.

Generally Accepted Accounting Principles (GAAP or US GAAP) is the accounting standard adopted by the U.S. Securities and Exchange Commission (SEC)[2]. The GAAP are a common set of accounting principles, standards and procedures that companies must follow when they compile their financial statements. GAAP is a combination of authoritative standards and the commonly accepted ways of recording and reporting accounting information.

---

1 *"The International Accounting Standards Board (IASB) is an independent, private-sector body that develops and approves International Financial Reporting Standards (IFRSs). The IASB operates under the oversight of the IFRS Foundation. The IASB was formed in 2001 to replace the International Accounting Standards Committee"* [DEL 17].

2 The U.S. Securities and Exchange Commission (SEC) is an independent agency of the United States federal government. The SEC holds primary responsibility for enforcing the federal securities laws, proposing securities rules, and regulating the securities industry, the nation's stock and options exchanges, and other activities and organizations in the United States. *"During the peak year of the Depression – passed the Securities Act of 1933. This law, together with the Securities Exchange Act of 1934, which created the SEC, was designed to restore investor confidence in our capital markets by providing investors and the markets with more reliable information and clear rules of honest dealing"* [SEC 34].

The US GAAP are the accounting standards used in the USA, while IFRS is the accounting standard used in over 110 countries around the world. GAAP is considered a more "rules based" system of accounting, while IFRS is more "principles based".

IFRS standards were proposed to harmonize accounting across the EU, but then these standards quickly became very attractive around the world. While the SEC has stated that it intends to move from US GAAP to the International Financial Reporting Standards (IFRS), the latter differs considerably from US GAAP.

Convergence between IFRS and US GAAP has looked increasingly uncertain over the past few years and now, with the International Accounting Standards Board (IASB) and the Financial Accounting Standards Board (FASB)[3] pursuing their own, independent agendas and today US GAAP converge more and more to IFRS, the most used accounting standards in the world.

Consequently, it continues to be essential for the US to be involved in the development and application of IFRS because of: (1) the number and significance of foreign private issuers using IFRS in the US capital markets; and (2) the number of US companies investing abroad and having either to issue IFRS financial statements within the group, or use and analyze IFRS financial statements to manage their joint arrangements and other investment opportunities.

Thus, an understanding of the differences between IFRS and US GAAP continues to be important for preparers and users of financial statements. In this book, we attempt to present and analyze financial statements and financial analysis differences. This book does not discuss every possible difference; rather, it is a summary of those areas encountered frequently where the principles differ or where there is a difference in emphasis or specific application guidance.

---

3 *"Established in 1973, the Financial Accounting Standards Board (FASB) is the independent, private-sector, not-for-profit organization based in Norwalk, Connecticut, that establishes financial accounting and reporting standards for public and private companies and not-for-profit organizations that follow Generally Accepted Accounting Principles (GAAP). The FASB is recognized by the Securities and Exchange Commission as the designated accounting standard setter for public companies. FASB standards are recognized as authoritative by many other organizations, including state Boards of Accountancy and the American Institute of CPAs (AICPA). The FASB develops and issues financial accounting standards through a transparent and inclusive process intended to promote financial reporting that provides useful information to investors and others who use financial reports"* [FAS 17].

Following US GAAP, we discuss some of the financial ratios that investors and analysts use to assess a firm's performance and value. Recall that U.S. public companies are required to file their financial statements with the SEC on a quarterly basis on form 10-Q and annually on form 10-K. They must also send an annual report with their financial statements to their shareholders each year. Private companies often prepare financial statements as well, but they usually do not have to disclose these reports to the public. Financial statements are important tools through which investors, financial analysts, and other interested outside parties (such as creditors) obtain information about a corporation. They are also useful for managers within the firm as a source of information for corporate financial decisions. Every public company is required to produce four financial statements: the balance sheet, the income statement, the statement of cash flows and the statement of stockholders' equity. These financial statements provide investors and creditors with an overview of the firm's financial performance.

This review can be read continuously or sequentially according to the needs of the readers.

Each chapter, relatively independent of the others, alternates between theoretical elements, practical elements and corrected application exercises.

In the first chapter, we approach the notion of value, a basic element, essential for a good understanding of the rest of the book.

Chapter 1 – Value: IFRS vs. US GAAP

We will see successively the notions of time, risk and information:

– Value and time, where the following notions will be addressed:

  - Costs of money (interest rates);

  - Value of money according to US GAAP;

  - Future value and present value (simple interest and compound interest);

  - Future value and present value under US GAAP;

  - Annuities and unearned income: IFRS;

  - Calculation of net and future values in accordance with US GAAP;

  - Market value (valuation of debt);

  - Actuarial rate of return;

– The value and risk of the notions of:

- Probabilities and expected returns;

- Expected uncertain rate of return;

- Profitability–risk couple;

- Introduction to diversification;

- Diversification and non-diversifiable risks;

- Modeling randomized profitability with a two-factor model;

– Value and information, where the following notions will be addressed:

- Information and uncertainty, (financial market, value, information and market price (stocks and bonds);

- Information efficiency.

To analyze in detail the financial states used in Corporate Finance (in France with the PGC or abroad with IFRS standards), we will follow the six steps taken by financial analysts that will constitute the different chapters of this book.

Chapter 2 – Diagnosis of Financial Statements: IFRS

The classical approach to an investigation takes place in four stages:

– the analysis that identifies the nature of a problem, a situation, etc., by interpreting the elements;

– the diagnosis which consists of a thorough examination of the elements to make them more accessible, determine the content, study their relative autonomy, and assess their purpose and their efficiency;

– the prognosis that aims to predict the evolution of a situation based on the study of theoretical and practical data and information;

– a preconization that proposes advice and recommendations for the perpetuation or even the liquidation of an entity.

We shall detail in turn:

– economic and financial analysis of company data;

– the financial reading of the balance sheet.

Chapter 3 – Analysis of the Financial Structure: IFRS vs. US GAAP

Functional analysis of financial statements relates to the balance sheet structure and operating flows in the income statement. The asset is presented in an ascending order of liquidity and the liabilities per growing demand.

We will discuss in turn:

– The main functions in the French chart of accounts (assets and liabilities), Finance, Investment, Operations and Allocation, which are presented in the order of possible liquidity (Financing, Operations).

– The analysis of working capital requirements (WCR), which can be carried out over one year (static) or over several years (dynamic) and deals with the structural analysis of the balance sheet.

– The treasury, which consists of cash availabilities and equivalents. The treasury is composed of immediate availability and cash equivalents of highly liquid short-term investments that are readily convertible to cash.

– Balance sheet analysis in accordance with US GAAP.

Chapter 4 – Analysis of Activity: Analysis of Profit and Loss Account: IFRS vs. US GAAP

The analysis of the company's activity, which is the starting point for any diagnosis, is based on the short term, and allows us to appreciate the growth of the company and measure its profitability.

We shall analyze in turn the following points:

– The notion of profitability and managerial performance: profitability, the propensity to yield a profit (profit margin), relates to the net accounting result and to performance indicators such as intermediate balances of management of the PCG or the few indicators under IFRS. It should not be confused with efficiency which, in turn, yields the result on invested capital and is strictly based on a balance sheet analysis (balance sheet profit and balance sheet capital).

– The Banque de France's (Bank of France) management indicators: they are based on the analysis of the behavior of companies grouped together in different sectors of activity, and are therefore closer to the logic of IFRS than to that of PCG.

– The correspondence of the PGC-Bank of France indicators: the Banque de France complies with the analysis of the PCG for the allocation of accounts, taxes and similar payments and interest which are no longer considered systematically as remuneration of the State in the first case or of personnel in the second.

– Cash flow: profit sheets consist of two types of cash flows, those having an influence on the cash position during the year and those that have no influence. We will discuss the approach by the PGC and then by the Order of Chartered Accountants.

– Renewed management indicators (IFRS): management accounts have been renewed by the ascendancy of IFRS. EBITDA, ROA, ROE, NOPAT, ROCE, COFROI, FREE CASFLOW and EVA MVA have been added to the old indicators without any standardization.

– Analysis of results in accordance with US GAAP standards.

Chapter 5 – Analysis of Operational Profitability and Risk: IFRS

Efficiency, profitability, cash flow, etc., depend on the financial accounting results (balance sheet and income statement). However, these come from the elements of the social accounts which themselves are composed of items that do not all originate from an invoice.

We shall therefore see successively the following elements:

– The tree structure of the models for calculation of costs.

– Profitability depending on the full cost model chosen: company profit depends on the sales of the products and the necessary expenses. Since expenses are components of costs, the way they are calculated influences the outcome.

– The budget: a distinction is made between budgets in partial costs and those in full cost. The resulting performance varies according to the budgetary choice.

– Break-even point: profitability is determined by the ratio between two items in the income statement variable cost margin VCM/Sales Turnover.

– Operating leverage: leverage allows us to multiply an action. There is an operating leverage effect that measures the sensitivity of the current result Cr, compared with a Δ of the turnover and the leverage effect that depends primarily on the financial burden on the company's profitability.

– Return on equity: profitability is calculated by dividing the annual net profit of the income statement and the balance sheet into equity; this ratio is called Return on Equity (ROE).

Chapter 6 – Analysis by Ratios: IFRS

The diagnosis must be enriched by the determination of the relative values allowing us to situate the company in space and in time.

We will detail the following:

– Composition and evolution ratios: ratio analysis compares data on the Balance Sheet and the restated income statement for financial analysis, in order to derive relevant data for diagnosis and recommendations (Flux/Level, Level/Level, Level/Flux, Flux/Flux, Flux/Level).

– The database of the Central Balance Sheets, CBS. The information managed by the BdF constitutes "a database of companies monitored individually over time". The CBD is based on the French NAF Activity List, which codifies the activity of the different companies according to their main activity code EPA.

Chapter 7 – Analysis by Flux Tables: IFRS vs. US GAAP

Dynamic analysis of fund flows and cash flows is used to judge the company's ability to prevent potential failures. The tables explaining the change in the cash position of the balance sheet can be classified into two main categories:

– The financing chart of the PCG General Chart of Accounts explains the change in treasury by the difference between the change in working capital and the change in the working capital requirement.

– The cash flow tables explain the change in fund flows by its origins in the main functions: current, investment and financing.

We will discuss the different financing and existing cash flow tables:

– the PGC functional funding table;

– the Banque de France's financing table is typical of a comparative analysis. It falls between the functional analysis of the General Chart of Accounts and the IFRS for the purposes of international comparison;

– the cash flow chart for the Ordre des Experts Comptables explains the change in the cash position of the balance sheet, not as recommended by the PCG but by finding cash flows within each of the functions that generated them: activity, financing and investment;

– the multi-annual Free Cashflow table: the current activity of a company generates cash, but also consumes a portion of this cash through the necessary maintenance of fixed assets and the financing of the positive variations in the working capital requirement;

– the synthesis of the restatements of the financing tables and the useful flows to compare the different components that constitute them;

– analysis of the statement of cash flows according to US GAAP;

– the statement of equity.

This book will end with a Glossary of Economic and Financial Concepts

We hope this book is useful to you. Do not hesitate to go back to some chapters and start the exercises again if necessary.

Enjoy!

1

Value: IFRS vs. US GAAP

"... *value does not wait for the number of years ...*" wrote P. Corneille. This may be true for humans but certainly not for capital. It is of course not equivalent to have a sum of money now or later. If we invest this amount, we will not hold it until maturity and we lose the opportunity to invest it elsewhere. This time lost opportunity has a cost. The latter, which would make immediate or later provision equivalent, is called interest. The legal or normal person who needs money and the person who wants to make capital available will agree on the price, that is to say, the equivalent interest rate. Therefore, value and time (1.1) are functions of the interest rate. As in the future, there is no certainty that the expected value carries a share of risk (1.2) that is paid in proportion to the risk incurred, so there will be a risk premium to pay. The better the investor is informed about the readability of his investment horizon, the better he can adjust the requested rate. Therefore, the value and the information (1.3) available are correlated. Thus, the interaction between value, time, risk and available information is discussed in this chapter.

1.1. Value and the time[1]

"*Is it worth the cost*" – is this common sense often referred to? For financial investment, this cost of money is an expected profit, called interest rate.

---

[1] A portion of the French version of section 1.1 was written by David Heller, professor at ISC Paris.

1.1.1. *Cost of money, interest rate (nominal and real)*

The rates fixed for financial transactions are annual. If the latter takes place on a space–time less than the year (months, quarters, semesters), the rate is pro-rated at the annual rate.

EXAMPLE.– An annual rate of 5% is equivalent to the following rates:

– monthly: 5% / 12 = 0.42%;

– quarterly: 5% / 4 = 1.25%;

– half-yearly: 5% / 2 = 2.5%.

The economic agents can choose a fixed rate (rate unchanged until the end of the transaction) or a variable rate (rate revised according to a reference rate based on the money or bond market).

The real interest rate corresponds to the nominal interest rate adjusted for inflation. Let:

$$1 + n = (1 + r) \times (1 + i)$$

$$1 + r = \frac{1+n}{1+i}$$

where:

– n: nominal rate

– r: real rate

– i: inflation rate

EXAMPLE.– The one-year inflation rate is 1.5%. What is the real interest rate for a paid investment at 4%?

$$1 + r = \frac{1+4\%}{1+1.5\%} = 1.0246$$

r = 2.46% Only

The non-disposition of annual sums at a cost results in interest. If an amount is saved each year for retirement, e.g. in order to dispose at the end of a capital, this is called capitalization. If, on the other hand, we wonder how much they will have at the end if they invest a sum of money at present at a certain rate over a certain period of time, this is called discounting.

1.2. The time value of money: US GAAP

A timeline is a linear representation of the timing of potential cash flows. Thus, drawing a timeline of the cash flows will help you visualize the financial problem.

Example 1

Assume that you expect to receive two payments, one at the end of each year over the next two years.

The time line of your inflows is the following:

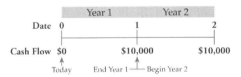

It is very important to differentiate between two types of cash flows

– Inflows are positive cash flows;

– Outflows are negative cash flows, which are indicated with a – (minus) sign.

Example 2

Assume that you are investing $10,000 today and that the project will generate two annual $6,000 cash flows. The first cash flow at date 0 (today) is represented as a negative sum because it is an outflow (investment). The expected profits for the two next years are Inflows. The timeline of this project can be represented as follows:

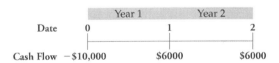

Example 3

You have a bank loan and you make monthly payments of $2000. The mortgage has 26 years to go. Show the timeline from your perspective. How would the timeline differ if you created it from the bank's perspective?

Answer

You make a monthly payment (Outflows) of $2000 over 26 years (26*12 = 312 months):

0	1	2	3	4			312
	−2000	−2000	−2000	−2000			−2000

From the bank's perspective, the timeline would be identical except with opposite signs (inflows).

1.3. Future value and present value: capitalization and discounting in discrete time

Capitalization corresponds to the value acquired from an initial amount, placed at rate i, after n periods. Actualization results from the inverse process, that is to say, from a known amount at a future date, hence it is possible to determine the present value (at the date of the decision).

Two methods of calculating remuneration via interest rates can be envisaged: simple interest for investments of one-year duration and compound interest for investments with a maturity of more than one year, including interest from previous years.

1.3.1. Simple interest

In principle, interest is paid once, when the funds are repaid to the investor at maturity. The interest rate is necessarily nominal, that is to say, annual.

Figure 1.1. *Future value of a placement by simple interest*

If the term of investment is one year, the compensation is equal to the product of the nominal rate multiplied by the amount of the investment and the final value of the investment is:

$$V_1 = V_0 + V_0 i = V_0(1 + i)$$

where:

– V_1: value of the final placement after one year;

– V_0: initial offering amount;

– i: interest rate (investment compensation).

EXAMPLE.– An investor invests €150 over one year at a nominal rate of 2%. What is the final value of the investment at the end of the year?

$$V_1 = 150 \times (1 + 2\%) = €153$$

If the duration of the investment is less than one year, a remuneration proportional to that period (pro rata temporis) should be calculated. Thus, if the duration of the investment is one month, it is legitimate for the compensation to be 12 times lower than the remuneration of a one-year investment since the term of the capital is not the same. Moreover, in the case of treasury operations lasting up to one year, French banks consider a 360-day business year with a 30-day period each month. Only banks in Great Britain and the former Commonwealth countries assume one year to be 365 days. Therefore, we have:

$$V_n = V_0 \left(1 + \frac{ni}{360}\right)$$

where:

– V_n: final value of the financial investment after n days;

– V_0: initial value of financial capital;

– i: interest rate = return on investor investment = cost of borrower;

– n: number of days before maturity.

Conversely, if we know the value that will be acquired V_n of an investment after n days, we can deduce its current or updated value V_0.

Figure 1.2. *Value of a simple interest investment*

In this case, the formula is:

$$V_0 = \frac{V_n}{1+\frac{ni}{360}}$$

We can then deduce n and i:

– The profitability or the annualized return in which the rate i of an investment for n days:

$$V_n = V_0\left(1+\frac{ni}{360}\right)$$

$$\frac{V_n}{V_0} - 1 = \frac{ni}{360}$$

$$i = \frac{360}{n}\left(\frac{V_n}{V_0} - 1\right)$$

– The duration in n days allowing an initial capital V_0, placed at nominal rate i, to become V_n:

$$n = \frac{360}{i}\left(\frac{V_n}{V_0} - 1\right)$$

These formulae are used in particular to value securities issued by companies wishing to take on a debt without resorting to the bank loan called negotiable debt instrument (NDI). Investors (individuals, companies, UCITS, etc.) of excess liquidity then subscribe. The name of the TCN varies according to the issuer, and it is called:

– a treasury bill when the issuer is an industrial or commercial enterprise;

– a certificate of deposit where the issuer is a bank;

– a treasury bill when the issuer is a state.

To the extent that the investor needs to regain liquidity, it is possible for the investor to resell his NDI before the end of the investment.

EXAMPLE.– An investor with €500,000 of cash to invest for 4 months subscribes to the issuance of a Treasury bill from Alpha. The characteristics of the equity are as follows:

– the nominal value is € 500,000. This is the amount borrowed by Alpha and will therefore have to be repaid at maturity (without taking interest into account);

– the nominal rate of the investment is 3%. This is the rate on the basis of which the interest will be paid by Alpha at maturity to the bearer of the Treasury. Note that this is regardless of the evolution of rates on the money market;

– the lifetime of the NDI is 4 months. In other words, the maturity date of the Treasury Note is 4 months after its issue.

After 3 months, liquidity needs lead the investor to resell his NDI. At that date, the reference rate on the money market increased to 5%.

1) Determine the amount received if the security is held to maturity.

$$V_n = V_0 \left(1 + \frac{ni}{360}\right)$$

$$V_n = 500\,000 \times \left(1 + \frac{3\% \times 120}{360}\right) = €505,000$$

NB: 4 months correspond to 120 days (4 × 30 days)

2) Determine the resale price of the Treasury bill after three months.

Let P be the resale price after 3 months. P ratio must be set so that the return that will be provided to the new NDI buyer is the same as the return they would obtain from a money market investment (5%) over the same period as that remaining before the deadline (30 days). To the extent, Alpha pays the sum of € 505,000 at the due date, regardless of whether the holder of the security (calculated in question 1), P, satisfies:

$$P\left(1 + \frac{5\% \times 30}{360}\right) = €505\,000$$

Knowing that:

$$V_0 = \frac{V_n}{1 + \frac{ni}{360}}$$

Here, V_0 corresponds to P. We then have:

$$V_0 = \frac{505\,000}{1 + \frac{5\% \times 30}{360}} = €502{,}905$$

3) Determine the rate of return of the investment during these three months.

The initial investor placed €500 000 for 90 days and resold the NDI at €502, 905. Let 'i' be the effective return of his investment:

$$500\,000 \left(1 + \frac{90 i'}{360}\right) = 502\,905$$

$$\frac{360}{n}\left(\frac{V_n}{V_0} - 1\right) = i$$

$$i' = \frac{360}{90}\left(\frac{502\,905}{500\,000} - 1\right) = 2.32\%$$

Rising rates lead the initial investor to obtain a lower yield than he would have obtained by retaining his title until maturity.

Conversely, if the reference rate had been reduced to 1% 30 days before maturity (the date of resale of the NDI), the resale price P 'of the Treasury Note would have been:

$$P'\left(1 + \frac{1\% \times 30}{360}\right) = €505{,}000$$

Knowing that:

$$V_0 = \frac{V_n}{1 + \frac{ni}{360}}$$

Here, V_0 corresponds to P'. We then have:

$$P' = \frac{505\,000}{1 + \frac{1\% \times 30}{360}} = €504{,}580$$

Let i' be the return on investment:

$$500\,000 \left(1 + \frac{90 i}{360}\right) = €504{,}580$$

$$\frac{360}{n}\left(\frac{V_n}{V_0} - 1\right) = i$$

$$i = \frac{360}{90}\left(\frac{504\,580}{500\,000} - 1\right) = 3.67\%$$

In this case, the decline in interest rates benefits the original investor who gets a higher return on his investment by reselling his NRS rather than retaining it until maturity.

1.3.2. Compound interest

To the extent that compound interest consists of investments or borrowings with a maturity date of more than one year, interest earned in each year will in turn be of interest. This involves capitalization or the composition of interests.

If V_0 corresponds to the amount invested at the nominal rate i for n years and V_n is the value of the investor's assets after n years, then V_n bears the name of the acquired value.

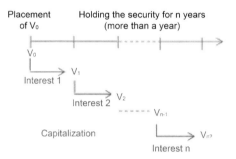

Figure 1.3. *Future value of an investment by compound interest*

$$V_1 = V_0 + iV_0 = (1+i)V_0$$

$$V_2 = V_1 + iV_1 = (1+i)V_1 = (1+i)(1+i)V_0 = (1+i)^2 V_0$$

...

$$V_n = V_{n-1} + iV_{n-1} = (1+i)V_{n-1} = \underbrace{(1+i)\ldots(1+i)}_{n \text{ times}} V_0 = (1+i)^n V_0$$

$$V_n = (1+i)^n V_0$$

EXAMPLE.– An investor places €10, 000 in a savings book A for 5 years at 1%. The amount of its assets at the end of the 5 years is as follows:

$$V_5 = (1 + 1\%)^5 \times 10\,000 = €10,510$$

So, €510 interest.

Conversely, if we know the acquired value Vn of an investment after n years, it is possible to deduce its current (or updated) value V_0.

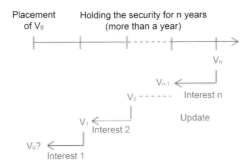

Figure 1.4. *Value of an investment by compound interest*

In this case, the formula is:

$$V_0 = \frac{V_n}{(1+i)^n}$$

The construction of repayment plans is part of this logic of compound interest.

People are called annuitants if they have no need to work and receive investment income previously earned from their annuities.

Thus, the annuity is constituted by sums perceived as annuities, following investment and the fact that the beneficiary has paid work or not is not taken into consideration in our work.

1.4. US GAAP: future value and present value of rules of time travel

The three rules of time travel are used in the same manner using either US GAAP or IFRS.

Financial decisions often require combining cash flows or comparing values. Three rules govern these processes:

1) Only values at the same point in time can be compared or combined.

2) Move a cash flow forward in time: *Future Value of Cash Flow* $= FV_n = C*(1+r)^n$

3) Move a cash flow backward in time: *Present Value of Cash Flow* $= PV = C/(1+r)^n$

Example 1

Calculate the future value of $4000 in:

a) Five years at an interest rate of 5% per year.

b) Ten years at an interest rate of 5% per year.

c) Twenty years at an interest rate of 10% per year.

d) Why is the amount of interest earned in part (a) less than the amount of interest earned in part (b)?

Answer

a) Timeline:

0	1	2			5
4,000					FV = ?

$FV_5 = 4,000 * 1.05^5 = \$5,105.126$

b) Timeline:

0	1	2			10
4,000					FV = ?

$FV_{10} = 4,000 * 1.05^{10} = \$6,515.578$

c) Timeline:

0	1	2			5
4,000					FV = ?

$FV_5 = 4,000 * 1.1^5 = \$6,442.04$

d) Because in the last 5 years you get interest on the interest earned in the first 5 years as well as interest on the original $4,000.

Example 2

What is the present value of $20,000 received:

a) Twelve years from today when the interest rate is 5% per year?

b) Twenty years from today when the interest rate is 10% per year?

c) Six years from today when the interest rate is 3% per year?

Answer

a) Timeline:

0	1	2	3			12
PV = ?						20,000

$PV = 20,000/1.05^{12} = \$11,137.097$

b) Timeline:

0	1	2	3			20
PV = ?						20,000

$PV = 20,000/1.1^{20} = \$2,972.872$

c) Timeline:

0	1	2	3	4	5	6
PV = ?						20,000

$PV = 20,000/1.03^6 = \$16,750.418$

Example 3

For your birthday, you hesitate between two options, either receiving $8000 today or $20,000 in 10 years. If the interest rate is 6% per year, which option is preferable?

Answer

Timeline:

0	1	2	3	4			10
PV = ?							20,000

PV (option 1) = $8,000

PV (option 2) = $20,000/1.1^{10}$ = $11,173.184

Thus, the $20,000 in 10 years is preferable because it is worth more.

1.4.1. US GAAP: Effective annual rate and annual percentage rate

The Effective Annual Rate (EAR) presents the actual amount of interest that will be earned at the end of 1 year. For instance, with an EAR of 10%, at the end of the first year a $200,000 investment is expected to grow by:

200,000* (1 + EAR) = $200,000*(1,1) = $220,000.

In two years it is expected to grow by:

$200,000* (1 + EAR)^2 = 200,000*(1,1)^2 = $242,000

Earning a 10% return every year is not the same as earning 5% every six months.

The general Equation for Discount Rate Period Conversion is the following:

Equivalent **n**-Period Discount Rate = $(1 + r)^n - 1$

$(1,1)^{0.5} - 1 = 1.0488 - 1 = 0.0488 = 4.88\%$

Note n = 0.5 refers to six months or ½ year.

Example 1

– Suppose an effective annual rate (EAR) of 15%. What is the amount of interest earned each quarter?

– How much will you need to save at the end of each quarter in order to accumulate $100,000 in 10 years?

Answer

– An effective annual rate (EAR) of 15% is equivalent to earning $(1.15)^{1/4} - 1 = 0.0355 = 3.55\%$ per quarter.

– Determine the quarterly payment C in order to know the amount to save each quarter to have $100,000 in 10 years. Thus:

C = FV(Annuity)/(1/EAR)*((1 + EAR)^{10} – 1)
= 100,000/(1/0.0355)*((1.0355)^{10} – 1) = $8,507.0183 per quarter

Annual percentage rate (APR)

According to Berk and DeMarzo [BER 14], banks quote interest rates in terms of annual percentage rate labeled (APR), which represents the amount of simple interest earned in one year. To calculate the actual amount that will be earned in one year, convert the APR into an effective rate.

Example 2

Suppose a bank interest rate of 5% APR with a monthly compounding. Thus, it is expected to earn 5%/12 months = 0.4166% every month. Therefore, the interest compounds every month to:

$\$1*(1.004166)^{12} = \$1.05115$

Thus, the effective annual rate (EAR) is 5.115%, which is higher than the bank interest rate of 5% APR with a monthly compounding.

Consequently, the APR does not incorporate the true amount earned over one year, so it is not used as a discount rate. The actual interest earned each compounding period is:

Interest Rate per Compounding Period = APR/k periods/year

Then, from APR to EAR:

$1 + EAP = (1 + APR/k)^k$

Example 3

Suppose you have 3 investments options for a 1-year deposit: 5% APR compounded monthly, 5% APR compounded annually, and 5% APR compounded daily. Calculate the EAR for each investment option. Assume that there are 365 days in the year.

Answer

For a one dollar invested in an account with 5% APR with monthly compounding, you will receive:

$(1 + 0.05/12)^{12} = \$1.05116$

Thus, EAR = 5.116%.

For one dollar invested in an account with 5% APR with annual compounding, you will receive:

$(1 + 0.05) = 1.05\%$

Thus, EAR = 5%.

For one dollar invested in an account with 5% APR with daily compounding, you will receive:

$$(1 + 0.05/365)^{365} = 1.05126$$

So, EAR = 5.126%.

Example 4

What is the APR for an account based on semi-annual compounding if the EAR is 5%? What is the APR with monthly compounding?

Answer

Using the formula for converting from an EAR to an APR quote:

$$\left(1 + \frac{APR}{k}\right)^k = 1.05$$

Solving for the APR:

$$APR = \left((1.05)^{\frac{1}{k}} - 1\right)k$$

With annual payments k = 1, so APR = 5%

With semiannual payments k = 2, so APR = 4.939%

With monthly payments k = 12, so APR = 4.889%

1.4.2. US GAAP: the determinants of interest rates

Fundamentally, interest rates are determined in the market based on individuals' willingness to borrow and lend. In this section, we look at some of the factors that may influence interest rates, such as inflation, government policy and expectations of future growth.

Inflation and Real Versus Nominal Rates

– *Nominal Interest Rate*: the rates quoted by financial institutions and used for discounting or compounding cash flows.

– *Real Interest Rate*: the rate of growth of your purchasing power, after adjusting for inflation.

The rate of growth of your purchasing power, after adjusting for inflation, is determined by the real interest rate, which we denote by r_r. If r is the nominal interest rate and i is the rate of inflation, we can calculate the rate of growth of purchasing power as follows:

$$\text{Growth in Purchasing Power} = 1 + r_r = \frac{1+r}{1+i} = \frac{\text{Growth of Money}}{\text{Growth of Prices}}$$

We can rearrange the equation to find the following formula for the real interest rate, together with a convenient approximation for the real interest rate when inflation rates are low:

The Real Interest Rate:

$$r_r = \frac{r-i}{1+i} \approx r - i$$

Example 1

Suppose that the average one-year Treasury Constant Maturity rate is 2% and the rate of inflation is 0.5%. What is the real interest rate?

Answer

The real interest rate is $(2\% - 0.5\%)/(1 + 0.5\%) = 1.4925\%$

It is then approximately equal to the difference between the nominal rate and inflation.

An increase in interest rates will typically reduce the NPV of an investment. Consider an investment that requires an initial investment of $10 million and generates a cash flow of $3 million per year for four years. If the interest rate is 5%, the investment has an NPV of:

$$\text{Growth in Purchasing Power} = 1 + r_r = \frac{1+r}{1+i} = \frac{\text{Growth of Money}}{\text{Growth of Prices}}$$

If the interest rate rises to 9%, the NPV becomes negative and the investment is no longer profitable:

$$NPV = -10 + \frac{3}{1.09} + \frac{3}{1.09^2} + \frac{3}{1.09^3} + \frac{3}{1.09^4} = \$0.281 \text{ million}$$

The yield curve and discount rates:

Term structure: The relationship between the investment term and the interest rate.

Yield curve: A graph of the term structure.

The term structure can be used to compute the present and future values of a risk-free cash flow over different investment horizons.

$$PV = \frac{C_n}{(1+r_n)^n}$$

Present value of a cash flow stream using a term structure of discount rates:

$$PV = \frac{C_1}{1+r_1} + \frac{C_2}{(1+r_2)^2} + \cdots + \frac{C_N}{(1+r_N)^N} = \sum_{n=1}^{N} \frac{C_N}{(1+r_n)^n}$$

Example 2

What is the present value of a risk-free 2-year annuity of $300 per year? Use the following yield curve:

Treasury rates	
Term (years)	Rate
1	1%
2	2%

Answer

Discounting each cash flow by the corresponding interest rate:

Present Value (PV) = 300/(1.01) + 300/(1.02)² = 297.029 + 288.35 = $585.379

1.5. Annuities and unearned income: IFRS

1.5.1. *Value of a sum of constant annuities*

Assuming that an investor places an amount a each year at rate i.

The first payment a is made on the date t = 0.

The last payment a is made on the date t = n.

Assuming that the investment horizon coincides with the date t = n, the last payment a has no time to accumulate interest.

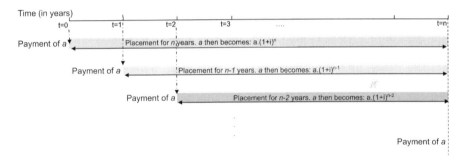

Figure 1.5. *Capitalization of an investment by constant annuity*

By adding up the capitalized values of all the sums paid, the acquired value V_n of the investor's assets in t = n satisfies:

$$V_n = a(1+i)^n + a(1+i)^{n-1} + a(1+i)^{n-2} + \cdots + a(1+i)^0$$

$$V_n = \sum_{t=0}^{n} a(1+i)^t$$

$$V_n = a \sum_{t=0}^{n} (1+i)^t$$

Now the sum of the n+1 first terms of a geometric sequence of reason equal to q is written:

$$\sum_{t=0}^{n} q^t = q^0 \frac{1-q^{n+1}}{1-q} = \frac{1-q^{n+1}}{1-q}$$

Here q = 1+i.

$$V_n = a \frac{1-(1+i)^{n+1}}{1-(1-i)}$$

$$V_n = a \frac{1-(1+i)^{n+1}}{-i}$$

$$V_n = a \frac{(1+i)^{n+1}-1}{i}$$

$$V_n = \sum_{t=0}^{n} a(1+i)^t = a \frac{(1+i)^{n+1}-1}{i}$$

EXAMPLE.– An investor places each year, at the beginning of January, a sum of € 1,000 into an account remunerated at 3% per year. What is the value of their assets after 10 years?

It is a matter of determining the value gained by the 11 payments, of which only the first 10 generate interest. In this case, the value V10 after 10 years confirms:

$$V_{10} = 1\,000 \; \frac{(1+3\%)^{10+1}-1}{3\%} = €12{,}808$$

1.5.2. Current value of a sum of constant annuities

We seek to determine V_0 that satisfies:

$$V_0 = \frac{a}{1+i} + \frac{a}{(1+i)^2} + \cdots + \frac{a}{(1+i)^n}$$

$$V_0 = \sum_{t=1}^{n} \frac{a}{(1+i)^t} = \sum_{t=1}^{n} a(1+i)^{-t}$$

$$V_0 = a \sum_{t=1}^{n} [(1+i)^{-1}]^t$$

Now the sum of the first n terms of a geometric sequence of reason equal to q is written:

$$\sum_{t=1}^{n} q^t = q \frac{1-q^n}{1-q}$$

Thus, replacing q by $(1+i)^{-1}$, we have:

$$V_0 = a(1+i)^{-1}\frac{1-(1+i)^{-n}}{1-(1+i)^{-1}}$$

$$V_0 = \frac{a}{1+i}\frac{1-(1+i)^{-n}}{1-\frac{1}{1+i}}$$

$$V_0 = \frac{a}{1+i}\frac{1-(1+i)^{-n}}{\frac{1+i-1}{1+i}}$$

$$V_0 = \frac{a}{1+i}\frac{1-(1+i)^{-n}}{\frac{i}{1+i}}$$

$$V_0 = a\frac{1-(1+i)^{-n}}{i}$$

EXAMPLE.– A company makes a loan of €1,000,000 refundable over 4 years by constant annuities. The nominal interest rate is 3%. What is the amount of the annuity?

$$a = V_0 \frac{i}{1-(1+i)^{-n}}$$

$$a = \frac{1\,000\,000 \times 3\%}{1-(1+3\%)^{-4}} = €269,027$$

1.5.3. *The updating of constant sums over an infinite period: the return*

When an investor holds a share (share of the capital of an enterprise), the flows he obtains through dividends (remuneration of the shareholder) persist as long as he retains his financial title. This situation corresponds to an annuity. The current value of the security confirms:

$$V_0 = d(1+i)^{-1} + d(1+i)^{-2} + \cdots + d(1+i)^{-(n-1)} + d(1+i)^{-n} + P_n(1+i)^{-n}$$

$$V_0 = d\frac{1-(1+i)^{-n}}{i} + P_n(1+i)^{-n}$$

If $n \to \infty$, then $(1+i)^{-n} \to 0$. Thus:

$$V_0 = \frac{d}{i}$$

EXAMPLE.– An investor acquires one share with an annual dividend of €5. Assuming a 2% rate, what is the current value of the stock?

$$V_0 = \frac{5}{2\%} = €250$$

1.6. Calculating net present value and future value: US GAAP

1.6.1. *Constant annuities of cash flows*

After establishing the rules of time travel and determining how to compute present and future values, we are ready to address our central goal: comparing the costs and benefits of a project to evaluate a long-term investment decision. We define the net present value (NPV) of an investment decision as follows:

$$NPV = PV(benefits) - PV(costs)$$

The benefits are the cash inflows and the costs are the cash outflows. We can represent any investment decision on a timeline as a cash flow stream where the cash outflows (investments) are negative cash flows and the inflows are positive cash flows. Thus, the NPV of an investment opportunity is also the present value of the stream of cash flows of the opportunity.

Present value of a cash flow stream:

$$C_0 + \frac{C_1}{(1+r)} + \frac{C_2}{(1+r)^2} + \ldots + \frac{C_N}{(1+r)^N}$$

$$PV = \sum_{n=0}^{N} PV(C_n) = \sum_{n=0}^{N} \frac{C_n}{(1+r)^n}$$

Future value of a cash flow stream with a present value of PV:

$$FV_n = PV \times (1+r)^n$$

Net present value compares the present value of cash inflows (benefits) to the present value of cash outflows (costs).

Annuities: When a constant cash flow occurs at regular intervals for a finite number of N periods, it is called an annuity.

– *Present value of an annuity is the following*:

$$PV = \frac{C}{(1+r)} + \frac{C}{(1+r)^2} + \frac{C}{(1+r)^3} + \ldots + \frac{C}{(1+r)^N} = \sum_{n=1}^{N} \frac{C}{(1+r)^n}$$

For the general formula, substitute P for the principal value and:

PV(annuity of C for N periods)
= P − PV(P in period N)

$$= P - \frac{P}{(1+r)^N} = P\left(1 - \frac{1}{(1+r)^N}\right)$$

– *Future value of an annuity*

$$FV \text{ (annuity)} = PV \times (1+r)^N$$

$$= \frac{C}{r}\left(1 - \frac{1}{(1+r)^N}\right) \times (1+r)^N$$

$$= C \times \frac{1}{r}\left((1+r)^N - 1\right)$$

Example 1

You have invested in a business that will pay you $5,000 at the end of this year, $10,000 at the end of the following year, and $25,000 at the end of the year after that (three years from today). The interest rate is 6% per year.

a) What is the present value of your project?

b) What is the future value of your project in three years (on the date of the last cash flow?

Answer

a) Timeline:

0	1	2	3
	5,000	10,000	25,000

$PV = 5{,}000/1.06 + 10{,}000/(1.06^2) + 25{,}000/(1.06^3) = 4{,}716.981 + 8{,}899.96 + 20{,}990.482 = \$34{,}607.423$

b) Timeline:

0	1	2	3
	5,000	10,000	25,000

$FV = PV*(1+r)^n = 34{,}607.423*(1.06)^3 = \$41{,}217.994$

Example 2

A company is thinking of developing a new composite road bike. Development will take six years and the cost is $400,000 per year. Once in production, the bike is expected to make $600,000 per year for 10 years. Assume the cost of capital is 8%.

a) Calculate the NPV of this investment opportunity, assuming all cash flows occur at the end of each year. Should the company make the investment?

Answer

a) Timeline:

0	1	2	3		6	7		16
	−400,000	−400,000	−400,000		−400,000	600,000		600,000

$$NPV = -\frac{200{,}000}{r}\left(1 - \frac{1}{(1+r)^6}\right) + \left(\frac{1}{(1+r)^6}\right)\frac{300{,}000}{r}\left(1 - \frac{1}{(1+r)^{10}}\right)$$

$$= -\frac{200{,}000}{0.1}\left(1 - \frac{1}{(1.1)^6}\right) + \left(\frac{1}{(1.1)^6}\right)\frac{300{,}000}{0.1}\left(1 - \frac{1}{(1.1)^{10}}\right)$$

=$169,482

NPV = PV (benefits) – PV(costs)
= 600,000/0.08*(1–1/(1.08)^{10})– 400,000/0.08 *(1–1/(1.08)^6) = 4,026,048.839
– 1,849,151.865 = $2,176,896.97

NPV > 0, so the company should make the investment.

Example 3

You have been offered a unique investment opportunity. If you invest $20,000 today, you will receive $800 one year from now, $3000 two years from now, and $19,000 ten years from now.

a) What is the NPV of the opportunity if the interest rate is 10% per year? Should you take the opportunity?

b) What is the NPV of the opportunity if the interest rate is 2% per year? Should you take it now?

Answer

Timeline:

0	1	2	3			10
–20,000	800	3,000				19,000

a) NPV = – 20,000 + 800/1.1 + 3,000/(1.1^2) + 19,000/(1.1^{10})
= – 20,000 + 727.2727 + 2,479.3388 + 7,325.3224
= – 9,468.0661

Because the NPV < 0, don't take it.

b) NPV $= -20{,}000 + 800/1.02 + 3{,}000/(1.02^2) + 19{,}000/(1.02^{10})$

$= -20{,}000 + 784{,}313 + 2{,}883.506 + 15{,}586.618 = -745.563$

Even with 2% interest rate the project is not profitable, thus, you refuse this investment.

Example 4

When you purchased your house, you took out a 30-year annual-payment mortgage with an interest rate of 8% per year. The annual payment on the mortgage is $20,000. You have just made a payment and have now decided to pay the mortgage off by repaying the outstanding balance. What is the payoff amount in the following situations:

a) You have 18 years left on the mortgage?

b) You have 10 years left on the mortgage?

c) There are 18 years left on the mortgage and you decide to pay off the mortgage immediately before the twelfth payment is due?

Answer

a) Timeline:

12	13	14	15			30
0	1	2	3			18
	20,000	20,000	20,000			20,000

To pay off the mortgage you must repay the remaining balance. The remaining balance is equal to the present value of the remaining payments. The remaining payments are an 18-year annuity, so:

$PV = 20{,}000/0.08 * (1 - (1/(1.08)^{18})) = \$187{,}437.7427$

b) Timeline:

21	22	23	24			30
0	1	2	3			10
	20,000	20,000	20,000			20,000

To pay off the mortgage you must repay the remaining balance. The remaining balance is equal to the present value of the remaining payments. The remaining payments are a 10-year annuity, so:

$$PV = 20,000/0.08 * (1 - (1/(1.08)^{10})) = \$134,201.628$$

c) Timeline:

12	13	14	15			30
0	1	2	3			18
20,000	20,000	20,000	20,000			20,000

If you decide to pay off the mortgage immediately before the twelfth payment, you will have to pay exactly what you paid in part (a) as well as the twelfth payment itself.

Example 5

What is the present value of $6000 paid at the end of each of the next 100 years if the interest rate is 5% per year?

Answer

Timeline:

0	1	2	3			100
	6,000	6,000	6,000			6,000

The cash flows are a 100-year constant annuity, thus the annuity formula is the following:

$$PV = 6,00/0.05 * (1 - 1/(1.05^{100})) = \$119,087.461$$

1.6.2. Perpetuity

The value of a perpetuity is simply the cash flow divided by the interest rate.

Present Value of a Perpetuity

$$PV(C \text{ in Perpetuity}) = \frac{C}{r}$$

Example 1

Suppose you invest today $200,000 in a project at 5% cost of capital. This project is expected to generate $20,000 each year forever. What is the present value (PV) of this project? What is the net present value (NPV) of this project?

Answer

This is a perpetuity of $20,000 per year.

Thus,

$$PV = C/r = 20,000/0.05 = \$400,000$$

Then, the $NPV = PV - C_0 = 400,000 - 200,000 = \$200,000$

Example 2

Suppose a bond outstanding pays $250 per year forever. Assume the current interest rate is 6% per year.

a) What is the value of the bond immediately after a payment is made?

b) What is the value of the bond immediately before a payment is made?

Answer

Timeline:

0	1	2	3	
	250	250	250	

a) The value of the bond is equal to the present value of the cash flows. By the perpetuity formula:

PV = 250/0.06 = $4,166.66

b) The value of the bond is equal to the present value of the cash flows. The cash flows are the perpetuity plus the payment that will be received immediately.

PV = 100/0.04 + 100 = £2,600

PV = 250/006 + 250 = $4,416.66

Example 3

You have the opportunity to invest $250,000 in an apartment. Then, you expect to rent it and earn $15,000 every year forever. If the discount rate is 5% per year, what should you do?

Answer

Timeline:

0	1	2	3	
−250,000	15,000	15,000	15,000	

To decide whether to buy the apartment you need to calculate the NPV. The cash flows the rent of the apartment generates are a perpetuity, so by the PV of a perpetuity formula:

PV = 15,000/0.05 = $300,000

NPV = 300,000 – 250,000 = $50,000

You should invest in this project since the NPV is positive.

1.6.3. *Growing cash flows*

A) *Growing perpetuity*

Assume you expect the amount of your perpetual payment to increase at a constant rate, g.

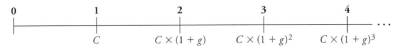

Present value of a growing perpetuity

$$PV \text{ (growing perpetuity)} = \frac{C}{r - g}$$

Example 1

Suppose you invest today $200,000 in a project at 5% cost of capital. This project is expected to generate $20,000 each year and will grow every year by 3% forever. What is the present value (PV) of this project? What is the net present value (NPV) of this project?

Answer

This is a growing perpetuity of $20,000 by 3% every year.

Thus:

PV = C/(r – g) = 20,000/(0.05 – 0.03) = $1,000,000

Then:

$$NPV = PV - C_0 = 1{,}000{,}000 - 200{,}000 = \$800{,}000$$

Example 2

Suppose you had inherited a growing perpetuity. The first payment will occur in a year and will be $3,000. Each year after that, it is expected that your payments grow by 6% forever. If the interest rate is 10% per year:

a) What is today's value of the heritage?

b) What is the value of the heritage immediately after the first payment is made?

Answer

a) Timeline:

0	1	2	3	
	3,000	3,000(1.06)	$3{,}000(1.06)^2$	

Using the formula for the PV of a growing perpetuity gives:

$$PV = 3{,}000/(0.1 - 0.06) = \$75{,}000$$

b) Timeline:

	1	2	3	4	
0		1	2	3	
		3,000	$3{,}000(1.06)^2$	$3{,}000(1.06)^3$	

Using the formula for the PV of a growing perpetuity gives:

PV = 3,000*(1.06)/(0.1 − 0.06) = 3,180/0.04 = $79,500

Example 3

You are thinking of a project that will save you $2,000 in the first year. It is expected then that the savings decline at a rate of 3% per year forever. What is the present value of the savings if the interest rate is 7% per year?

Answer

The timeline is the following:

0	1	2	3
	2,000	2,000(1 − 0.03)	2,000(1 − 0.03)^2

We must value a growing perpetuity with a *negative* growth rate of −0.03:

PV = 2,000/(0.07 − 0.03) = $20,000

Example 4

A pharmaceutical company has developed a new drug. The patent on the drug will last 20 years. It is expected that the drug's profits will be $5 million in its first year and that this amount will grow at a rate of 4% per year for the next 20 years. What is the present value of the new drug if the interest rate is 15% per year?

Answer

Timeline:

0	1	2	3			20
	5	5(1.04)	5(1.04)²			5(1.04)¹⁶

This is a 20-year growing annuity. Using the growing annuity formula we have:

PV = 5,000,000/(0.15 – 0.04)*(1 – (1.04/1.15)²⁰) = $42,566,168.632

B) Growing annuity

The present value of a growing annuity with the initial cash flow *c*, growth rate *g* and interest rate *r* is defined as:

– *Present value of a growing annuity*

$$PV = C \times \frac{1}{(r-g)} \left(1 - \left(\frac{1+g}{(1+r)}\right)^N\right)$$

Example 1

You want to save for your retirement. You plan to contribute $23,000 to the account at the end of this year. You anticipate you will be able to increase your annual contributions by 2% each year for the next 50 years. If your expected annual return is 10%, how much do you expect to have in your retirement account when you retire in 50 years?

Answer

The present value of the series of deposits is:

PV = $23,000 × (1 ÷ (0.1 – 0.02)) × (1 – (1 + 0.02 ÷ 1 + 0.1)⁵⁰) = $284,998.75

The future value of the series of deposits is:

FV = $284,998.75 × (1.1)⁵⁰ = $33,456,246.332

Example 2

Suppose that a private school's tuition is $20,000 per year, payable at the beginning of the school year. It is expected that tuition will increase by 3% per year over the 13 years of schooling. What is the present value of the tuition payments if the interest rate is 3% per year? How much would you need to have in the bank now to fund all 13 years of tuition?

Answer

Timeline:

0	1	2	3		12	13
20,000	20,000(1.03)	20,000(1.03)^2	20,000(1.03)^3		20,000(1.03)^{12}	0

Two parts of this problem: today's tuition payment of $20,000 and a 12-year growing annuity with first payment of 20,000(1.03). However, we cannot use the growing annuity formula because in this case $r = g$. We can just calculate the present values of the payments and add them up:

$$PV = 20,000\,(1.03)/(1.03) + 20,000\,(1.03)^2/(1.03)^2 + 20,000\,(1.03)^3/(1.03^3) + \ldots + 20,000(1.03^{12})/(1.03^{12}) = 20,000 + 20,000 + 20,000 + \ldots + 20,000 = 20,000*12 = \$240,000$$

Adding the initial tuition payment gives:

$$240,000 + 20,000 = \$260,000$$

Example 3

You are running a Fintech company. Analysts predict that its earnings will grow at 50% per year for the next five years. After that, as competition increases, earnings growth is expected to slow to 5% per year and continue at that level forever. Your company has just announced earnings of $2,000,000. What is the present value of all future earnings if the interest rate is 10%?

Answer

Timeline:

0	1	2	3	4	5	6	7
	2(1.5)	$2(1.5)^2$	$2(1.5)^3$	$2(1.5)^4$	$2(1.5)^5$	$2(1.5)^5(1.05)$	$2(1.5)^5(1.05)^2$

This problem is composed of two parts:

(1) A growing annuity for 5 years;

(2) A growing perpetuity after 5 years.

First we find the PV of (1):

PV = 2,000,000/(0.1 − 0.5) * (1 − $(1.5/1.1)^5$) = $18,575,606.485

The PV of (2). The value at <u>date 5</u> of the growing perpetuity is the following:

PV = 2,000,000 *$(1.5)^5$(1 − 0.05)/(0.1 − 0.05) = $96,187,500

Adding the present value of (1) and (2) together gives the PV value of future earnings:

$18,575,606.485 + $96,187,500 = $114,763,106.485

1.7. Market value

The market value of a financial security (share or bond) is the price at which it can be purchased or sold, in particular, on the secondary market (the Stock Exchange). Theoretically, i.e. in equilibrium markets, the market value corresponds to the present value of the future cash flows generated by financial security.

EXAMPLE.– An investor holding an Alpha share must receive a dividend of 50 at the end of year N, a dividend of 40 at the end of year N + 1 and at the value of year 3 one dividend of 30. Based on this information and with a discount rate of 3%, what is the value of the share?

$$V = \frac{50}{1+3\%} + \frac{40}{(1+3\%)^2} + \frac{30}{(1+3\%)^3} = €113.7$$

1.7.1. *Relation required rate: value*

The current value of a sum decreases as the rate retained is high and the duration is low.

EXAMPLE.–

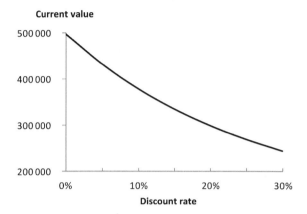

Figure 1.6. *Current value based on discount rate*

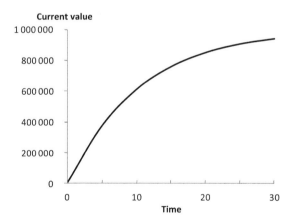

Figure 1.7. *Current value as a function of time*

1.7.2. *Valuation of fixed rate debt*

A company that wants to take out a loan can turn to two types of funding providers:

– Banks: in this case, the company contracts an undivided loan, which means that the creditor is unique (bank or banking syndicate).

– Bondholders: in this case, the company becomes indebted to a plurality of lenders by issuing bonds. A bond is a generally marketable negotiable debt security that represents a fraction of a long-term loan. The value of a bond is the sum of the discounted cash flows that the security must provide to its owner in the future, namely interest (or coupons) and the redemption value.

EXAMPLE.– An investor subscribes to the issuance of a bond redeemable at maturity (the principal repayment is made at maturity), the characteristics of which are as follows:

– nominal value of the bond: €100;

– fixed nominal rate: 5%;

– refund in 3 years.

Immediately after issuance, the reference average rate of return bonds (TMO) is raised to 6%. At what price level does the price of the bond then rise?

The bond represents a credit of €100 to 5%. Consequently, the bondholder receives, at the end of each year, a coupon (payment of interest) of 100 x 5% = €5. Let V be the value of the bond. V confirms:

$$V = \frac{5}{1+5\%} + \frac{5}{(1+5\%)^2} + \frac{5+100}{(1+5\%)^3}$$

$$V = \frac{5}{1+5\%} + \frac{5}{(1+5\%)^2} + \frac{5}{(1+5\%)^3} + \frac{100}{(1+5\%)^3}$$

$$V = \sum_{t=1}^{3} \frac{5}{(1+5\%)^t} + \frac{100}{(1+5\%)^3}$$

$$V = 5\frac{1-(1+5\%)^{-3}}{5\%} + \frac{100}{(1+5\%)^3}$$

$$V = 100$$

If the TMO is increased to 6%, the bond value V' is obtained by discounting the future flows (coupons and repayment of capital) to 6% instead of 5%. However, the interest owed by the company is unchanged (€5) since it corresponds to a fixed rate of 5% applied at a nominal value of €100. In this case, the market value V' of the bond is as follows:

$$V' = 5\frac{1-(1+6\%)^{-3}}{6\%} + \frac{100}{(1+6\%)^{3}}$$

$$V' = €97.33$$

As a result, an increase in the TMO of 1 point results in a decrease in the value of the bond of 100 - 97.33 = €2.67 or 2.67/100 = 2.67%.

This result highlights the sensitivity of the value of the bond to changes in interest rates and illustrates that a rise in interest rates results in a decrease in the value of the security. Indeed, the new buyer is not going to invest €100 at 5%, whereas with his same €100 he could get a remuneration at 6% on the market. Therefore, in order for the initial investor to sell his security, the market value of the security must be lowered.

1.8. Actuarial rate of return

In order to compare two borrowing or investment conditions with different timings of payments, the interest rate that would have been announced in the context of annual payments should be determined. The aim is to determine the annual equivalent rate or actuarial rate, denoted by r. It must be equivalent to placing an amount M for one year:

– at the actuarial rate r. In this case, the investor receives interest after one year;

– at the nominal rate i. The investor then receives interest at the end of each of the m periods, which are in turn placed in order to generate interest. Interest earned at the end of each period is calculated on an i/m basis.

Therefore:

$$M(1+r) = M\left(1+\frac{i}{m}\right)^m$$

$$1+r = \left(1+\frac{i}{m}\right)^m$$

EXAMPLE.– A company is targeting three banks with a view to obtaining a credit of €1 million over 10 years. The proposals of the three banks are summarized below:

Bank	A	B	C
Nominal rate	4.06%	4.08%	4.10%
Periodicity of payments	Monthly	Biannual	Annual

Which offer is appropriate? The objective here is to determine the actuarial rate; in other words, the rate that would have been posted by each bank if the payments had to be annual.

Let r_x be the actuarial rate of the bank X.

– with regard to bank A:

$$1 + r_A = \left(1 + \frac{4.06\%}{12}\right)^{12}$$

$$r_A = \left(1 + \frac{4.06\%}{12}\right)^{12} - 1 = 4.14\%$$

– with regard to bank B:

$$1 + r_B = \left(1 + \frac{4.08\%}{2}\right)^{2}$$

$$r_B = \left(1 + \frac{4.08\%}{2}\right)^{2} - 1 = 4.12\%$$

– with regard to bank C:

$$r_C = 4.10\%$$

It is therefore more appropriate to retain the proposal drawn up by Bank C in: $r_A > r_B > r_C$

In the beginning, we considered that the future was understandable (and not certain). As a result, the interest rate made equivalent a current sum, and the same sum alienated for a certain time, magnified by interest.

Only the globalized and tumultuous future makes any investment more or less risky if only by the solvency of the borrower. Only the State is always solvent and this is one of the reasons why it borrows at very low rates therefore without risk. Otherwise, the return on investment is possible. In order to take account of the uncertainties, the account is taken of the risk to the creditor, the remoteness of the maturity, and so on, in short, the risk of illegibility by making the operation no longer possible but more likely.

1.9. Value and risk

1.9.1. *Probabilities and expected returns*

Certain returns associated with an insured repayment, such as 10-year government bonds, define risk-free assets. They present a zero risk.

Moreover, it is possible to determine the profitability R of an action between two past periods. It is the sum of the rate of return of the share (the ratio between the dividend paid per share and the initial share price) and the increase in its value between the two dates (the ratio of the capital gain or impairment loss on disposal, even the initial market price):

$$R = \frac{DPA}{V_0} + \frac{V_1 - V_0}{V_0}$$

$$R = \frac{V_1 - V_0 + DPA}{V_0}$$

where:

– DPA: dividend per share paid in period 1;

– V_0: value of the share (stock market price) at period 0;

– V_1: share price (stock market price) at period 1.

For *n* periods, the average profitability of a share is as follows:

$$R = \frac{\sum_{t=1}^{n} R_t}{n}$$

EXAMPLE.– The share price and dividend paid by Alpha were as follows between year N and N + 2:

Year	N–1	N	N+1	N+2
StockMarket Price	€49 k	€50 k	€52 k	€55 k
Dividends paid	–	€2 k	€3 k	€1 k

From these data, calculate the profitability of the action of the company Alpha between the period N and N + 2.

The profitability for year N is as follows:

$$R_N = \frac{50-49+2}{49} = 6.1\%$$

The profitability for year N + 1 is as follows:

$$R_{N+1} = \frac{52-50+3}{50} = 10\%$$

The profitability for year N+2 is as follows:

$$R_{N+2} = \frac{55-52+1}{52} = 7.7\%$$

The average profitability between year N and N+2 is as follows:

$$R = \frac{6.1\% + 10\% + 7.7\%}{3} = 7.9\%$$

1.9.2. Uncertain expected rate of return

Financial assets have different levels of risk. Investors who hold them require a certain degree of profitability to pay for the risk incurred. Certainly, the shares may be subject to calculations as to their expected profitability. However, future unpredictable events modify the future flows generated by these assets, thus influencing their profitability. It is therefore necessary to calculate expected profitability based on forecasts of dividends paid and fluctuations in stock prices resulting from expectations in terms of economic and financial results.

1.9.3. Couple profitability, a risk: representation of expectation/standard deviation

The riskier the asset, the higher the expected return. In other words, a risky asset corresponds to the rate of return of a risk-free asset to which is added a risk premium that is synonymous with remuneration for the investor given the risk taken. Risk aversion is different for investors: some choose high levels of risk in an effort to capture high returns; others prefer to limit the risks incurred to the detriment of lower returns.

Risk is measured by the standard deviation or variance in the return on equity. It allows us to represent the dispersion of profitability around its expectation. Let VAR (R) be the variance of the profitability R of an action and σ (R) its standard deviation, we then have n periods:

$$VAR(R) = \frac{\sum_{t=1}^{n} R_t^2}{n} - \overline{R^2} \text{ and}$$

$$\sigma(R) = \sqrt{VAR(R)}$$

An efficient investor chooses between two portfolios with the same risk, in the hope of attaining the highest profitability. Similarly, between two investments with the same expectation of return, the investor retains the one with the lowest risk.

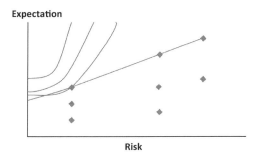

Figure 1.8. *The risk/return pair of an asset portfolio*

The choice between portfolios on the efficient frontier (in red) depends on the degree of risk aversion of the investor. The efficient frontier is the border below which the portfolios are rejected as inefficient or ineffective. This risk aversion can be represented by utility curves that express the requirement of additional profitability for any additional risk taking. Finally, the selected portfolio is that which is at the intersection of the utility curve of the decision maker and the efficient frontier.

1.9.4. Introduction to diversification: the case of two assets

The risk can be reduced by combining more or less risky assets within a portfolio.

Expectation of the profitability of a portfolio consisting of two assets:

$$E(R_P) = p_1 E(R_1) + p_2 E(R_2)$$

where p_1 and p_2 correspond to the weights of the two assets.

Variance in the profitability of a portfolio consisting of two assets:

– If the returns of the two assets are independent, we have:

$$VAR(R_P) = p_1^2 VAR(R_1) + p_2^2 VAR(R_2)$$

EXAMPLE.– A portfolio consisting of two A and B shares has the following characteristics:

Actions	Weights	E(R)	σ(R)
A	35%	20%	14%
B	65%	8%	17%

Calculate the expectation (the expected return) and the standard deviation (risk) of the portfolio assuming that the returns are independent.

$E(R_P) = 35\% \times 20\% + 65\% \times 17\% = 18.05\%$

$VAR(R_P) = 35\%^2 \times 14\%^2 + 65\%^2 \times 17\%^2 = 0.0146$

Let:

$\sigma(R) = \sqrt{0.0146} = 12.08\%$

NB: VAR (R) = σ²(R)

– If the returns of the two assets are not independent:

$VAR(R_P) = p_1^2 VAR(R_1) + p_2^2 VAR(R_2) + 2p_1 p_2 COV(R_1, R_2)$

where $COV(R_1, R_2) = E(R_1 R_2) - E(R_1) E(R_2)$

EXAMPLE.– Using the data from the previous example and having a covariance between assets A and B of -0.23, calculate the standard deviation (risk) of the portfolio.

$VAR(R_P) = 0{,}0146 + 2 \times 35\% \times 65\% \times (-0.23) = -0.09005$

$\sigma(R) = \sqrt{-0.09005} = 30\%$

1.9.5. *Notions of diversification and non-diversifiable risk*

Global risk = Market risk + Specific risk

The overall risk of an action is measured using the standard deviation of the profitability of the share. Market risk, known as systematic risk, is the risk of general market fluctuations. Thus, interest rates or economic conditions in particular affect the stock market price more or less. The specific risk, in turn, refers to the characteristics of the listed company.

By diversifying its portfolio of financial assets, an investor can only eliminate the specific risk. Therefore, market remuneration, through the risk premium, only pays for systematic risk (insofar as a heterogeneous portfolio has no impact on degree).

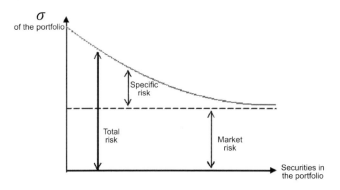

Figure 1.9. *The overall risk of a portfolio*

The tendency of the profitability of an action to fluctuate according to the market is measured using β. In other words, the beta expresses the extent to which a change in market performance affects the performance of the company's share:

– if β > 1, the share is said to be aggressive, that is to say that the variations in the return of the market are amplified at the level of the action of the company;

– if β < 1, the share is said to be defensive, i.e. the changes in market yield are attenuated at the level of the firm's action;

– if β = 1, the company share replicates the market.

The extent of the beta depends particularly on the sensitivity of the activity to the economic situation, the structure of expenses (the higher the fixed costs are, the more the beta values will be) and the uncertainty of predicting future results.

As a result, more betas in the insurance sector (around 1.7) and lower beta in the food consumer goods sector (around 0.6) are observed.

EXAMPLE.– Suppose that the β of a company S is 0.8. Therefore, when the stock market index (market) increases by 10%, the stock price of the S share increases by 8%.

1.9.6. *Modeling randomized profitability with a two-factor model*

By taking two factors, the expected profitability of an action is as follows:

$$E(R) = R_F + \beta_1[E(R_1) - R_F] + \beta_2[E(R_2) - R_F]$$

where R_F: risk-free rate.

EXAMPLE.– The profitability of the Vega share depends on the ABC stock index and the interest rate i. The risk-free rate is 2%. From the following, calculate the expected profitability of the Vega share.

Factors	β	Risk premium $E(R_i) - R_F$
Stock index ABC	1	7%
Interest rate i	0.8	5%

$$E(R) = 4\% + 1 \times 7\% + 0.8 \times 5\% = 15\%$$

Assuming a homogeneity of investor expectations and risk-taking, as well as their rationality and perfect market information, the equilibrium model of financial assets (CAPM) is used to justify the general equilibrium of the market. The profitability of an action is then:

$$E(R_i) = R_F + \beta_i[E(R_M) - R_F]$$

where:

– R_F: risk-free rate

– β_i: beta of the share representing its systematic risk which is remunerated (the specific risk is not remunerated because it can be eliminated by diversification)

– $E(R_M) - R_F$ = market risk premium.

We have seen the calculations to more or less control the uncertainties weighing on the return on investments.

When investing in the stocks of publicly traded companies, the historical value of the securities and the state of the economy are displayed. A Nobel Prize Winner E. Fama even admitted that the stock price included all relevant information about a company since the value of the stock at a time is a balance that satisfies everyone without anyone having any influence on it. Other Nobel laureates Ars Peter Hansen and Robert Shiller have been opposed to this theory but are known to be refutable and relevant at times [LEV 16].

1.10. Value and information

1.10.1. *Information and uncertainty*

Changes in the value of financial assets are the result of information available to investors in the market. The constant dissemination of quality information promotes the proper functioning of the latter. The uncertainty that characterizes the state of a market in times of crisis connotes mistrust and risk for investors.

1.10.1.1. *Financial market concept*

A financial system provides:

– information on prices and performance facilitating decision-making;

– means of financing resulting from the distribution between the resources and the needs of the economic agents;

– settlement and clearing mechanisms through means of payment;

– management and risk tools due to the diversity of financing and investment facilities.

With regard to capital markets, the external financing of the agents is direct. In other words, the agents in need of financing are directed without intermediaries to agents with financing capacity by placing securities or financial contracts (stocks, bonds, derivatives, etc.) in the markets. The financial system then connects applicants and fund providers.

Capital markets are split between the money market (short-term capital market) and the capital market (long-term capital market).

The financial market is organized around the listing and trading of securities and financial contracts. The primary market is the market on which the new financial instruments are issued and subscribed to by new investors (capital increase, bond issue, etc.). The issue prices are non-negotiable (set by the companies). This is the new market.

The secondary market is the market on which the securities previously issued are negotiable at market price. This is the opportunity market or stock market.

Consequently, the financial markets allow the financing of listed companies and the States thanks to the investments of the economic agents. In addition, they promote the valuation of listed companies and are beyond the takeover and consolidation between them. Finally, they provide the necessary framework for risk coverage.

1.10.1.2. *Value, information and market price*

1.10.1.2.1. The stock market

The stock price of a share corresponds theoretically to the present value of the future flows it will generate. In practice, it is the market through the play of supply and demand that determines its value. Two types of listing constitute the market:

– continuous listing, reserved for the most traded securities, means that the stock market prices adjust from the time of the arrival of stock exchange orders from a central order book;

– the fixing is a listing determined at specific times from the stock exchange orders collected since the previous fixing.

The volatility and performance of the action discussed above are essential information for the analysis of an action. It is also important to look at the liquidity of the security, i.e. whether it is trading rapidly given the daily trading volume. When an action is illiquid, significant price differences may occur.

In addition, the price-to-earning ratio (PER) is a financial tool for comparing companies in the same industry:

$$PER = \frac{\text{Stock price}}{\text{EPS}}$$

where:

– Stock price: share price.

– EPS: earnings per share net of tax and excluding special items.

If a company's PER is too high (in relation to a sectoral PER), this means that the share is overvalued. In this case, it would be necessary to separate from the action. If a company's PER is too low (in relation to a sectoral PER), this means that the share is undervalued. In this case, it would be a matter of acquiring the share to realize a future gain.

Finally, stock market indices are reliable indicators for measuring the performance of equity markets. They may come from national, international or sectoral markets.

EXAMPLE.– The CAC 40 is a French stock index that combines 40 French stocks from the top 100 market cap stocks in France. The constitution of the sample must satisfy a good representation of the set of values. The Dow Jones (30 stocks) and the

Nasdaq 100 are the equivalent in the US market; the Nikkei (255 stocks) is the Japanese stock index.

However, these very distant markets remain linked by globalization and the correlation of their variation is very strong to the point that the variation in one is predictive for the others [LÉV 15].

NB: Market capitalization is the market price of a company multiplied by the number of shares quoted. It is theoretical because if everyone sells their shares, the exchange rate collapses.

1.10.1.2.2. The bond market

Obligations are debts to the States and local authorities allowing companies with at least two years of existence to meet their medium- and long-term financing needs by going directly through the capital market, by reducing their dependency on banks.

There are different values when it comes to bonds. The issue value of the bond is the money the investor lends to the issuer. The nominal (or facial) value is the amount used to calculate the coupon, i.e. the interest.

Coupon = nominal value x nominal rate

Thus, the issue price may be different from the nominal value:

– If transmission value = nominal value, the transmission is said to be at par.

– If transmission value < nominal value, the transmission is below par. In accounting terms, the difference is the issue premium.

– If transmission value > nominal value, the transmission is above par (very rare).

The redemption value is the amount that the issuer reimburses the bondholder. It may differ from the nominal value by being higher (above par). In accounting terms, a redemption premium is then set up.

Market value represents the market value of an obligation, i.e. its market price. It should be noted, however, that the market price of a bond differs from its bond price.

The bonds are listed as a percentage of their par value and their accrued coupon.

The price of a bond is the amount to be paid by the investor who wishes to acquire the bond. The investor must then pay the bond price plus the accrued coupon. Indeed, the holder of the bond holds his security a certain number of days after the payment of the last coupon. It therefore requires the investor to remunerate the investor on a pro rata basis for its unpaid interest.

$$\text{Coupon accrued (expressed as a percentage of nominal)} = i \times \frac{n}{365}$$

where:

– i: interest rate;

– n: number of days the bond has been held since the last coupon payment;

Thus, the price = price + coupon accrued.

EXAMPLE.– An investor subscribes to the issue of a bond with the following characteristics:

– Date of issue: 06/09/N;

– Due date: 06/09/N+5;

– Nominal value: €500;

– Nominal rate: 3%;

– Payment of the coupon: every 06/09.

On 01/02/N+1, the investor wants to resell his financial security. At that date, the bond price is €505. Calculate the resale price of the bond.

Price at the footer of the coupon as a percentage of the nominal value: $\frac{505}{500} = 101\%$

The number of days of accrued interest is 147 days:

– 24 days in September N+1;

– 31 days in October N+1;

– 30 days in November N+1;

– 31 days in December N+1;

– 31 days in January N+2.

Coupon accrued as percentage of nominal: $3\% \times \frac{147}{365} = 1.21\%$

Coupon (in value): $500 \times 3\% \times \frac{147}{365} = €6.04$

Bond price as percentage of nominal: 101% + 1.21% = 102.21%

Bond prices (in value terms): 505 + 6.04 = €511.04.

1.10.2. Information efficiency

Informational efficiency refers to the ability of stock exchanges to integrate any new information, enabling them to indicate at any time a rational value. In order to tackle this situation, market authorities should fight insider trading, which involves profitable trades because of the availability of proprietary information. On the other hand, the market must be liquid, i.e. the securities can be exchanged easily with low barriers, such as low transaction costs.

1.10.3. Exercises

Exercise 1

An investor has cash to invest and wishes to purchase a commercial paper issued by company X. The characteristics of the security are as follows:

– nominal value: €2,500,000;

– facial rate: 4%;

– lifetime: 6 months.

After 2 months, liquidity needs lead the investor to resell the commercial paper. At that date, the money market reference rate is 5%.

Questions

1) Determine the amount received by the investor if the NDI is held to maturity.

2) Determine the selling price if the investor wishes to separate the security after 2 months.

3) Determine the rate of return of the investor's investment during these 2 months.

Answers

1) Let V_6 be the amount received by the investor if the TCN is held to maturity. It corresponds to the repayment of the principal plus the interest due on the investment for 6 months and calculated according to the principle of simple interest.

In other words, at maturity, the investor receives an amount equal to the capitalization at the rate of 4% (pro-ratised 180 days) of its initial capital of €2,500,000. Therefore:

$$V_6 = 2,500,000 \times \left(1 + 4\% \times \frac{180}{360}\right) = €2,550,000$$

2) Let V2 be the resale price after two months. V2 must be set in such a way that the yield that will be provided to the buyer is the same as that it would obtain from a money market investment (i.e. 5%) over the same period as that which remains until it reaches maturity (i.e. 120 days). In addition, to the extent that the issuer of the NDI pays the holder of the security at the end of the term the sum of 2,550,000 (determined in question 1), V2 checks:

$$V_2 = \frac{2\,550\,000}{1+5\%\frac{120}{360}} = €2,508,196.72$$

3) The initial subscriber finally placed €2,500,000 for 60 days and recovered € 2,508,196.72 by reselling the NDI. Let i be the return of his investment; i' satisfies:

$$i' = \frac{360}{60}\left(\frac{2\,508\,196,72}{2\,500\,000} - 1\right) = 1.97\%$$

Exercise 2

An investor invests €5,000 for 4 years. The bank in which he invests his funds offers him a nominal (necessarily annual) interest rate of 2.5%.

Questions

1) Calculate the value of this investment at the end of the 4 years.

2) Knowing that the assumed inflation rate is 1.5% per annum, calculate the value of this investment in constant euros at the end of the 4 years.

Answers

1) $5\,000 \times (1 + 2.5\%)^4 = €5,519.06$

2) $\frac{5\,000 \times (1+2.5\%)^4}{(1+1.5\%)^4} = €5,199.98$

Exercise 3

An investor invests at the beginning of each year an amount of €15,000 into an account paid at 3% for 8 years.

Question

1) Calculate the value of this investment at the end of the 8 years.

Answer

$$15\,000 \frac{(1+3\%)^{8+1}-1}{3\%} = €152\,386.59$$

Exercise 4

An investor wants to dispose in 4 years of an amount of €35,000.

Question

How much should he place knowing that the bank offers to pay his investment at 2% per year?

Answer

$$35\,000 \frac{1-(1+2\%)^{-4}}{2\%} = €133,270.5$$

Exercise 5

In year N, an investor acquired 1,000 shares of a company for a total amount of €65,000. In N + 1, the investor received a dividend of €8 per security; in N + 2, a dividend of € 9 per share. For liquidity purposes, the investor resold his portfolio of shares at the end of year N + 2 for €70,000.

Question

1) Determine the rate of return of the investor's investment throughout the holding period of the shares.

Answer

Let i be the expected rate of return

$$65\,000 = \frac{1\,000 \times 8}{1+i} + \frac{1\,000 \times 9 + 70\,000}{(1+i)^2} => i = 16.57\%$$

The solution of the equation can be determined from the TRI function in Excel.

Exercise 6

One company addresses three banks to obtain a credit of €100,000 over 5 years. The proposals of the three banks are summarized below:

Bank	A	B	C
Nominal rate	5.34%	5.36%	5.38%
Periodicity of payments	Monthly	Biannually	Quarterly

Question

1) Which offer is appropriate?

Answer

Let r_x be the actuarial rate of the bank X.

$$r_A = \left(1 + \frac{5{,}34\%}{12}\right)^{12} - 1 = 5.47\%$$

$$r_B = \left(1 + \frac{5{,}36\%}{2}\right)^{2} - 1 = 5.43\%$$

$$r_B = \left(1 + \frac{5{,}38\%}{4}\right)^{4} - 1 = 5.49\%$$

It is therefore more appropriate to retain the proposal of Bank B.

Exercise 7

Months	Share price A at the end of the month	Level of the stock index at the end of the month
1	550	321
2	558	333
3	570	341
4	562	338
5	575	345

Questions

1) Calculate the monthly returns of the A share and the stock index.
2) Determine the total risk for action A.

Answers

1)

Months	Profitability of share A	Profitability of the stock index
2	$\left(\frac{558}{550} - 1\right) \times 100 = 1.45\%$	$\left(\frac{333}{321} - 1\right) \times 100 = 3.74\%$
3	$\left(\frac{570}{558} - 1\right) \times 100 = 2.15\%$	$\left(\frac{341}{333} - 1\right) \times 100 = 2.40\%$
4	$\left(\frac{562}{570} - 1\right) \times 100 = -1.40\%$	$\left(\frac{338}{341} - 1\right) \times 100 = -0.88\%$
5	$\left(\frac{575}{562} - 1\right) \times 100 = 2.31\%$	$\left(\frac{345}{338} - 1\right) \times 100 = 2.07\%$
Average profitability	$\frac{1.45 + 2.15 - 1.4 + 2.31}{4} = 1.13\%$	$\frac{3.74 + 2.4 - 0{,}88 + 2{,}07}{4} = 1.83\%$

2) $\text{VAR}(R_A) = \frac{1.45^2 + 2.15^2 + (-1.4)^2 + 2.31^2}{4} - 1.13^2 = 2.2284$

$\sigma_{R_A} = \sqrt{2.2284} = 1.49\%$

Exercise 8

For year N, you are presented the average monthly price of two listed shares:

SLV share price

Months	Jan	Feb	March	April	May	June	July	Aug	Sept	Oct	Nov	Dec
Course	12	16	18	10	14	15	13	16	18	20	17	22

CSM share price

Months	Jan	Feb	March	April	May	June	July	Aug	Sept	Oct	Nov	Dec
Course	30	28	26	24	25	28	23	32	28	31	27	25

You are told that a dividend of €2 was paid in September N for the SLV share and that no dividend was paid for the CSM share.

Questions

1) Calculate the monthly returns as well as the average monthly profitability of the two shares.

2) Calculate the standard deviation of the profitability for the two equities.

3) Comment.

Answers

1)

SLV share

Month	Jan	Feb	March	April	May	June	Jul	Aug	Sept	Oct	Nov	Dec	Average profit
Profit		33.33%	12.50%	-44.44%	40.00%	7.14%	-13.33%	23.08%	25.00%	11.11%	-15.00%	29.41%	9.89%
Dividend paid			2										

CSM share

Month	Jan	Feb	March	April	May	June	July	Aug	Sept	Oct	Nov	Dec	Average profit
Profit		-6.67%	-7.14%	-7.69%	4.17%	12.00%	-17.86%	39.13%	-12.50%	10.71%	-12.90%	-7.41%	-0.56%

Examples of calculating monthly profitability (SLV share):

– May: $\left(\frac{14}{10} - 1\right) \times 100 = 40\%$

– September: $\left(\frac{18+2}{16} - 1\right) \times 100 = 25\%$

Example of average profitability (SLV share):

$$\frac{33.33 + 12.5 + \cdots + 29.41}{11} = 9.89\%$$

2) $\sigma(R_{SLV}) = \sqrt{\frac{33.33^2 + 12.5^2 + \cdots + 29.41^2}{11} - 9.89^2} = 25.23\%$

$\sigma(R_{CSM}) = \sqrt{\frac{(-6.67)^2 + (-7.14)^2 + \cdots + (-7.41)^2}{11} - (-0.56)^2} = 16.29\%$

3) The average monthly profitability and the standard deviation for year N is higher for the SLV share. The risk of this action is illustrated by a greater volatility. It is then normal that the profitability of the SLV action is higher.

Exercise 9

A listed company wants to estimate the rate of return required by its shareholders. You will receive the following information:

– Rate of return on risk-free assets: 0.5%

– β of the company: 0.9

– Average rate of return of the benchmark stock index: 4%

Question

Calculate the cost of equity using Medaf.

Answer

$$k = 0.5\% + 0.9(4\% - 0.5\%) = 8.15\%$$

2

Diagnosis of Financial Statements: IFRS

The classical approach of an investigation must be structured as follows:

a) Analysis: identification of the nature of a problem, a situation, etc., by the interpretation of the elements: analysis of a problem, a situation...

b) Diagnosis: thorough examination of the elements, to make them accessible, to determine their content, to study their relative autonomy, to assess their purpose, their efficiency... diagnosis of a dysfunction, a structure, a profitability...

c) Prognosis: prediction of a situation based on the study of data, theoretical and practical information, which requires modeling and simulation...

d) Recommendation: advice, recommendations for the sustainability or even the liquidation of an entity: refrain from continuing in this way if... continuation in such a strategy or policy if...

2.1. Economic and financial analysis of business data

2.1.1. *Principles and levels of study*

A financial analysis consists of presenting a study of the pair: risk-profitability

It must follow a coherent method of investigation to:

1) look for *symptoms* that are favorable or worrying;

2) find the *causes* of these *symptoms*;

3) alert about *risks*;

4) consider probable future *solutions* for endemic problems.

According to the principle that we find only what we seek and that we seek only what we know, there are several levels of examination of the financial situation according to the competence of the analyst and the degree of investigation required:

– *The beginner*, student... bases himself on an inductive method limited to the study of the financial statements where:

1) He investigates the risks of failure at the level of:

- structural imbalances in the balance sheet; working capital fund, working capital requirement, current funding requirement, etc.;

- cash flows; cash flows, net cash flows, cash flows from operating activities, investments, financing, changes in the cash position of the balance sheet, etc.;

- financing tables, cash flow statements, free cash flows, etc.;

2) He determines the performance indicators of the company:

- standardized by the GAP: turnover, value added, gross operating surplus, operating profit, current result, etc., and by relative magnitudes, their ratios;

- not standardized by the GAP but used by USGaap or IFRS: income from ordinary activities, Ebit, Ebitda, profitability of capital, etc.;

- for example,[1]

Danone in M€ to	2014	2015	2016	2017	2018
Turnover	19,318	20,869	21,298	21,144	22,412
Revenue	19,318	20,869	21,298	21,144	22,412
Operating income	2,729	2,747	2,128	2,151	2,210
Cost of net financial debt	-174	-170	-193	-179	-152
Net profit	1,855	1,787	1,550	1,253	1,398
Net income (group share)	1,671	1,672	1,422	1,119	1,282

The beginner's analysis is based on a limited number of indicators that require selecting a number of data from the financial statements.

He then develops a multi-year analysis to see whether the indicators are expanding or declining.

3) Finally, he looks for other useful information to establish:

- a reliable analysis with information on the sector, the market, competitors, the economic situation, etc.;

- recommendations on the economic and financial management of risks, profitability and solvency.

---

1 file:///D:/%23opus/manfin/Danone_-_Rapport_financier_semestriel_2015.pdf

– The expert, orienting investors and often working in organizations outside of the companies he studies, has a more deductive approach. Based on his knowledge and professional experience, his judgment is influenced by the comparison with similar entities, his experience of the economic situation, forecasts on the environment, markets, etc.

For example: *"Danone's objectives in 2015 confirmed. Organic growth in net sales of between 4% and 5% like-for-like indicating a slight increase in operating margin on a comparable basis".*

"Consolidated sales of Danone increased by 8.8% on a historical basis to €11,392 million in the first half of 2015. Excluding the effects of changes in the basis of comparison, foreign exchange rates and the scope of consolidation, revenues increased by + 4.6%, driven by a + 0.7% increase in volumes and a + 3 increase in value, 9% foreign exchange effects of + 4.6% reflect the favorable impact of the evolution of certain currencies, including the US dollar, the Chinese yuan, the Argentine peso, the British pound and the Indonesian rupee."

His analysis is based on relative rather than absolute values (limited to financial statements). He establishes a relationship between the information he holds and the financial statement data that he investigates

For example, "With a growth of 4.6% and a margin increase of half a point in the first half, we are in line with our operating plan. In a context that remains volatile, we remain focused on our priorities: consolidating our profitable and sustainable growth model and strengthening the competitiveness of our brands and professions at the service of consumers. In Europe, where we are seeing a significant increase in margins and we are implementing our transformation program into the fresh dairy business and are finalizing the conditions for a return to growth. In China, we are strengthening our child nutrition business, building on both the success of our international brands and the strength of our partnership with Mengniu and Yashili. In the CIS and in North America, we are closely controlling our activities to revitalize the growth of these transition markets while continuing our investments to develop the category. In each region, the results for the half-year reflect the good execution of our plans and the quality of the work performed by the 100,000 employees of the company. With its unique strengths, culture, trademarks, geographic platforms, talent of its teams and the confidence of its partners, Danone continues to build the conditions for sustainable profitable growth every day and gradually sets up its business transformation plan "Danone 2020", for the creation of economic and social value in the service of our mission of enterprise."[2]

---

2 Emmanuel Faber, CEO of Danone in quoted annual report.

The Expert:

– researches financial statements, the elements that confirm or invalidate assumptions;

– cross-checks data, information, intelligence, opinions;

– does not give advice but provides recommendations to investors, guides the choices of mergers, acquisitions, participations, etc.

He is located at the level of major entities and works with the national reference system (GAP) and international IFRS, US Gaap, etc.

If you are not an expert, you will only conduct a relevant financial analysis if you:

– have a good understanding of the type of business you are analyzing;

– know precisely what you are looking for, or else you will not understand what you find;

– remain consistent with the followed investigation method;

– master the tools (financial functions of Excel®, charts and coefficients of determination, means and standard deviations, statistical laws, financial tables, current values and internal rates of return, etc.);

– keep in mind that your calculations are used to provide:

1) a diagnosis with a reasoned report on:

- the economic and financial strengths and weaknesses of the company in the face of threats from its market, sector, etc.;

- environmental events that can influence sustainability (Brexit, election of Donald Trump in the USA, embargoes, etc.).

2) a clear analysis in a *reasoned plan* of the short-term fate of the company.

3) a prognosis on the conditions for improving its situation resulting from a change in the data.

4) recommendations emphasizing strategic *means* to:

- implement the mitigation of the risks of failure (abandonment of product range, outsourcing, etc.);

- increase and sustain, profitability, default risk, solvency, etc. (sources of financing, mergers, etc.).

2.1.2. Typology of financial analysis

The analyst's recommendations relate to:

– the ability of the company to manage its growth for:

- generating sufficient cash flow;

- being economically and financially efficient. For this purpose, the analyst compares the significant management balances with:

– general accounting, turnover, or revenue (IFRS) to measure profitability;

– capital employed to measure profitability;

– major financial balances, i.e. the adequacy between the economic (passive) means used and the financial resources (assets);

– decision support to guarantee the granting of a loan to finance its growth. The analysis should determine risk assessment and the cost of:

- acquisitions of companies in the context of external growth;

- the purchase, sale or held securities of the company studied and of guiding investors;

– alerts and recommendations that must address the problem of:

- insufficient margins;

- poor control of the operating cycle or activity;

- lack of equity;

- over or under investment;

- unbearable salary cost, skill deficit;

- etc.

Under IFRS or the updated GAP, the financial statements may keep the same:

– denomination, which means a balance sheet, income statement, flow charts, cash flow statement, related documents;

– structure, but without having the same contents or the same values.

The financial study covers the same elements: risk (cash), profitability, solvency but the diagnosis relates to accounts whose values are different under GAP standards or under IFRS.

EXAMPLE OF A BRIEF ANALYSIS.–

SOLID RESULTS IN 2016[3]			
	The SCOR company recorded solid results in 2016, confirming the excellent start of its "vision in action" plan. In 2016, the group achieved very good results, in line with the profitability and solvency objectives of its new "vision in action" strategic plan. The company is expanding its business, notably with the department of life division in Asia and the gain of new market shares by the US division. The company continues to lead innovative initiatives and to develop new tools to improve its management activities. The company is on track to achieve its strategic goals in the "vision in action" plan, actively pursuing its shareholder compensation policy by raising its dividend to €1.65 and is now considering share buybacks. The following figures relate to the 2016 financial year at current exchange rates.
€13.8 Bn	GROWING SALES	€603 million	SOLID NET INCOME (excluding exceptional items, 2016 net income amounted to €660 million)
€6.7 Bn	SHAREHOLDERS' EQUITY INCREASES (+ 5% compared with 2015 after the payment of 278 million euros of dividends in May 2016)	9.5% (10.6% excluding exceptional items)	A HIGH ROE, in line with "vision in action" 883 basis points above the risk-free five-year rate, in line with the goal set in the "vision in action" plan
€43.3 Bn	A BALANCE SHEET IN EXPANSION (plus 4% compared with the end of 2015)	€1 Bn	A HIGH STANDARDIZED OPERATIONAL CASH FLOW.
225%	EXCELLENT SOLVENCY, slightly above the optimal solvency zone of 185%-220%	Stable or positive outlook AA- (S & P) Aa3 (Moody's) Fitch AA-	FIRST FINANCIAL STRENGTH FOR CUSTOMERS
€ per share	AN ATTRACTIVE DIVIDEND (up 10% compared to 2015, representing a distribution rate of 50.7%)	PLUS 5.4% at constant exchange rate	EXCELLENT RENEWALS P & C USA ON JANUARY 1st A well-controlled growth of the activity, a satisfactory expected profitability, in line with the plan "vision in action".

---

[3] Score the Art & Science of Risk Les Échos, p. 27, 23/2/2017.

These concepts must be absolutely clear. Their calculation should not be a problem neither should their advantages nor their limits.

2.1.3. *Destination of the financial statement analysis*

The individual accounts are the financial statements published by unconsolidated companies. They are also called: social accounts, summary documents, accounting tax declaration known as Cerfa, etc., and they consist of: the balance sheet, the income statement and supporting documents providing additional information. Two financial analyses are complementary, temporal and spatial:

– Temporal, i.e.:

- static: over a single year, thus qualified as static;

- dynamic: over several years, called dynamic because we analyze the evolution of positions.

– Spatial, which can be either:

- structural: which is based on balance sheet and cash flow analyses to check whether the structure meets generally accepted equilibrium standards. Several approaches are possible: functional, financial wealth, IFRS and also the Banque de France, fund pool, etc.;

- fixed income: which is based on the flows of the year, therefore on the analysis of the income statement or the cash flow statement. In one year, the distortion of posts does not have time to be important. However, the reclassification of flows to determine intermediate results (intermediate management balances) remains important for judging economic and financial performance.

• the IFRS conceptual framework states that financial statements should "provide a fair presentation of an entity's financial position, financial performance and cash flows" that may be useful to a broad range of users who have to make "IAS1" economic decisions. The object differs but not the subject. Indeed, the financial analysis must be able to be presented to the stakeholders:

1) internal partners:

- the managers whose objective is to ensure the profitability of the capital invested and the durability of the organization, by developing the employment and the growth of the means of production;

- the human capital needed for productivity gains and organizational competence.

2) external partners:

– minority investors who wish to minimize risks and make their investments profitable;

– credit institutions such as banks that want to ensure solvency (the granting of loans without solvency guarantee was the cause of the stock market crash of 2007 and other problems);

– the State concerned by a faithful presentation of the assets, the result and the financial situation, because its mission is:

– to levy taxes and duties,

– to pay subsidies, direct aids.

These State measures, as we saw during the crisis of 2008 and following [LEV 10], are sources of financing for companies, as are the tax breaks and deferred settlements of taxes and other expenses to be paid to the State.

– Central balance sheets such as the Banque de France, European harmonized data banks, etc., collect, classify, analyze billions of information about companies. Their methods of analysis serve as references and this is particularly the case for the Banque de France, which helps its members to position themselves within their sector and to establish a diagnosis (Geode). Since 2007, it has been recognized as an external credit assessment agency, which allows financial institutions to rely on its expertise to calculate their capital requirements.

FIBEN (Fichier Bancaire des Entreprises) (French Banking Database of Enterprises) and its 28 modules in 2007 are a database that provides information and risk analyses on companies. The most frequent questions to help external financial analysis concerns the ability of companies to honor their commitments within three years, payment incidents, commercial judgments, details of indebtedness, etc. The credit rating, based essentially on the financial analysis of the Banque de France, that focuses in particular on the following elements:

– profitability: review of company performance (main aggregates: value added, net income, gross operating surplus);

– financial autonomy: appreciation of the capacity of the company to release resources to repay its debts (main aggregates: cash flow);

– non-current financial debts; interest and similar expenses...;

– solvency: appreciation of the level of own funds (main aggregates net own funds, financial indebtedness, total balance sheet...);

– balance sheet equilibrium: review of liquidity to verify adequacy between resources and financed assets (main aggregates: Global Net Working Capital Fund, Assets less than one year and Liabilities under one year....).

The credit rating is calibrated as follows:

– rating 0: no adverse information but no collection of recent accounting documentation.

– rating 3++: appreciated financial position, satisfactory profitability and solvency, excellent ability to withstand adverse developments in its environment.

– rating 4+: the company's ability to meet its fairly high financial commitments. Financial situation appreciated in view of recent accounting documents but does not present a financial strength allowing a more favorable rating. The company is in a context of starting the activity. A continuation plan, a safeguarding plan or an approval of the conciliation agreement has been recently adopted while the examination of the accounting documents would normally have resulted in a more favorable rating.

– rating 5: ability to meet its fairly low financial commitments, and financial situation with relative imbalances (low earnings capacity or unbalanced balance sheet structure but limited). The company holds the capital of companies whose importance appears significant and which are rated 5+ or 5. An interim administrator has been appointed. A legal representative, a natural person, calls for strong attention. Majority partners, natural persons, have received an indicator or majority shareholders, legal persons, have received a credit rating of 5+ or 5.

– etc.

There is also an appreciation of the management team.

– rating 000: the information collected about the manager or the individual entrepreneur does not call for comment and no information is unfavorable.

– rating 040: the information gathered about the manager or the individual entrepreneur requires special attention; the natural person performs a legal representative role in a company in liquidation for less than 3 years. The natural person acts as a legal representative in at least two companies and is assigned a credit rating 9. The individual entrepreneur is passed on the quotation of his sole proprietorship when he has received a credit rating of 4+, 4 or 8.

– rating 050: special attention required. The natural person acts as a legal representative in two companies, each of which is subject to a bankruptcy judgment of less than five years from the date of the last judgment pronounced, unless such companies are the subject of a joint judgment, or an extension of judgment. The individual entrepreneur is passed on the quotation of his sole proprietorship when it has been assigned a credit rating of 5+, 5 or 9. As part of a legal redress, a recovery plan has been abandoned.

– rating 060: very strong or particularly strong attention required. The person is a legal representative in at least three companies, each with a court-ordered liquidation order of less than five years from the date of the last judgment pronounced. The person is the subject, in a personal capacity, of one of the judicial decisions of personal bankruptcy, prohibition to direct, to manage, to administer, to control, or judgment of judicial recovery or judicial liquidation. The individual entrepreneur is passed on a credit score of 6 or P assigned to his sole proprietorship.

A company is said to be:

– failing, in the event of the opening of legal proceedings (recovery or liquidation) against it. The company then receives a rating of P. Even when this rating is later replaced by a more favorable rating, following the adoption of a continuation plan, e.g. the company remains in the category of default for calculating statistics;

– in default of payment, if it satisfies the previous condition (legal proceeding) or if the company receives a rating 9 during the observation period due to major payment incidents reported by one or more credit institutions. The period considered for the attribution of this rating is that of the last 6 months. Thus, after the attribution of a rating, if a company sees its payments become regular again, it can leave the category in default and be given a more favorable rating, after a global study of the file by the analyst.

2.2. Financial reading of the balance sheet

Are the elements taken into account in the financial statements recorded on the assets side of the balance sheet or as expenses in the income statement? The principle is as follows:

The element is identifiable ⇨	No ⇩	In expenses	In the income statement
Yes			
⟡ The element is a carrier of future economic advantage ⇨			
Yes			
⟡ The element generates a resource that the company controls ⇨			
Yes			
⟡ The cost of the item is reliably assessed ⇨			
Yes			
⟡ The item is for sale or production ⇨			
Yes			
⟡ The item is in the inventory	No ⇨	Immobilization	To the assets
Yes			
⟡ The element has a physical substance			
Yes			
⟡ Tangible capital			
Yes	No		
Intangible capital			

2.2.1. Principles of financial statement preparation

The principles were established in the updated French General Chart of Accounts in 2014. The following principles are consubstantial with IFRS except the principles of the French General Chart of Accounts:

– of prudence that becomes the principle of neutrality in IFRS;

– nominalism which accounts for items at their acquisition value;

– the intangibility of the opening balance sheet according to which the opening balance sheet for a year must correspond to the closing balance sheet of the previous year;

– the predominance of the substance over the appearance of the consolidated accounts.

The following General Chart of Accounts principles forms the financial statements that serve as the analyst's database:

– *Continuity of operation*

This principle precludes the valuation of the liquidation company. This value would be fair and it is a difference with IFRS where the balance sheets are to be valued at a fair value (market value or probable realization value).

For example, the amortization expense of depreciable assets has a significant share in the determination of cash flow. Its traceability assumes that the basis of calculation (the value of the good) is stable. Under IFRS, it would be possible to modify the valuation of the property, so its amortization over the estimated value at the balance sheet date.

– *Caution*:

Every accountant and financial manager must have an attitude that leads him to reflect on the scope and consequences of his actions. He must take all measures to avoid mistakes, possible malpractices, refraining from all that he believes can be a source of damage.

EXAMPLE.– As the calculation of risk is a key element of financial analysis, the precautionary accounting principle is essential for the determination of default risks and other risks, as for the application of financial instruments with IFRS9.

– *Comparability and permanence of methods*:

The presentation of the published company accounts and the valuation methods cannot be changed without exception. One of the purposes is to allow comparisons over time, which is essential for dynamic financial analysis.

– *The permanence of the methods*:

This is a condition *sine qua non* to ensure comparability. It allows a comparability of performance over time. However, with IFRS the methods change and are at the managers' discretion. Comparability can become more difficult.

– *Faithful image*:

The faithful image is the sole purpose of financial accounting. It replaced the diptych "regularity, sincerity", which were means. It expresses an obligation to fairly provide all useful and relevant information to enable third parties to have, through the financial statements, an accurate perception of the economic and financial reality of the company.

– *Sincerity*:

The reality and the truth, therefore the authenticity, of the financial statements cannot be challenged, therefore there is an absence of any malicious act.

EXAMPLE.– The balance sheet and profit and loss account are indispensable and these three elements form an inseparable whole.

The principle of sincerity is based on the leadership of the company, the responsibility to present the real economic and financial situation of the company in a fair manner.

– *Non-compensation*:

Assets and liabilities, expenses and revenues. If we depart from this principle, then everything would be offset in accounting and the only flow that would remain is the only flow that is created by the company as the result. We would go back to a cash accounting that did not explain the operations that generated them and was completely opaque. Even if the trend is to give back its letters of nobility to the treasury, this does not prevent the accounting traceability of all operations.

EXAMPLE.– An example of this principle applied in finance is that of the financing table. Self-financing = cash flow - dividends paid. We are obliged to not put self-financing with resources, which would be mathematically fair, but not to compensate for a position by others.

– *Intangibility of the opening balance sheet*:

This principle specifies that the state in which the company's balance sheet is left at the end of a year is the one in which it must be found in the opening balance sheet for the following year.

It is therefore essential for a financial analysis that it can be found in the previous closing balance sheet with identical data and information.

– *Autonomy of accounting years*:

The principle of continuity of operation does not mean collision or interference. Each accounting year must be independent. This implies that any event connected with it must be inscribed in it, and one should not suppose that according to the principle of continuity, previous facts can be put back to the next exercise.

It is essential that a financial analyst can find in the income statement and balance sheet the result of an exercise in its entirety, without it being tainted by some inexplicable events.

– *Historical cost*:

This involves respecting the nominal value of the currency without taking into account the variations in its purchasing power. This implies that the monetary unit is stable and that the monetary units of different epochs can be added together. Keeping a property in nominal value on the balance sheet means that the value remains apparent and does not necessarily correspond to the real or market value of the property.

EXAMPLE.– A loan of €100,000 made in 2017 will have to be repaid as €100,000 in 2027. Keeping the value of the assets in the balance sheet at their date of entry into the assets makes it possible to keep a simple reference system, especially in case of stability of the currency, as currently with the euro. However, the historical view of the balance sheet does not give an immediate assessment. With the IFRS an assessment at the balance sheet date is preferred. This creates, of course, interpretation problems for the financial analyst.

2.2.2. Mechanism

The balance sheet is a giant with feet of clay. Its history is certified, solid, but cash is its weak point. Indeed, the level of cash at the bottom of the balance sheet concentrates the major risk of failure. The value of this cash is a constant, whatever the financial accounting standards used, since its variation between the initial balance sheet (previous year) and the final (year studied) remains the same.

– in the balance sheet (PCG, IFRS, etc.);

– in the financing tables (PCG) and cash flow (IFRS, Order of Chartered Accountants, Banque de France, etc.).

The balance sheet is made up of two parts: on the right, the liability that has made it possible to finance all the resources for the activity located on the left, on the assets side. Therefore, whatever the accounting standard used: total assets = total liabilities.

2.2.2.1. Asset

"An asset is an identifiable element that has a positive economic value that generates a resource that the entity controls and from which it expects future economic benefits". To qualify as an asset, a property must be:

1) an identifiable element of the assets;

2) controlled by the entity;

3) a source of future economic benefits.

If even one of the conditions is not respected, it is not an asset.

• According to this principle, assets held in financial leases should be capitalized. This is true in IFRS but not yet authorized in the French General Chart of Accounts; the analyst can restate this difference as many others in order to compare companies. Likewise, with IFRS, some financing is deducted from the financed assets such as investment grants, premiums, the non-called part of the capital, etc. This blurs the principle of "non-compensation of assets and liabilities" of the General Accounting Plan.

However, there are no comparisons between companies as it is not necessary to restate the financial statement items from one year to the next.

The business, by expanding its activity, increases its assets and must necessarily increase its liabilities to finance its growth.

2.2.2.2. Liability

On the liabilities side, we group together economic assets that have a "negative" economic value. They are therefore "obligations" (debts) towards third parties. These liabilities correspond to the amount of outflow of resources that the entity must bear in order to extinguish its obligations (debts) towards third parties.

The counterparts to these disbursements are economic benefits expected from third parties to whom the company has "obligations".[4]

These liabilities or debts that the company will have to repay sooner or later (equity on liquidation) can be either:

– (own) funds contributed by the owners, shareholders, if it is a corporation per share;

– debt, by borrowing from credit institutions or directly on the market, but their cost in relation to dividends is an important element of the financing strategy;

– grants received, which add the amortization to the taxable profit each year, while it cashed them at once;

– debts generated by the activity, such as undistributed profits put in reserve that allow the company to self-finance. They do not hurt the shareholders because they give the company more resources to finance its development and even foreshadow more substantial dividends in the future;

– current debts of the operation, contracted from creditors (suppliers, State, social organizations, etc.), paid with a certain delay.

Thus, all debts are recorded as liabilities, and liabilities are only debts, the very long term (capital) and the very short term (overdraft). Maturities vary, from the capital repaid to the dissolution of the company, to the very short-term bank overdraft.

---

4 http://www.plancomptable.com/titre-II/titre-II_chapitre-I_section-2_212-1.htm.

The study of the liabilities makes it possible to trace the sources of past funding and to consider those still possible as desirable.

Arbitration between each of these sources of funding may conflict with:

– managers (who would be refused applications for refinancing);

– lenders (who see the risk of insolvency increasing);

– shareholders (who would refuse to commit new funds to the company).

Therefore, the financing strategy goes hand in hand with the sharing of solvency risks. This contingent aspect is important to study for the predictions and recommendations of the analyst.

Indeed, the company during its development was necessarily brought to appeal to:

– old or new shareholders, to increase shareholders' equity. This is not the same strategy because in the latter case there is a risk of dilution of the powers of the former shareholders, the balance of powers in the governance being a risk factor of conflict whose hidden or proven cost is to be considered by the analyst as a risk of governance as treated by the Banque de France:

– to other investors such as:

  - institutional proposing resources such as:

    – long-term borrowings, the cost of which depends on the risk and profitability estimates to be estimated;

    – short-term hedges for the purpose of cash overdrafts, which are generally more expensive in terms of interest because they are urgently needed but not amounted to because of very short durations;

  - capital markets for groups, that are:

    – long term, where these companies issue bonds;

    – short term. The money market makes it possible to meet the short-term financing needs of banks, the state and also companies with negotiable debt securities (certificates of deposits, commercial paper, negotiable medium-term notes, etc.) and goods of the Treasury.

2.2.2.3. *General principles of balance sheet presentation*

The functional analysis of the balance sheet is part of a continuity of activity. The financial analyst must compare the recorded value of the assets according to the financial accounting standard and that of the liabilities. Despite the principle of non-offsetting asset items and liabilities, the balance sheet study is done horizontally to check the ability of the company, to finance its non-current assets, by non-current debts of the company. Thus, the functional assessment highlights the following major balances:

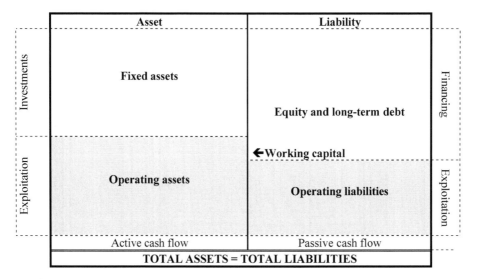

In the General Chart of Accounts, the functional approach makes major balances. It:

– allocates balance sheet items in three main functions: financing, investment (non-current) and operation (current);

– values the balance sheet items at their historical cost (first accounting entry), adjusted for the corrections that have accounted for them each year (depreciation, provisions for depreciation, etc.);

– has the advantage of:

　- maintaining a consistency between the balance sheet of one year (at the beginning) and that of the following year (closing), whereas in IFRS the intangibility of the balance sheet is no longer required;

　- enabling the financial analyst to better monitor the flows that have changed their positions in the financial statements: income statement, cash flow statement, changes in equity, etc.;

　- being able to automatically be presented using Cerfa bundles (tax-accounting documents that can be written, scanned, downloaded, viewed, stored and transferred at will). The CERFA bundles consist of all the pre-printed documents sent by the tax authorities each year at the beginning of March. These documents are intended for companies to transcribe their summary documents.

All these documents provided by the Tax Directorate (DGI) and filled by companies provide a wealth of information.

The presentation of the IFRS balance sheet, which classifies the assets and liabilities as "non-current" or "current", shows them at market value and not as in the General Accounting Plan at accounting value.

– An asset is classified as current if it should be realized within 12 months, or if it is useful for normal operations, or if it is held for transactions or if it is cash or the equivalent.

– A liability is classified as current if the company expects it to be settled within 12 months, or as part of normal operations, or if it is held for transactions, etc.

		Asset	Liability		
Filed by: Increasing liquidity	**Long term**	Non-current assets	Non current liabilities or non-current debt	**Long Term**	*Filed by: Increasing demand*
	Short term	Current assets	Current liabilities or current debts	**Short Term**	
		Active cash flow	Passive cash flow		
		TOTAL ASSETS = TOTAL LIABILITIES			

– It is possible to classify liabilities by increasing the due date and assets by the order of increasing liquidity. It is a search for liquidity that is often used by funding institutions.

The IRS (Fisc) has a significant influence on financial statements in the General Chart of Accounts (depreciation, special amortization, etc.). Therefore, corporate wealth is still under legal influence although it is defended by speaking of economic heritage.

• Under IFRS, only financial assets are mentioned.

Depreciation allowances are a possibility of accelerated depreciation allowed by the tax authorities.

• Accelerated depreciation is not allowed under IFRS. Thus, between two amortizable assets capitalized in the General Chart of Accounts and in IFRS, the balance sheet value will not be the same and neither will the amount of self-financing which includes the expenses.

Thus, when a company acquires tangible property, it must activate it and establish a depreciation plan that takes into account its acquisition value and its estimated life. The French Accounting Plan provides for several depreciation methods that will affect the amount of annual depreciation (allocation to the income statement).

EXAMPLE.– Amortization of an asset of €10,000 N, bought on April 15 and put into service on April 20, depreciable in 5 years.

– Admitted to French Accounting Plan and IFRS

- Constant amortization

Duration of amortization = 5 years, therefore the depreciation rate = 20%. The first year, the duration of use of the machine is calculated over a year of 360 days, it is (30 - 20) = 10 days in April and 7 months of 30 days = 220 days.

Year	Depreciable base	Duration of use (number of days)	Annuity amount	Residual value
N	10000.00	220	1222.22	8777.78
N+1	8777.78	360	2000.00	6777.78
N+2	6777.78	360	2000.00	4777.78
N+3	4777.78	360	2000.00	2777.78
N+4	2777.78	360	2000.00	777.78
N+5	777.78	140	777.78	0.00

- Variable amortization depending on the use of the property

It consists of determining the amount of the amortization annuity based on the actual use of the purchased property. If a machine is intended to produce a total number of parts, its depreciation will be prorated to what it produced in a year on what it is expected to produce during its lifetime.

EXAMPLE.– If a machine is bought at €45,000 to produce 100,000 pieces in total and 12,250 pieces were produced during the year, the annuity will be: €45.000 x 12,250 / 100,000 = €5512.5.

This type of depreciation can apply to projects. In public works, new equipment is purchased which is amortized according to the mileage completed.

– Admitted to French Accounting Plan but not allowed in IFRS

- Decreasing or accelerated depreciation

Overweighting depreciation over the first years of acquisition will reduce the expense of a tangible investment.

Not all assets can benefit from this depreciation. It is only applicable to rapidly obsolete equipment (IT, etc.) and allows decreasing annual depreciation.

Only newly purchased industrial or office equipment with a shelf life greater than or equal to 3 years may have declining balance. The declining balance rate is calculated by applying a coefficient to the linear (constant) depreciation rate. The coefficient is a function of the depreciation period, it is (2017) of:

- 1.25 for a depreciation period between 3 and 4 years;

- 1.75 for a depreciation period between 5 and 6 years;

- 2.25 for a depreciation period of ≥ 7 years.

To end this decreasing function at the end of depreciation, when the ratio of the annuity/number of years remaining to be amortized becomes lower than the net book value/the number of years remaining to be covered, we take this constant value.

EXAMPLE.– Keeping with the previous example with, for simplicity, the purchase on January 1 of year N, we obtain the following degressive depreciation table:

Year	Depreciable base	Annuity amount	Residual value
N	10000.00	3500.00	6500.00
N+1	6500.00	2275.00	4225.00
N+2	4225.00	1478.75	2746.25
N+3	2746.25	1373.13	1373.13
N+4	1373.13	1373.13	0.00

– Abnormal or exceptional depreciation (tax) in French accounting plan

If the company wants to acquire or manufacture a particular investment and allocate its cost over a few months, it can ask the tax authorities for exceptional (accelerated) depreciation. The extraordinary amortization allows us to amortize over a year or two a particular investment.

NOTE.– The amount of cash flow (gross cash flow) including the calculated expenses (endowments) differs according to the method of amortization and, as we will see, the calculation of the profitability of investments based on this cash flow is different.

2.2.2.4. *Financial and systematic accounting system flows/levels*

The faithful image presents itself through several documents which form an inseparable whole, linked by a homogeneous economic and financial mechanism. Schematically:

– the balance sheet contains assets and liabilities accumulated over the years, therefore levels;

– the profit and loss account contains the corresponding annual economic and financial flows;

– the annexes explain the determination of the balance sheet and income statement items and provide additional information;

– the chart of financing of the French Accounting Plan explains the variation Δ of the cash position of the balance sheet by the variation of the Levels of the Working Capital Fund and Working Capital Requirement of the balance sheet ($\Delta FR - \Delta BFR$).

• The IFRS cash flow statement explains the change in the balance sheet's cash flow by the variation in cash flows: activity, investments and financing.

Since it takes a certain amount of time for a flow to fill or empty a level, what binds a Level and its Fill or Dump Flow is the flow's delay. Therefore:

$$\boxed{\text{Level reached} = \text{Flow intensity} \times \text{Flow time}}$$

EXAMPLE.– Fixed assets that are 1.000 in the balance sheet (Level) are amortized linearly in 5 years and depreciate (by a flow) of 200 per year. Therefore:

Starting Level (Assets) 1000 - Closing Level (Assets) 800 = 200 Level decrease in the balance sheet = 200 impairment loss (recorded with expense in the income statement).

Active Balance Sheet		Recordings Accountants 1st year:	CR income statement	
			Charges	Products
+ assets	1.000	← Balance sheet amortization = Depreciation at the CR →		
- amortization	- 200		+ 200	
= book value	= 800			
→ Results	-200		→ Results-200	

This depreciation of the asset is a consumption of capital (the 1,000 initially necessary to finance it becomes 800), which translates into a loss of -200. This is why the result on the balance sheet is recorded in shareholders' equity.

In general, suppose that a Level (balance sheet item) is at the beginning of the exercise equal to N0 and that it reaches after a certain time, a Level N1. Therefore, to go from Level N0 to higher Level N1, it took:

– one or more entries that have increased the level of fixed assets;

– maybe also one or more output streams:

So that in the end, the differential ($\neq$) of flux has increased the Level of: N1-N0.

Suppose now that we place

– on the one hand, an indicator ΔN of variation of the Levels of the balance sheet;

– on the other hand, an indicator ($\neq$) measuring the flow differential of the income statement; these two indicators then indicate the same difference, therefore the same result, and they verify the following relation:

ΔN (balance sheet items) = Σ *algebraic flows* (income - t expenses from the income statement)

Therefore, the result of the company appears at the same time in the:

– balance sheet as the variation in the Levels;

– income statement as the algebraic sum of flows; without it being necessary to defer the result of the profit and loss account in the balance sheet or vice versa.

This flow dynamic creates causal links between the balance sheet and the income statement flows. It is on this analysis of the flows of the profit and loss account and the variations in the balance sheet items on which a large part of the analyst's work is based. We can therefore state the following four principles of analysis:

1) *variation of Levels (ΔN) in time is a flow*, therefore: $\Delta N = f$

• *acquisitions, disposals, production, depreciation of fixed assets, changes in inventories, increases or repayments of loans, etc. (basis of the cash flow statement)*;

2) *flow variation (Δf) in time, is a flow*, therefore : $\Delta f = f$

• *changes in expenses and income statement income, interim management balances for the GIC or financial indicators under IFRS, etc.;*

3) *balance sheet Level difference ($\neq N$) is a Level*, therefore: $\neq N = N$

• *Level of Working Capital, Level of Working Capital Requirement, Level of Cash, etc.;*

4) *Flow difference of the income statement ($\neq f$) is a flow*, so: $\neq f = f$

• *Calculation by differences of Value Added, Operating Surplus, Ebit, Ebitda, Net Profit and Loss, Caf Self-Financing Capacity, Cash Flow, etc.)*

The balance sheet is the memory of the previous periods (storage) and it prefigures the following Levels (balance of opening and closing). However, since a flow does not exist before starting, the income statement at the beginning of the period has no value, and its accounts have been settled, except the record that is said to be the memory of the company.

2.2.3. *Functions: financing, investment, exploitation and distribution*

The separation of functions remains essential for the financial analyst.

2.2.3.1. Funding

These are transactions that adapt liabilities to the needs of the assets. This function guarantees the solvency of the company.

• Financing activity is, according to IFRS, an activity that changes the size and structure of equity and borrowed capital.

2.2.3.2. Investments

The difference between an expense and an investment is that one leads to an outflow of cash for a consumable good or service in the year and is therefore charged to the profit and loss account and the other is to make an expense in year or more in order to receive future benefits over the year.

Investment consists of long-term or non-current assets (including financial investments for IFRS), assets that have been acquired or created by the enterprise and that contribute to the production of a result. Investment is often confused with "capital" ("my capital, these are my machines, my buildings, my stock, etc."), which has led to a confusion in the notion of resource assets and liabilities.

The investment function therefore only concerns high-level assets (non-current). These investments concern tangible and intangible fixed assets (personnel training, branding, development) as well as the financing of activity (BFR) requirement.

2.2.3.2.1 Tangible assets

Their analysis helps to observe how the company is growing. Growth is said to be internal when the company has invested in property, and external when it has invested in shares of companies holding the assets it needs.

– Organic growth refers to non-financial investments that can be of three kinds:

1) Renewal. In other words, without major consequences on the activity. They do not really affect the structure of the income statement since the activity will continue in a similar way;

• *changing a machine or equipment because the former is at the end of its life does not change the business; depreciation will increase if the property is depreciable.*

2) Of growth. In this case, the activity will be improved, it will change the production processes and thus change the expenses and income statement;

• *purchasing machines or new data processing equipment modifies the activity of the company and the organization of work.*

3) Strategic. In this case, the company will have another activity, new products, new services, new horizons, etc., and rebuild all its organization. The income statement will not have much to see in this case and the future is no longer fed by the past.

• *Investing in new equipment for a new activity changes the company strategically.*

– External growth is achieved by applying a strategy of investments and financial disinvestments. These operations on financial fixed assets may relate to:

- *Participation*, securities whose long-term possession is considered useful for the company's activity, in particular because it makes it possible to exert an influence on the company issuing the securities or to control them, implying a search for power and control of the company from which the company acquired these securities. For example, securities acquired, in whole or in part, by a takeover bid or securities representing at least 10% of the capital of a company.

- *Capitalized*, portfolio activity (TIAP) intended for the portfolio activity, that is to say "activity which consists of investing all or part of its assets in a portfolio of securities to withdraw, at more or less short term, sufficient profitability [...] and which is exercised without intervention in the management of companies whose securities are held".

- *Other locked-in securities*; securities, other than the two previous ones, that the company intends to hold on a long-term basis and that represent long-term investments.

- *Investments* classified as current or current assets are acquired with a view to making a gain in the short term.

The French Accounting Plan pays greater attention to the historic cost because the precautionary principle, which was so lacking during the 2007 crisis and subsequent crises or the 2010 debt crisis, is still fundamental.

• Investment properties exist only in IFRS (because the French Chart does not include the destination of a building but rather its nature: corporeal, intangible or financial).

2.2.3.2.2. Intangible assets

An intangible asset is a non-monetary asset, identifiable (separable) but without physical substance. They are valued at their cost.

Business capital is an intangible asset in the General Chart of Accounts:

• However, not in IFRS, development expenses are either capitalized or expensed.

• Under IFRS, necessarily to the assets.

Research expenses are recorded as expenses in French Accounting Plan and in FRS.

The difference in value between the market value on the balance sheet and the estimated value is entered in an amortizing account. The revaluation of these fixed assets is not planned.

• Under IFRS, this value is estimated annually which may result in reversible impairment (provision).

2.2.3.3. Investment choice methods

In the foreseeable future, investment choices will be made by simple methods and known financial functions.

The classification of securities as assets and liabilities and their annual valuation is intended to inform the analyst of the financial strategy implemented and to enable him to measure the impact of this strategy on shareholders' equity and profit or loss.

Schematically, according to the French Accounting Plan, the securities, whatever their rank, are registered with their:

– acquisition cost, if acquired for value;

– market value, if acquired for free, by way of exchange or received as contributions.

• Under IFRS, the initial recording of a financial asset is at fair value.

2.2.3.3.1. Fair value

This is the price that would be received for the sale of an asset or paid for the transfer of a liability in a normal transaction on the valuation date; it is close to the selling price of the elements of the company.

In financial statements in the French Accounting Plan, fair value is almost never used.

2.2.3.3.2. IFRS 9, classification and valuation of financial assets

• IFRS 9, which replaced IAS 39 in early 2018, and is intended to be less complex and with more "fair value" valuations in the balance sheets.

Schematically IFRS 9 distinguishes only three categories of financial assets and no longer four, has a wider range of risk-opening strategies and sets relaxed accounting principles to reduce the volatility of earnings.

For bonds, liability debt instruments and other asset receivables, classification is based on the management model or business model of these instruments and the complexity of the cash flows that flow from them.

The business model is a proactive management of financial instruments. It shows whether the company is willing to hold the financial instruments to receive future expected income or sell at fair value prior to maturity to earn capital gains.

Thus, a financial asset is either[5]:

– cash flow;

– an equity instrument (shares…) of other companies;

– a right,

 - to receive cash, or other financial assets of companies,

 - to exchange financial assets or financial liabilities with another company if the exchange is favorable to the company studied;

– a contract that will have to be settled in equity instruments (shares, etc.) of the company studied.

The initial value of the financial asset, its cost price = fair value + any transaction costs (except for those that will subsequently be measured at "fair value through profit or loss")

EXAMPLE.– *An asset is acquired for 105 with a purchase commission of 5 in the category "fair value through equity". The company increases the asset by 105. If the asset is resold, it will be with a commission of 10. At the end of the year, the asset is worth 100. The entity then records a loss of 5 inscribed in the equity in "Other comprehensive income", without taking into account possible 10 collectible in case of sale of the asset.*

---

5 http://www.apdc-france.fr/wp-content/uploads/Analyse-critique-de-la-transition-vers-norme-IFRS-9.pdf

With IFR9, the notion of Business Model BM determines whether a financial asset is to be valued according to its "amortized cost" (less risky in the event of a financial crisis) or according to its "fair value, through the profit and loss account" or "fair value through shareholders 'equity'".

1) *Amortized cost*

To apply it, the asset must first be held in the LBM that contains the asset until maturity to collect the income and secondly the financial asset must give rise to fixed dates of the compound's income capital and interest on the outstanding capital.

EXAMPLE.– A bond is issued on 1/01/N at a nominal value of 1,000, repayable in 3 years for 1,000, with an annual interest rate of 5% and with direct acquisition costs of 28. Interest and repayment are settled at the end of the year.[6]

The valuation of the obligation using the amortized cost method consists of determining the discount rate, known as the effective interest rate, which is used to equalize the future flows and the initial value, then to apply each year to the cash flow remaining to be cashed or disbursed to obtain the amortized cost to be shown on the balance sheet.

Calculation of the effective interest rate:

$$1.000 + 28 = 1.028 = \frac{50}{(1+i)} + \frac{50}{(1+i)^2} + \frac{1.050}{(1+i)^3} = 4\%$$

• Early amortized cost:

N	N1	N2
1 028	$= \frac{50}{(1+0.04)} + \frac{1.050}{(1+0.04)^2} = 1\ 019$	$\frac{1.050}{(1+0.04)} = 1\ 010$

2) Fair value through the JVCR or Fair Value Through Profit and Loss FVTPL

Financial instruments that do not meet one of the two criteria, that of the business model or according to the contractual characteristics of cash flows, for an amortized cost valuation are then measured at their fair value. Exceptionally, in the case of financial instruments held as assets and liabilities, it is possible to offset them for assets and liabilities, if this reflects their financial compensation.

---

[6] Barbe-Dandon O., Didelot L., "Le portefeuille titres en IFRS et en règles françaises dans les comptes individuels", *Revue Française de Comptabilité*, no. 403, October 2007.

3) *Fair value through equity FVTOCI or Fair Value through Other Comprehensive Income*

When the company acquires equity instruments (shares etc.) and wants to sell them or buy them back in the short term to make a profit, it must classify them as FVTOCI. The evaluation is done instrument by instrument. The choice of valuation from a financial asset to the FVTOCI is irrevocable.

IAS39 had to hold the assets until maturity to qualify as a "held-to-maturity investment" PDE or a Held To Maturity HTM. This category has disappeared with IFRS 9.

Synthesis:

	Classification of Financial assets		
Rating categories	Derivative instruments	Equity investment	Debt investment
Cushioned cost			X
FVTPL Mandatory	X	X	X
FVTPL by option			X
FVTOCI		X	

2.2.3.3.3. IFRS 9, classification and valuation of financial liabilities

– *Classification in equity or financial debt*:

Financial liabilities relate to any liability that is either:

- a contractual obligation to remit income or another financial asset to another company, to exchange financial assets or liabilities on terms potentially unfavorable to the company;

- a contract that can be settled in equity instruments of the company studied.

– *Composite financial instruments (hybrid)*:

These instruments contain a share of equity and a share of financial debt. For example, a bond convertible into shares must be recognized in part as a financial debt (obligation to discharge the debt with cash) and partly in shares (shares, etc.) of the issuing company.

The French Accountant Plan shares it at the end when the creditor chooses his way to be paid.

• There is no hybrid capital in the IFRS balance sheets because the imputation choice has to be determined at the beginning.

– *Financial debts to release capital gains FVTPL*:

They are divided into two, the financial debts:

1) held for speculative purposes Held For Trading (HFT). The fact of incurring a financial debt to finance its activities with capital gains (trading) is not enough to place it in HTF;

2) designated by the company to be measured at "fair value through profit or loss" FVTPL.

It is difficult to establish a precise correspondence between the classification of French Accounting Plan securities and IFRS. However, according to the General Chart of Accounts, transfers between categories are obligatory when securities cease to fulfill the conditions of belonging to the category in which they have been classified, e.g. securities listed as "held to maturity", which may be reclassified as "available-for-sale"; or "available-for-sale" securities, which may be reclassified as "held-to-maturity", if there is a change in intent.

However, neither securities recognized as "loans and receivables" nor "financial assets at fair value through profit or loss" can be reclassified as another category.

The inclusion in the top or bottom of the balance sheet of the values, according to one or the other of the reference standards, modifies the necessary surplus of the Financing on the Investments (except the financial or assimilated institutions) without judging the optimal level of the excess. This difference between these two main functions that are essential for solvency is called the Working Capital Fund.

2.2.3.4. *Exploitation*

Operational activities are those that generate income and do not fit into the two previous categories: Investment and Financing.

The cash flows in this section include amounts received from customers and paid to suppliers (including internal, i.e. employees).

It is the activity of the operating cycle or the current activity under IFRS, which results in cash flow offsets. Indeed for accrual accounting, an accounting immutation has as a generator the document and not the regulation.

Figure 2.1.

The activity is uninterrupted (cycle) and subject to the risks of the rule shifts called commercial outstanding. It must therefore be financed in part by non-current resources in excess of the Working Capital Fund, at the risk of:

– a link in the short term (current) giving way and leading to a break in cash flow;

– a failure for non-payment by the cash grow.

These great functions are not as homogeneous and coherent as they seem.

• *the financing of a capital asset for which only 6 months remain will remain in the financing function, whereas a customer debt of more than one year will remain in the operating cycle. By nature, one is a means of financing and the other a line of "loans and receivables issued by the company", which relates to the current activity, and therefore, the operating cycle. This is why other analyses treat the balance sheet differently.*

This operating cycle is continuously modified with the activity and analyzed at the level of two types of accounts:

– on the assets side: "stocks", "receivables and related accounts";

– on the liabilities side: "suppliers and related accounts".

2.2.3.5. Division

This is the distribution of value created by and for stakeholders:

– dividends to shareholders;

– the financial costs to the lenders;

– taxes and social charges to the State;

– participation, salaries and other payments to persons;

– and self-financing for the company.

This breakdown does not appear clearly in financial statements. It is dynamic because it is located between two balance sheets: before and after distribution in the General Chart of Accounts.

• For IFRS, there is only one balance sheet to report - the one after distribution. Therefore, this last function is not displayed. The financial analyst can determine it from the variation in the items concerned by it, in the balance sheet after distribution.

This functional financial analysis of the balance sheet focuses on its structure, i.e. the proportions of each major function. It reveals:

– the strategies, policies and financial tactics followed;

– the conditions for the development of the company;

– the balance of the means necessary to achieve the objectives;

– the distribution of the created value;

– the presentation.[7]

Operations of function **Division**				
Balance sheet BEFORE distribution		Balance sheet AFTER distribution	
Elements of the function **Investment**	Elements of the function **Funding**	Elements of the function **Investment**	Elements of the function **Funding**
Elements of **Exploitation**		Elements of **Exploitation**	

---

7 PCG 2006.

The Breakdown is dynamic because it is located between two situations and is therefore detailed in the Glossary of Economic and Financial Concepts. The financial analyst can find it from the variation in the items concerned in the balance sheet after distribution.

The financial analysis of these four functions traces the decisions that have been made. The functional approach of the balance sheet is interested in the proportions of each function in an absolute way compared with the balance sheet total and relative between them, and reveals:

– the *strategies*, *policies* and financial *tactics* followed;

– the implementation of the company's development resources;

– respect for the major balances necessary to achieve the objectives.

A financial replay of asset and liability items can never be exhaustive. However, according to the General Chart of Accounts, certain main principles must be followed, such as the principle of prudence or precaution, which evaluate the elements of the balance sheet at a minimum, at the risk of presenting illusory resources. The values entered in the balance sheet thus remain in historical cost gross value, that is to say, at the cost of entry, with a column for the deductions of expected accounting depreciation and in a column other than the net value.

The balance sheet of individual accounts that meet the standard of the PCG is a balanced inventory of resources the company owns. This inventory contains two major performance indicators:

– cash as an indicator of the risk of default;

– the result as an element of profitability and profitability (since the result is the only element that the balance sheet and the profit and loss account hold reciprocally);

– solvency: assets – financial debts.

2.2.3.6. *Balance sheet formats*

The structure of the balance sheet is composed equally of assets and liabilities.

2.2.3.6.1. The assets in the French Accounting Plan

Basic System

521-1. BALANCE SHEET (in table)

ASSET	Exercise N			Exercise N-1
	Gross	Amortization and provisions	Net	Net
Uncalled committed capital				
IMMOBILIZED ASSETS (a)				
Intangible assets:				
Administration fees				
Research and development costs				
Concessions, patents, licenses, trademarks, processes, software, rights and similar securities				
Commercial Fund (1)				
Other				
Intangible assets in progress				
Advances and deposits				
Tangible fixed assets :				
Grounds				
Construction				
Technical installations, equipment and industrial tools				
Other				
Investments in progress				
Advances and deposits				
Financial fixed assets (2):				
Participations (b)				
Receivables related to equity investments				
Fixed securities in portfolio activity				
Other locked-in securities				
Loans				
Other				
Total I				

		Exercise N		Exercise N-1
ASSETS (continued)	Gross	Amortization and provisions	Net	Net
CIRCULATING ASSETS				
Stocks and works in progress (a):				
Raw materials and other supplies				
In production (goods and services) (c)				
Intermediate and finished products				
Merchandise				
Advances and prepayments on orders				
Receivables (3):				
Accounts receivable (a) and related accounts (d)				
Other				
Subscribed capital – called, unpaid				
TREASURY				
Marketable securities (in):				
Own shares				
Other equities				
Treasury instruments				
Availability				
Prepaid expenses (3)				
Total II				
Expenses to be spread over several financial years (III)				
Loan Repayment Premiums (IV)				
Active conversion differences (V)				
GRAND TOTAL (I+II+III+IV+V)				
(1) Including right to lease				
(2) Of which is less than one year (gross)				
(3) Of which is less than one year (gross)				

(a) *Assets with retention of title clause are grouped on a separate line marked "with... with retention of title clause".*

If it is impossible to identify goods, a reference to the foot of the balance sheet indicates the amount remaining to be paid on these goods. The amount to be paid includes that of the unmatured effects.

If securities are valued by equivalence, this item is subdivided into two sub-items, "Equivalent Share Interests" and "Other Participations".

(b) For equities, the "Gross" column presents the global equivalence value if it is greater than the acquisition cost. Otherwise, the purchase price is retained. The provision for overall depreciation of the portfolio is included in the 2nd column. The "Net" column shows the overall value of positive equivalence or a null value.

(c) A breakdown, if any, between goods, on the one hand, and services, on the other hand.

(d) Receivables resulting from sales or services.

(e) Position to be used directly if there is no buyback by the entity of its own shares.

2.2.3.6.2. Balance sheet liability in the French Accounting Plan before the distribution of the result

Basic system
BALANCE SHEET

LIABILITY BEFORE DISTRIBUTION	Exercise N	Exercise N-1
SHAREHOLDER'S EQUITY		
Capital (of which paid...) (a)		
Issue premiums, mergers, contribution		
Revaluation gap (b)		
Equivalence gap (c)		
Reserves:		
Legal reserve		
Statutory or contractual reserves		
Regulated reserves		
Other		
Report again (d)		
Profit for the year under allocation (profit or loss) (e)		
Investment grants		
Regulated provisions		
Total I		
Other equity*		
PROVISIONS FOR RISKS AND EXPENSES		
Risk provisions		
Provisions for expenses		
Total II		

DEBTS (1) (g)		
Convertible bonds		
Other bonds		
Loans and debts with credit institutions (2)		
Loans and other financial debts (3)		
Advances and down payments received on orders in progress		
Accounts payable and accounts receivable (f)		
Social and tax debts		
Debts on fixed assets and accounts receivable		
Other debts		
Treasury instruments		
Prepaid income (1)		
TOTAL III		
Liabilities translation differences **(IV)**		
GRAND TOTAL (I+II+III+IV)		
(1)	More than one year		
	Less than one year		
(2)	Including current bank overdrafts and credit balances of banks		
(3)	Including participatory loans		

* with the opening of the items constituting this heading on separate lines (amount of equity issues, conditioned advances).

 A Total I bis shows the amount of other equity between Total I and Total II of the balance sheet liabilities. The Grand Total is completed accordingly.

(a) Including subscribed but not uncalled capital.

(b) To be detailed in accordance with the legislation in force.

(c) Position to be submitted when securities are valued by equivalence.

(d) Amount in brackets or preceded by a minus sign (-) in case of deferred losses.

(e) Amount in brackets or preceded by a minus sign (-) in case of loss.

(f) Debts on purchases or services.

 With the exception, for the application of (1), advances and down payments received on orders in progress.

2.2.3.6.3. Balance sheet liability in French Accounting Plan after the distribution of the result

Basic system

BALANCE SHEET TEMPLATE (in table, after distribution)

LIABILITY AFTER DISTRIBUTION	Exercise N	Exercise N-1
SHAREHOLDERS EQUITY		
Capital (of which paid) (a)		
Issue premiums, merger, contribution		
Revaluation gap (b)		
Equivalence gap (c)		
Reserves:		
Legal reserve		
Statutory or contractual reserves		
Regulated reserves		
Other		
Report again (d)		
SUB-TOTAL: NET SITUATION		
Investment grants		
Regulated provisions		
Total I		

* Where applicable, the heading "Other equity" is inserted between "Equity" and "Provisions for liabilities and expenses".

With opening of the items constituting this item on separate lines (amount of equity issues, conditioned advances, etc.).

A Total I bis shows the amount of other equity between Total I and Total II of the balance sheet liabilities. The Grand Total is completed accordingly.

(a) Including subscribed uncalled capital.
(b) To be detailed in accordance with the legislation in force.
(c) Position to be submitted when securities are valued by equivalence.
(d) Amount in parentheses or preceded by a minus sign (-) for deferred losses.

2.2.4. *Investment study*

2.2.4.1. *Principles*

Should the analysis of investment choices separate the cost of financing or include the financial burden in the cost of the investment project? Should the comparison of several projects include the burden of their financing?

Those who advocate for the separation of investment and financing support their analysis on the fact that an investment must by its profitability cover the cost of financing and the risks involved. Those who argue for a global analysis say that integrating financing into investment leads to a financially attractive investment. The competition between the offerers makes sense only for equivalent investments of the same risk.

Schematically, if the investment chosen can be financed by a set of already existing resources or is planned as part of the financing of growth, then the programmed financial burden should not influence the choice of investments. If, on the other hand, a specific investment is backed by a particular financing, then the cost of the resource must interfere with profitability and the choice of projects.

The non-financing choice makes sense only if the consequences on the risk for the company are equivalent. If the choice incorporates a calculation of discounted net income flows, it is the choice of the discount rate that determines the breakeven point of the projects. The margin depends on whether the company has access to the financial market and intermediation. In this case, the cost of equity is more easily determined relative to the stock price. Otherwise, the cost of equity is the one used from an estimate of capital market rates over the duration of the projects.

In the case where the projects influence the overall risk of the company, the possible discount rate emanates from an estimated weighted average rate of the different sources of financing of the balance sheet or of a future market capitalization. Finally, if strategic-type investments have a higher risk than business risks, the discount rate must be increased to incorporate this risk differential.

If the investments involve the use of additional indebtedness, then the additional financial cost must be integrated into the projects and it is necessary to differentiate the discount rates according to the self-financing of each project. Projects are almost never financed 100% by external resources, so each project has its own self-financing percentage. The discount rate for each project will therefore be weighted by the proportion of the project's own financing to the internal rate of remunerations of capital employed in the company.

Finally, if a project increases the risk of the company by the size of the indebtedness that it provokes, the increase in the overall risk is to be included in the investment.

– The Weighted Average Cost of Capital WACC is the average annual rate of return expected by shareholders and creditors in return for their investment.

With:

- Equity P

- Debt D

- CP equity cost

- Cost of CD debt

- Then the CMPC = $\frac{(P*CP+D*CD)*(1-t)}{P+D}$.

EXAMPLE.– A company is 40% financed from external investors and 60% from its own funds. If investors require 15% profitability and the financial weight of the debt is 10%, then the WACC for a rate of income tax t of 33% = 60% × 15% + 10% × 2/3 × 40% = 11.6%.

Therefore, as long as the company has little debt, its overall risk is low, and it can choose the cost of new, low external financing. However, if new investments seriously increase the overall solvency risk, it is necessary to increase the rates of return and thus the cost of financing the capital invested. Thus, if the shareholders have the opportunity, the choice of investments will be focused on projects financed as much as possible without self-funding.

PROGNOSIS.– The calculation of the WACC involves a precise assessment of the cost of equity. Several methods make it possible to determine this cost.

The investment includes a set of capital held by the company or that it can obtain and that it will immobilize for a specified period. This level of invested capital will secrete flows of capital consumption called depreciation as well as income flows resulting from an increase in productive capacity and exploitation activity.

2.2.4.1.1. Typology

There is an accounting typology and other financial investments.

The first classifies them as intangible, tangible and financial assets, which has the advantage of being well-circumscribed and quantified in the company accounts. However, it limits the investment to the accounting valuation of a sum registered according to the rules and procedures of the general chart of accounts or IFRS.

If the technical capital is listed there, on the one hand, it ignores the human capital which is just as much a consumer of financial resources and, on the other hand, it impliquates the financing of financial fixed assets, which are potentialities of resources.

The second typology corresponds more to the decision to invest and retains the conditions that gave rise to the investment.

– Maintenance investments allow the conservation of the potential of the company and although they are never renewed identically, they do not change the growth or structure of social accounts.

– Growth investments that have the effect of significantly increasing the growth of the company, the human potential, the quality of products and communication, reduce costs and deadlines, and keep the company's competitive strength.

– Strategic investments that modify the structure of the business, products, production processes and operating modes make profound changes in the financial statements and underpin a strategic shift of diversification, integration or even conglomerate growth.

In France, capital substitution, which is based on a hypothetical high cost of labor, has led companies to make employees redundant to reduce costs, but the revival of productive investments has not been as high as expectations.

Financial investments that have been able to express the strategies of external growth by merger or absorption have often only had speculative and non-productive designs. Anyway, any investment can only come into being in a multi-criteria project that integrates the maximum of parameters.

2.2.4.1.2. Sequential process of an investment

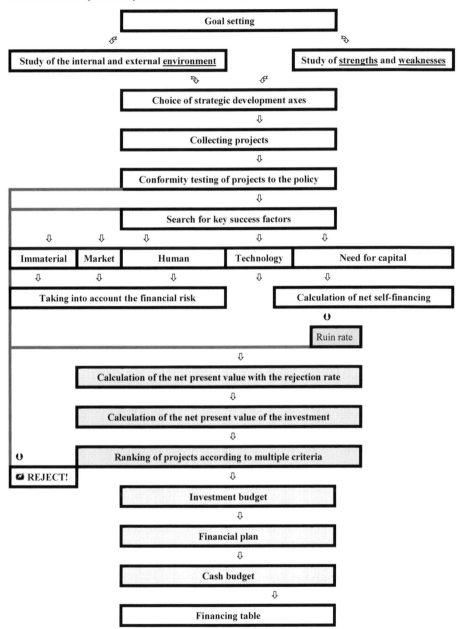

2.2.4.2. Parameters

2.2.4.2.1. Amount invested

The capital invested includes the main and incidental expenses of the investment as well as the flows of variation of the working capital requirement.

– The main expense includes the purchase price of the property, construction and demolition costs, installation and transportation installation costs, study, development, adjustment and commissioning costs.

– The change Δ in working capital requirements is strongly correlated with the growth in activity due to the increase in inventories and receivables. There is nothing to prevent a well-planned investment linked to the distribution of products generating a working capital resource deductible from the capital invested.

– Goods are disposed of if part of the company's assets are allocated to the exclusive use of the investment. The value of the investment must include the value in use of the capitalized asset.

– A new investment can lead to the sale of obsolete assets and the result of the sale should be included in the initial value of the investment.

– Specific external resources are granted for goods such as those involved in the fight against nuisances and the protection of the environment, which provide companies with bonuses and subsidies, in addition to tax advantages which lighten the burden of financial effort.

– The lifetime of the property is often wrong because many factors, including obsolescence, may interfere with the estimate of the property's life. However, it is crucial because the reasons for the strategic investment are halted in a changing environment and readjustments take place. It makes it possible to evaluate the duration of the expected self-financing or net income. Many lifetimes exist. We can use the shorter tax life, but leave the goods at the end of depreciation for a few years of use. The economic life is the longest. The technical lifespan is to be modulated according to the intensity of use and technological progress. In this case, commercial life is linked to the product life curve. Finally, the financial life is limited to the time required for the return on the investment.

– The residual value is included in the investment income. It concerns the sale of the property at the end of the period and the recovery of the increase in the working capital required to maintain the property in the portfolio. Indeed, the good in the final phase does not always have a redeemable value and can even be negative in the case where the destruction requires dismantling costs. As regards the recovery of the working capital requirement, the idea is that once the product range has been stopped, stocks, receivables and trade payables generated by the investment will also cease. This must be taken into account in the last self-financing generated by investments.

2.2.4.2.2. Income streams

Income is difficult to estimate, because the investing company is confronted with an increase in commercial, human production activity, which will be reduced to a simple calculation of turnover in cashable quantities and prices. The revenue forecasts are closely linked to the projected sales budget based on advanced marketing and statistical analyses.

For any new equipment, there is a new cost structure. Therefore,

– the direct costs of materials, direct labor, energy, etc., are quickly quantifiable and a policy of rigor of the prices is a serious help to the forecasting. However, it is not said that new equipment will use the same material, labor, etc., and a drift of charges cannot be excluded;

– indirect expenses includes advertising or promotional expenses to support sales of existing but differently manufactured products, as well as new customer loyalty expenses, reductions, discounts, rebates, cashing, etc.

2.2.4.2.3. Net self-financing

When we balance for each investment the generated income and expenses, we derive, as in any operating account, a generally profitable result. Otherwise, the project would be hard to maintain. The configuration of this account is as follows:

cashable receipts - disbursable expenses = result + calculated expenses - calculated products

In the first approach, the net cash flows are easily updatable and manageable as in a cash flow schedule, and in the second case, despite the mathematical equality, we seem to amalgamate the excess of income generated by the investment and the consumption of this cash flow capital is depreciation.

2.2.4.3. *Project selection*

To make a selection in the investment projects, it is enough to judge their profitability and for that to compare the cost of the investment with the sum of the incomes which it will secrete. This comparison can be done either:

– without discounting, then we proceed to an algebraic sum of expected revenues and expenses during the life of the property.

– with discounting, and reconcile revenues and expenses by period and bring them back to the date of the choice of the investment, taking into account their spreading.

2.2.4.3.1. Method without discounts

– Average rate of profitability:

This criterion is equal to the ratio of the "average profit" on the investment amount. It seems very basic and yet well-used, because it has the advantage of simplicity. It includes data that can be extracted directly from the accounts and allows you to compare projects with identical incomes every year. It can be refined using a more subtle numerator of type GOS net of IS and before Ebitda financial expenses.

The average rate of return can be used in large companies structured as business or profit centers, business units, etc., and where all projects do not emanate from a centralized financial department. They go back to the profit centers and then compare the expected revenues with the amounts of the investments desired by the managers. If the average rate of return is higher than the rate of return on capital employed in the business, then the project is granted, otherwise it is rejected. This makes it possible not to interfere in the management of each center, but to delegate it completely under exclusive control of the average profitability.

EXAMPLE.–

Years	A1	A2	A3	A4	A5
Earnings	-100	50	130	150	200

For an initial investment of 50, the average rate of return is 430/5 = 86.

Therefore, the summary of profitability would be 86/500 = 17.2%.

– Recovery period of invested capital (risk):

It is a criterion based on the time required for the income of an investment to recover the initial investment. In times of crisis and instability, opportunities may be short-lived in some regions and this criterion can be widely demanded for support.

The interest and the profitability of the project are ignored by this method. This is in fact a delay different from that required for financial profitability and less than the period of economic viability. This criterion applies quite well to technological projects that become obsolete before the end of the economic period, Start ups...

ANALYSIS.– However, this criterion is not very effective in the case of a choice between projects of unequal duration. Between a five-year investment that recovers capital after three years, and a ten-year project that recovers capital after five years, we cannot seriously choose between 3/5 and 5/10.

EXAMPLE.– For an investment of 100:

Years	A1	A2	A3	A4	A5
Earnings	20	30	40	50	10
Accumulation	20	50	90	140	150

The recovery time is 3 years (90) + $\frac{(100-90)12}{140-90}$ = 3 years 2 months and 2 weeks

We see how these criteria remain incompatible with a search for profitability, and only risk matters.

EXAMPLE.– For an investment of 100:

Years	A1	A2	A3	A4	A5	A6
Investment 1	20	40	80	20	0	0
Investment 2	20	20	40	80	80	70

According to this criterion of risk, it is preferable at I2, I1 >> I2 because the initial investment of 100 is recovered more quickly, while I2 will secrete another one and a half times the capital in two years (profitability).

2.2.4.3.2. Discounted method

REMINDERS.– Capitalization consists of pushing all these values back to the final date.

Discounting is to reduce to the current day of the decision a sum of future values.

EXAMPLE.– with C = capital, i = interest, A = annuities

Capitalization

A1= C+iC = **C(1+i)** = Capital + interest at the end of year 1

A2= C(1+i) + i[C(1+i)] = (1+i) (C+iC) = (1+i) (1+i) C = **C(1+i)** ^{2} = Capital + interest at the end of year 2

An = $\boxed{C(1+i)^n}$ Capital + interest at the end of year n

A1 = 6%	Rate
A2 = 15	Number of refunds
A3 = -300	Payment value
A4 = -600	Current value
A5 = 1	= beginning of period
5 331 =	Future value with the Excel® formula = VC (A1/12; A2; A3; A4; A5)

Actualization

With actualization, it is the opposite, at the end of the year:

1) $C(1+i)$ brought back at the beginning of year 1 becomes: $C/1+i$ ou $C(1+i)^{-1}$

2) $C(1+i)^2$ brought back at the beginning of year 1 becomes: $C/(1+i)^2$ ou $C(1+i)^{-2}$

...n: $C(1+i)^n$ brought back to the beginning of year 1 becomes: $C/(1+i)n = C(1+i)^{-n}$

If the capitalization is done using discount rates that vary because of rates, inflation, exchange, markets, etc.:

the capitalization $C/(1+i)^2$ becomes $C/(1+i) + (1+i_2) + ...(1+i^n)$

EXAMPLE.– Cell:

A1 = 1851	Amount
A2 = 8%	Rate
A3 = 8	Years

A4 =A1*POWER (1+A2; -A3) = 1.000 or

A5 =VA (A2; A3; A1) = 1.000

Monthly income:

A2	100	Monthly income
A3	10%	Rate
A4	10	Years
A5	-7567,12*	Current value of Investment

*=VA (A3/12; A4*12; A2;0)

– Inflation and other monetary drifts:

There is a case where, indeed, it seems that to the discount rate chosen, we must add another rate, that of inflation and other derivatives. This assumes that rate i does not take all of these factors into account.

– Constant prices:

Future revenues can be discounted, not in value, but in volume or constant prices, which will result in choosing a deflated discount rate id such as $1+id = (1+i)/(1+d)$.

Basically, this inflation rate d would depend more on how the project is financed than on the price index. If internal resources are subject to price drift and penalize the company, repayments of external resources in current currency benefit the company in case of inflation.

– Period of time less than one year:

So i annual becomes all the weaker as the period in months m is short, so:

$C(1+i)^n$ becomes $C(1+i/m)$ at the end of a year and at the end of n years, $C(1+i)^n$ becomes $C(1+i/m)^{n.m}$

If the division of the year is so large that the variable becomes almost continuous, then $C(1+i/\infty)_{n\infty} = C \cdot e^i$ (exponential) for the update.

This method corrects the assumption of discounting at the annual rate where income flows reach the end of the period.

These discounting techniques are well understood and many financial products such as stock savings plans, life insurance, etc. encourage potential investors to lock into long-term funds (of 8 years). In other words, we deprive ourselves in this case of any opportunity during this period. The longer the duration, the higher the risk, and the higher the risk premium must be to offset the attraction for liquidity.

In practice, projects are still suitable, even if they are no longer financially viable. This stems from the fact that it is necessary to dissociate, on the one hand, the financial profitability and the actuarial calculation and, on the other hand, the productivity of the investment once it is integrated into the enterprise. A financial return will only be corroborated if the investment generates economic productivity gains. Any sub-activity resulting from this investment is an added cost to be deducted from the discounted income.

– Other difficulties may appear:

- If the investment takes place over a long period of time, it is unrealistic to properly forecast income streams over 15 years and to choose a serious discount rate.

- Some projects that require extremely large real estate investments cannot be linked to their operating account because of the disproportion between the flow of operations and the level of capital employed. For example, there is no common measure between an investment budget for a nuclear site and the annual operating budget.

Whatever the bias of each analysis, by using the same method to compare similar projects, it can be concluded that the biases introduced largely offset each other and that the ranking between each project is permitted.

The criteria for choosing investments has a more ordinal than cardinal virtue, without the latter being negligible.

Updated payback period (UPP)

This method consists of discounting the investment for which disbursements and income generated by the investment can be spread over several periods. This allows for this criterion based on the urgency of the recovery of funds, a financial dimension from the discount rate chosen. Thus, it can be much more in line with the rate policy chosen by the company, while maintaining its preference for liquidity and not profitability.

Net present value (NPV)

The question is whether the amount of the investment is less than the sum of the discounted income it is secreting. This positive or negative difference is called the NPV. We consider that the discount rate has already been chosen and that the Excel ® function or the reading of the financial tables gives the result.

The update does not compare two projects, it only compares a capital today and the capital in the future, so the NPV can be comparable, not the projects. The procedure for calculating the NPV is as follows: once the discount rate, the amount of the capital invested and the duration of the financial profitability of the project have been determined, we calculate:

– the sum of discounted net revenues. We note that if the average incomes are identical each year, for a given rate we have $R_n(1+i)^{-n} = R[1-(1+i)^{-n}] / i$, which allows a simple use of the function financial a single reading in the table and simplifies the calculation. We often talk about a financial table, while many calculators can find these calculations at the touch of a button;

– the NPV of the project = $[\Sigma R_n(1+i)^{-n}] - I$ or $\{R [1-(1+i)^{-n}]/i\} - I$

The NPVs of each project are compared with each other. According to this criterion, the most profitable project is the one with the highest NPV.

EXAMPLE.– A computer acquisition project for 300 with a 100 BFR increase. The goods are depreciable in five years, and technically will be worth nothing after this period and will be at the end of warranty. The net income from this project is estimated at the amount of the investment each year, given the increase in service activity and a reduction in staff. What is the NPV of the project for a return on capital rate fixed at 10%?

Actualization 10%: invested capital 300 + 100 = 400

Project income: result = 300 - Amortization = 60 = (300 × 20%) = income before tax = €240 k

Tax 33% × €240 k = €80 k → net revenue = €160 k

Self-financing, cash flows or annual revenues:

Years	A1	A2	A3	A4	A5
Revenues	160	160	160	160	160
Amortization	60	60	60	60	60
Recovery of BFR					100
Self-financing	220	220	220	220	320

Self-financing, cash flows, or annual revenues discounted at 10%:

Years	A1	A2	A3	A4	A5
Self-financing	220	220	220	220	320
Update at 10%*	0.91	0.83	0.75	0.68	0.62
Total = 896	200	183	165	150	198

* *Reading of the update table at 10%*

n	7%	8%	9%	10 %	12%
1	0.934 580	0.925 926	0.917 431	0.909 091	0.892 857
2	0.873 439	0.857 339	0.841 680	0.826 446	0.797 194
3	0.816 298	0.793 832	0.772 183	0.751 315	0.711 780
4	0.762 895	0.735 030	0.708 425	0.683 013	0.635 518
5	0.712 986	0.680 583	0.649 931	0.620 921	0.567 427

etc.

- NPV = 896 - 400 = €496 k

This NPV is higher than the cost of the initial project and shows that the project remains valid even with a profitability of 10%.

The calculation of the NPV shows that the plan to invest 400 at 10% makes it possible to secrete each year, flows with a discounted sum greater than 400, but on the condition that self-financing is reused at a rate of 10%. Suppose that each year we reinvest inside the company or outside at a different rate, the NPV will automatically no longer be the same. Since the purpose of the NPV is not to determine the rate, we cannot blame them for confirming if NPV = 0. However, at the limit, a slightly positive NPV may become slightly negative with different reinvestment assumptions.

EXAMPLE.– Suppose that two projects P1 and P2 give:

$NPV1 = -100 + 20(1.15)^{-1} + 20(1.15)^{-2} + 120(1.15)^{-3} = 11.4$

$NPV2 = -100 + 70(1.15)^{-1} + 35(1.15)^{-2} + 30(1.15)^{-3} = 7$

PROGNOSIS.– Are you going to choose P1 because NPV1 > NPV2, while capital recovery is different? Should P1 be preferred to P2 because the final bonus is different?

In fact, the stability of the rate makes this conventional NPV only a special case of an integrated NPV where the reinvestment rates are variable.

Suppose a project has a deficit in the first year, it would have had to integrate the fact that they reduce the taxable profits.

Finally, the NPV does not manage incomplete alternatives, which is why, in the case of a project with a different duration, the support of the recovery period is desirable.

Constant annuity method

A sum of identical incomes simplifies the calculations since $(1+i)^{-1} + ... + (1+i)^{-n} = [1-(1+i)^{-n}]/i$ we will seek to transform into a constant annuity disbursed capital and income.

EXAMPLE.– An investment of 100 has an economic life of 5 years. After 3 years, it is given to acquire new equipment. The capital consumption of each year is equal to 40% the 1st year, 45% the 2nd year and 15% the 3rd year. The expenses are 24% the 1st year, 30% the 2nd year and 40% the 3rd year. What would be the equivalent amount to be disbursed for 3 years at 10%?

Years	A0	A1	A2	A3
Value	100	(1-40%) 60	27	4
Expense		24	30	40
Cost	100	84	57	44
Update at 10%		0.91	0.83	0.75
Discounted cost*	100	76.4	47.3	33
Accrued		76.4	123.7	156.7

We are trying to determine the amount of a constant payment each year that would give the same cumulative cost.

Let $C [1-(1.1)^{-3}]/10\% = 0.4C = 156.7 \Rightarrow C = 390$

Therefore, it is equivalent to disburse 390 for three years at 10%. This equivalence is seen in car advertisements that are offered with either monthly payments or a total to pay in cash.

IP profitability index

This presentation of NPV calculation is used to compare investments of very different amounts. In this case, flows have relative values only in terms of percentage.

With $\frac{NPV}{I}$ the unit margin of the investment

and as NPV = VA - I,

then $\frac{IP}{I} = \frac{NPV+I}{I} = 1 + \frac{NPV}{I}$

EXAMPLE.–

Years	A1	A2	A3	A4	A5
Revenues	40	40	20	20	15
Update at 10%	0.91	0.83	0.75	0.68	0.62
Total discounted income 107	36	33	15	14	9

Two P1 projects of 100 and P2 of 2000 with the following schedule:

IP1 = 107/100 = 1.07 → $\frac{NPV}{I} = 7\%$

Years	A1	A2	A3	A4
Revenues	400	600	1020	800
Update at 10%	0.91	0.83	0.75	0.68
Total revenue updated 2170	364	498	765	544

Then IP2 = 2171/2000 = 1.085 → $\frac{NPV}{I}$ = 8.5%

IP2 is preferable to IP1 according to this criterion, whereas the projects were not comparable at the beginning.

If IP > 1 then the NPV is positive.

Internal rate of return (IRR)

The problem is similar to that of the retail NPV that o does not fix i, we must look for the rate that balances the investment and its discounted income, so $I = \Sigma C(1 + i)^{-n}$ or NPV = 0

The NPV decreases with the increase in the rate I. This rate for which NPV = 0 is called the break-even point of the project or IRR (IRR in the Excel® function which calculates it automatically.)

EXAMPLE.– If a 2000 investment gives a residual value of 1% after 5 years, the net income is substantially constant and equal to a quarter of the investment. From what rate is this project profitable under this criterion?

We test:

1) first a base rate, e.g. 8%. Thus, 2000/4 [1- (1.08) -5 / 8%] + 2000/100 = 2011. So, this project is acceptable at 8%;

2) then with a different rate. It will not be necessary to choose this second rate so that the IRR is between the two rates. With 10%, this gives 500 [1-(1.1)$^{-5}$/10%] + 20 = 1908 < 2000. This project is not receivable at 10%.

To compute I accurately in the Excel® function that calculates it automatically, we use the linear interpolation, we calculate I by the following growth ratio:

$\frac{i1-i0}{I1-I0} = \frac{i-i0}{I-I0}$ let $\frac{10\%-8\%}{1908-2011} = \frac{i-8\%}{2000-2011}$ → i = 8.23%

The internal rate of return of the project is exactly 8.23%; however, it may seem very surprising to calculate it with extreme precision, whereas the model includes lax assumptions about the constancy of the rates, the reinvestment of the incomes, the approximate durations, a comparable capital that remains as complete alternatives. If these hypotheses are not all confirmed at the same time, the incomplete alternatives are taken into account in the integration method.

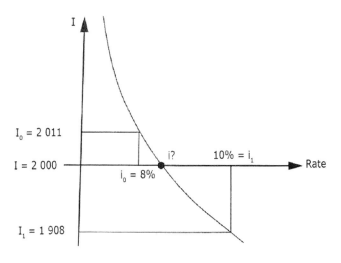

Figure 2.2.

Integration

Here, we are dealing with the case of disproportionate capital and dissimilar durations.

– Excessively invested capital

Let there be two 10% projects P1 and P2.

P1 = 1000:

Years	A1	A2	A3	A4	NPV	IRR	IP
Revenues	400	500	300	300			
10% discount	0.91	0.83	0.75	0.68			
Σ discounted revenue 1208	364	415	225	204	208	19%	21%

P2 = 500:

Years	A1	A2	A3	A4	NPV	IRR	IP
Revenues	250	250	150	125			
10% discount	0.91	0.83	0.75	0.68			
Σ discounted revenue 634	228	208	113	85	**134**	**21%**	**27%**

Let us test these projects at 16%:

P1	A1	A2	A3	A4
Revenues	400	500	300	300
16% discount	0.86	0.74	0.64	0.55
Total discounted revenue 1070	344	370	191	165

P2	A1	A2	A3	A4
Revenues	250	250	150	125
16% discount	0.86	0.74	0.64	0.55
Total discounted revenue 565	215	185	96	69

Let us confirm:

$$IRR1 = \frac{i1-i0}{I1-I0} = \frac{i-i0}{I-I0} \text{ let } \frac{16\%-10\%}{1070-1208} = \frac{i-10\%}{1000-1208} \rightarrow i = 19.1\%$$

IRR2 = ... = 21.2%

Similarly, for $IP = \frac{NPV}{I}$

$IP1 = \frac{208}{1000} = 20.8\%$

$IP2 = \frac{134}{500} = 26.8\%$

Criteria	NPV	IRR	IP
Comparison	P1>P2	P2>P1	P2>P1

In fact, none of these criteria is a panacea, because if:

– NPV 1 > NPV 2 of 208-134 = 64, it is not known that this bonus of 64 forces the company to invest 1000-500 = 500 more.

– IRR 2 > IRR 1, this means that we should prefer to win 21% out of 500, rather than 19% out of 1000. If we have to decide in this case, we have to imagine the differential flow of invested capital of 500.

This differential flow will have only one NPV and one TIR and will determine whether it is appropriate to invest this difference. If yes, we invest P2 and not P1.

P1 - P2 = 500

Years	A1	A2	A3	A4
Revenues P1	400	500	300	300
Revenues P2	250	250	150	125
Δ revenues	150	250	150	175
10% discount	0.91	0.83	0.75	0.68
Total discounted revenue 576	137	208	113	119

Excel® function = NPV (10%;150;250;150;175) = 575,20 # 576

- NPV = 576 - 500 = +76

Years	A1	A2	A3	A4
Δ revenues	150	250	150	175
16% discount	0.86	0.74	0.64	0.55
Total discounted revenue 480	129	185	96	69

NPV = 480 - 500 = -20

$$IRR = \frac{16\% - 10\%}{480 - 580} = \frac{i - 10\%}{500 - 580} \rightarrow i = 16.8\%$$

Or Excel® function = IRR (150;250;150;175) = 16.78%

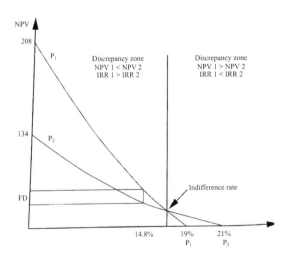

Figure 2.3.

Therefore, this differential investment is profitable at 16.8%, which is higher than the P1 discount rate. Therefore, you have to invest P2. However, we do not obtain maximum satisfaction, because the additional cost that is asked of the company, which would pass from the initial project cheaper, to another which would be more expensive, moreover supports all the criticisms already made on the relevance of this criterion single project.

– *Dissimilar durations*

An example was presented of projects with unequal duration. Among the possible solutions, some recommend repeating the shortest and longest projects n times to find a multiple delay. However, for two 5 and 7-year projects, it should be measured over 35 years and what are the interest rates, discount rates, revenues and expenses, not to mention the technology...? It is not conceivable economically, although it is still possible mathematically. The only solution for these projects before dissociating them completely is to try a study no longer on the main one, but on the opportunities for reinvestment of the income secreted until the end of the longest project.

– *Internal rate of return*

As the already seen NPV and IRR are characteristics of the integrated VANI NPV and the TIRI integrated internal rate of return, this method involves capitalizing the flows at a different rate corresponding to the reinvestment rate, then calculating the IRR that cancels the capitalized value.

EXAMPLE.– A project of 200 to 15% which would have investments considering the fall of the rates to 12%:

Capitalized values	n	10 %	12%	15 %
Value from	1	1,100 000	1,120 000	1,150 000
1 to the end	2	1,210 000	1,254 400	1,322 500
n periods	3	1,332 000	1,404 928	1,520 875
	4	1,464 100	1,574 100	1,749 006
	5	1,610 510	1,762 342	2,011 357

	A1	A2	A3	A4
Revenues	126	121	80	25
Capitalization at 12%	1.12	1.25	1.40	1.57
Total capitalized revenue = 444	141	151	112	40

$$TIRI = (1+i)^4 = 444/200 = 2.22 \Rightarrow i = -1 + \sqrt[4]{2.2} = 21.8\%$$ where

Excel® Function, = POWER (2,2;1/4) = 1.21788

– *Integrated net present value (INPV)*

It must be discounted at the rate used, e.g. 15%.

Present value of 1 at the end of n periods:

n	7%	8%	9%	10%	12%	15%
1	0.934 580	0.925	0.917	0.909 091	0.892 857	0.869 565
2	0.873 439	0.857	0.841	0.826 446	0.797 194	0.756 144
3	0.816 298	0.793	0.772	0.751 315	0.711 780	0.657 516
4	0.762 895	0.735	0.708	0.683 013	0.635 518	0.571 753
5	0.712 986	0.680	0.649	0.620 921	0.567 427	0.497 177

Let VANI = -200 + 444 x 0,57 ... = 53

2.2.5. *Random analysis*

We consider that certain investment parameters are variables.

REMINDER.–

The probability that an event noted $(X = x_i)$ is realized and is the number $P(X = x_i)$ with $P(X = x_i) \in [0\,;1]$.

Two random variables X and Y are said to be independent if:

$P((X = x) \cap (Y = y)) = P(X = x) \times P(Y = y)$

Arithmetic Average

Formulation:

Principles

$\overline{ax} = a\,\overline{x}$

$\overline{ax + b} = a\,\overline{x} + b$

$\overline{x + y} = \overline{x} + \overline{y}$

Covariance
Formulation:

Mathematical Expectation

Formulation

$\boxed{E(X) = \Sigma\, x_i \times P(X = xi)}$

Principles

$E(aX) = a\,E(X)$

$E(aX+b) = a\,E(X) + b$

$E(X + Y) = E(X) + E(Y)$

Covariance
Formulation:

$\boxed{Cov(X,Y) = E\left[(X - E(X))(Y - E(Y))\right]}$

$\boxed{Cov(X,Y) = E(XY) - E(X)E(Y)}$

Variance
Formulation

Variance
Formulation

$V(X) = E\left[(X - E(X))^2\right] = E(X^2) - E(X)^2$

$\boxed{V(X) = \Sigma\, x_i^2\, P(X = xi) - E(X)^2}$

Common principles:

$V(aX) = a^2 V(X)$
$V(aX+b) = a^2 V(X)$
If X and Y are independent, then: $V(X + Y) = V(X) + V(Y) = V(X-Y)$
General principle:

$V(X+Y) = V(X) + V(Y) + 2\,cov.(X, Y)$
$V(X-Y) = V(X) + V(Y) - 2\,cov.(X, Y)$

Standard deviation

Formulation: $\boxed{\sigma(X) = \sqrt{V(X)}}$

Common principles

$\sigma(aX) = |a|\,\sigma(X)$
$\sigma(aX+b) = |a|\,\sigma(X)$

2.2.5.1. *Without risk or discount*

Let x1 ... xn, be the values that can take a variable with p1...pn the associated variabilities.

The mean is equal to (x1 +x2+...xn)/ n

The weighted average or mathematical expectation is equal to E(x)=Spi xi

For example, we have the choice between two projects:

	A1	A2	A3
Revenues	200	400	600
Probability	25%	50%	25%
	50	200	150

I1 = 400

	A1	A2
Revenues	200	600
Probability	60%	40%
	120	240

I2 = 360

So I1 seems preferable to I2, I1 >> I2

2.2.5.2. *Without risk but with discount*

Two projects of the same value give the following revenues:

I1 is A1 =30 and A2 =20 with a probability of a half

Let A1 =20 and A2 = 40 with a probability of a half

I2 is A1 =60 and A2 =20 with a probability of a quarter

let A1 =10 and A2 = 20 with a probability of three quarters

The preferable investment at the rate of 10% is:

Present value of €1k at the end of n periods

n	7%	8%	9%	10%	12%	15%
1	0.934 580	0.925	0.917	0.909 091	0.892 857	0.869 565
2	0.873 439	0.857	0.841	0.826 446	0.797 194	0.756 144
3	0.816 298	0.793	0.772	0.751 315	0.711 780	0.657 516
4	0.762 895	0.735	0.708	0.683 013	0.635 518	0.571 753
5	0.712 986	0.680	0.649	0.620 921	0.567 427	0.497 177

	A1	A2
Revenues	30	20
Probability	50%	50%
10% Discount	0.909091	0.826446
	13.636365	8.26446

E1 = 21.9

	A1	A2
Revenues	20	40
Probability	50%	50%
10% Discount	0.909091	0.826446
	9.09091	16.52892

E1 = 25.62

Mathematical Expectation of I1 = 47.5

	A1	A2
Revenues	60	20
Probability	25%	75%
10% Discount	0.909091	0.826446
	13.636365	12.39669

E2 = 26.03

	A1	A2
Revenues	10	20
Probability	25%	75%
10% Discount	0.909091	0.826446
	2.2727275	12.39669

E2 = 14.67

Mathematical Expectation I2 = E2 = 40.70

So I1 seems preferable to I2, I1 >> I2

2.2.5.3. Expectation limit

2.2.5.3.1. Expectations of earnings with probability of loss

For example, if I1 has as revenue A1 = -5 with a probability of 80%, A2 = 0 with a 10% probability and A3 = 100 with a 10% probability, and I2 has an income of 5 with certainty, the expectation of gains of I1 = -5 × 80% -0 × 10% + 100 × 10% = 6

	A1	A2	A3	
Revenues	-5	0	100	
Probability	80%	10%	10%	
10% Discount	0.909091	0.826446	0.751315	
	-3.636364	0	7.51315	= 3.88
	A1	A2	A3	
Revenues	5	0	0	
Probability	80%	10%	10%	
10% Discount	0.909091	0.826446	0.751315	
	3.636364	0	0	= 3.64

Therefore, I1 seems preferable to I2, whereas with I2 we have a certainty of gains of 5 but with I1 a virtual certainty of loss during 2 years and a low probability of gains that are more risky in 3 years.

2.2.5.3.2. Expectations of earnings and financial ruin threshold

Risk can always be limited by setting a threshold below which the expected result is unacceptable. This threshold is an indicator of risk aversion for the investor. Any value falling below this threshold is considered ruinous.

For example, an investment provides income whose probability distribution follows a Normal law of expectation 23 and standard deviation 3. If we judge the situation of bankruptcy, the probability of reaching this threshold of bankruptcy is:

P(bankruptcy) < 20 = P(bankruptcy < 20) ⇔ P (R) < 20 = P(R < 20)

Since the centered and reduced Normal law indicates that $t = (x-m)/\sigma$, then $(X-m)/\sigma = (X-23)/3$ so:

Reduced centered law table:

X	↓0.00	0.01	0.02	0.03	0.04	0.05	0.06	0.07	0.08	0.09
0.0	0.5000	0.5040	0.5080	0.5120	0.5160	0.5199	0.5239	0.5279	0.5319	0.5359
0.1	0.5398	0.5438	0.5478	0.5517	0.5557	0.5596	0.5636	0.5675	0.5714	0.5753
0.2	0.5793	0.5832	0.5871	0.5910	0.5948	0.5987	0.6026	0.6064	0.6103	0.6141
0.3	0.6179	0.6217	0.6255	0.6293	0.6331	0.6368	0.6406	0.6443	0.6480	0.6517
0.4	0.6554	0.6591	0.6628	0.6664	0.6700	0.6736	0.6772	0.6808	0.6844	0.6879
0.5	0.6915	0.6950	0.6985	0.7019	0.7054	0.7088	0.7123	0.7157	0.7190	0.7224
0.6	0.7257	0.7291	0.7324	0.7357	0.7389	0.7422	0.7454	0.7486	0.7517	0.7549
0.7	0.7580	0.7611	0.7642	0.7673	0.7704	0.7734	0.7764	0.7794	0.7823	0.7852
0.8	0.7881	0.7910	0.7939	0.7967	0.7995	0.8023	0.8051	0.8078	0.8106	0.8133
0.9	0.8159	0.8186	0.8212	0.8238	0.8264	0.8289	0.8315	0.8340	0.8365	0.8389
⇨1	**0.8413**	0.8438	0.8461	0.8485	0.8508	0.8531	0.8554	0.8577	0.8599	0.8621

$P\{t £ (X-23)/3\} = P(t £ -1) = P(t>1) = 1 - 0.8413 = 15.87\%$

Therefore, there is about 16% chance or 1 out of 6 chances for the investor to be ruined. However, the degree of acceptability of a small loss is related to the degree of having high earnings.

2.2.5.4. Considering the risk

A risk measure is the assessment of the dispersion of the possible outcomes around the mean. The variance of the probabilities of a discrete variable is equal to $V(x) = \Sigma Pi\,[x-E(x)]^2$ and the standard deviation $\sigma = \sqrt{V(x)}$

I1	A1	A2	A3	
Revenues	20	50	80	
Probability	25%	50%	25%	
	5	25	20	E (I1) = 50

I2	A1	A2	A3	
Revenue	40	45	50	
Probability	25%	50%	25%	
	10	22,5	12,5	E (I2) = 45

By the formula	X	- E(I1)	X-E(X)	[X-E(X)]²	x P(x)	I1
	20	-50	-30	900	x 25%	225
	50	-50	0	0	X 50%	0
	80	-50	30	900	X 25%	225
				Variance of I1		**450**

By the formula	X	- E(I2)	X-E(X)	[X-E(X)]²	x P(x)	I1
	40	-45	-5	25	x 25%	6,25
	45	-45	0	0	50%	0
	50	-45	5	25	25%	6,25
				Variance of I2		**12,5**

so, $E(I1) > E(I2)$ and $\sigma^2(I1) > \sigma^2(I2)$ → I2 is preferred to I1 ⇔ I1>>I2

We can say that by associating the mathematical expectation E(x), which is representative of the expected profitability, and the standard deviation σ(x), that of the risk, we circumscribe the problem of any decision-maker, reducing the risk of which he has an aversion and increasing the profitability that he seeks.

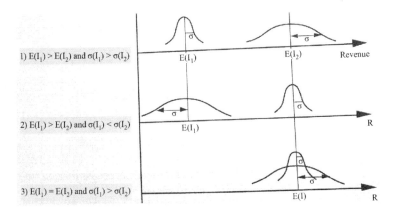

Figure 2.4.

All combinations of variation between expectancy and variance may exist as was the case for NPV and TIR. If the variance and the standard deviation are the same for two investments, they are not necessarily equivalent.

Let us assume identical incomes for two investments, and different probabilities:

I1	A1	A2	A3	A4	A5		
Revenues	20	60	100	140	180		
Probability	0%	30%	45%	20%	5%		
	0	18	45	28	9	100	E(I1)

I2	A1	A2	A3	A4	A5		
Probability	5%	20%	45%	30%	0%		
	1	12	45	42	0	100	E(I2)

Formulation	X	- E(X)	=	$(X-E(X))^2$	X P(x)	I1	
	20	-100	-80	6400	x 0%	0	
	60	-100	-40	1600	x 30%	480	
	100	-100	0	0	x 45%	0	
	140	-100	40	1600	x 20%	320	
	180	-100	80	6400	x 5%	320	
						1120	σ (I1)

Formulation	X	- E(X)	=	Square	x P(x)	I1	
	20	-100	-80	6400	x 5%	320	
	60	-100	-40	1600	x 20%	320	
	100	-100	0	0	x 45%	0	
	140	-100	40	1600	x 30%	480	
	180	-100	80	6400	x 0%	0	
						1120	σ (I2)

If we look at the curves of these two investments, we realize that despite everything, they are not equivalent. Curve 2 is obviously more risky than curve 1, because by tilting to the right, it presents a higher risk of lower earnings. However, this asymmetry cannot be measured by expected profitability or standard risk. For this purpose, it is necessary to calculate the semi variance which is a calculation of variance limited to the expectation.

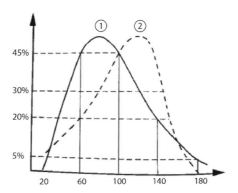

Figure 2.5.

Formulation	X	- E(X)	=	Square	P(x)	I1
	20	-100	-80	6400	x 0%	0
	60	-100	-40	1600	x 30%	480
						480 1/2σ² (I1)

Formulation	X	- E(X)	=	Square	P(x)	I1
	20	-100	-80	6400	x 5%	320
	60	-100	-40	1600	x 20%	320
						640 1/2σ² (I2)

I2 is riskier than I1, because its semi-variance is greater. Finally, let us note that the expectation of income of year n is equal to $E(x_n)$ and the variance $v(x_n)$, so:

The actual value of $E(x_n) = E[x_n(1+i)^{-n}] = (1+i)^{-n} E(x_n)$

and of $V(x_n) = V[x_n(1+i)^{-n}] = (1+I)^{-2n} V(x_n)$

Thus, the expectation of the present value of the incomes is equal to the present value of the expectations, but the variance of the present value of the incomes is not equal to the variance of the incomes at $(1+I)^{-2n}$.

However, these expectations and income variances cannot really be calculated because they are rarely independent. Indeed, when two events are independent, the probability of 2 does not pose any problems. P (A if B) = P (A) and P (B) if A = P (B) but, if the events are related P (A if B) = P(A) x P (B if A) = P(B) x P (A if B).

Given the lack of legibility of the geopolitical future, an organization must choose between two projects based on growth assumptions.

2.2.5.5. *The decision tree*

This is a network of probability occurrence when the investor is confronted with multiple and sequential decisions.

METHOD.– We indicate the alternatives or decisional nodes by squares, and the event nodes by circles.

EXAMPLE.– For a cost of capital of 10%, an investor must choose between two projects over 4 years, according to two possible future states:

E1: the activity will remain stable or will increase slightly (probability 0.6)

E2: the activity will regress (probability 0.4)

PROJECT 1.– Investment I1:

Date 0: of 6 000

Date 1: extension of the investment of 3 000 if E1

– Estimated cash flows

  - End of the 1st year 2000

  - Following:

    – If extension: 3 500 if E1 and 3 000 if E2

    – If not, 2 300 if E1 and 2 000 if E2

• If, at the date 1, E1 is not verified, expected annual cash flows of 2000

PROJECT 2.– Investment I2:

– Total at start of 8 000

– Potential annual cash flows of 2800 if E1 is confirmed or 2500 if E2 is confirmed

PROJECT 3.– Renunciation of any investment:

Should the investor achieve the extension according to the criterion E(NPV)?

0		1		...		4
					E1 60%	CF 3500
				Ext. 3000		
		E1 60%	D2		E2 40%	CF 3000
			CF 2000			
					E1 60%	CF 2300
I1	6000			Non-ext. 0		
					E2 40%	CF 2000
		E2 40%				CF 2000
		E1 60%				CF 2800
I2	8000					
		E2 40%				CF 2500

If extension

NPV at 10% over 3 years of 3500	€8, 704	x E1 60%	= 5 222
NPV at 10% over 3 years of 3000	€7, 461	x E2 40%	= 2 984
			= 8 207
			-Ext. 3000
		E(NPV)	**= 5 207**

If there is no extension

NPV at 10% over 3 years of 2300	€5, 720	x E1 60%	= 3 432
NPV at 10% over 3 years of 2000	€4, 974	x E2 40%	= 1 989
			= 5 421
			Ext. 0
		E(NPV)	**= 5 421**

According to the criterion of E(NPV) the investor should give up the extension.

The amount of the investment should amount to how much?

$$E(VAN_{I1}) = \{[(5421 + 2000) \times (1.1)\text{-}1 \times 60\%] + [2000 \times \frac{[1-(1.1)^{-4}]}{0.1} \times 40\%]\}$$
$$- \{6000\} = \textbf{584}$$

$$I2 = 8000 \rightarrow E(VAN_{I2}) = \{[2800 \times \frac{[1-(1.1)^{-4}]}{0.1} \times 60\%] +$$
$$[2500 \times \frac{[1-(1.1)^{-4}]}{0.1} \times 40\%]\} - \{8000\} = \textbf{495}$$

$$I3 = 0, \rightarrow E(VAN_{I3}) = 0$$

CONCLUSION.– According to the criterion of the mathematical expectation of the NPV, one must invest 6000 without extension in D1.

2.2.6. Undetermined analysis

This kind of situation arises when it is not possible to determine the vision of the future. We cannot extrapolate from the past.

The problem is knowing how to behave rationally in the face of a future in absolute ignorance. Two attitudes are possible depending on an indeterminate future in which the opportunities and threats are real but illegible.

2.2.6.1. Uncertainty

It is necessary to list the different states of the conjuncture and to associate, if possible, these occurrences with a probability of realization, intuitively or objectively. You can invest in a PEA for 8 years or in life insurance, or even for the purchase of a property with an estimate of the probability of not needing fixed amounts.

EXAMPLE.– A company wants to invest in a southern country whose economic and financial policy remains unstable. After a study of the possibilities offered, we consider five possible investments I1 to I5, taking into account the estimations of four scenarios. Based on these investments and these occurrences, the company hopes for the revenues presented in the following table.

Possible income from investments:

Projects	E 1	E 2	E 3	E 4	Business conditions
P 1	50	40	25	60	
P 2	30	55	20	35	
P 3	60	35	40	45	
P 4	25	65	10	30	
P 5	55	45	20	15	

2.2.6.1.1. Optimistic criterion or MaMa

This concerns maximizing the maximum income. This criterion that maximizes profitability also necessarily maximizes risk. This criterion would be justified in the case of a short investment such as for start-up companies, or speculative on the stock market.

In the example, given the conjunctural assumptions, the maximum income with the function = MAX (__:__), then with the function = MAX (__:__) again with these results we determine the highest.

P 1	60
P 2	55
P 3	60
P 4	**65**
P 5	55

However, if a loss of -1000 was in E4, e.g. P4 would have been chosen anyway. This criterion is therefore to be used with vigilance because, by choosing P4, we could have chosen the only investment that would have entailed a high risk of loss.

2.2.6.1.2. Pessimistic criterion or MAmi

The Wald criterion is more reasonable because among the investments that provide the minimum income, the Maximum minimum earnings (Mn) is chosen.

Therefore, the minimum income with the function = MIN (__:__) then with the function = MAX (__:__) we determine the highest.

P 1	25
P 2	20
P 3	**35**
P 4	10
P 5	15

This criterion is particularly suited to our problem where the environment can be ruinous for the investor. Apart from these unstable situations, it would be surprising to choose P3 in any case, according to this criterion instead of having for P1 50, 40, 25 and 60, we had 500, 400, 25 and 600, and this would lead to deprive ourselves of all high hope of very high profitability.

2.2.6.1.3. Laplace or Mamo Criterion

As we have no information, we can imagine that the forecasts made are not whimsical, but that all the economic conditions are all as likely to happen. It would be worth considering the average income of each investment and to retain the Maximum of the Mamo averages.

Let:

E(I1) =1/4x50+1/4x40+1/4x25+1/4x60=1/4x175=44

Where with the function = AVERAGE (__:__) the averages are obtained and then with the function = MAX (__:__) the maximum is determined.

P 1	44
P 2	35
P 3	**45**
P 4	33
P 5	34

Therefore, we choose P3 because, essentially, we refuse to decide and we let events decide for us in some way.

2.2.6.1.4. Hurwiecz [αM + (1-α)m] = OM + pm

In this criterion, the decision-maker specifies the probability of seeing the best situations occur and associates the maximum income and the opposite to the minimum income the rest (1-α).

If we think that the states will eventually end local uncertainties and risk areas will quickly move into the consensual movement, we can estimate α at 70%.

αM + (1-α) m

With the Max and min functions for each project, we obtain the extreme numbers. It is enough to weigh them by αM + (1-α) m and we obtain:

70%	α		
	M	m	
P 1	60	25	49.5
P 2	55	20	44.5
P 3	60	35	52.5
P 4	65	10	48.5
P 5	55	15	43

P3 is chosen. It is interesting to know what the degree of freedom of the estimate is that would lead to choosing another investment. For example, if by changing the percentage of the cell to 60% instead of 70%, we get 0.6, is the decision changed? It is a simple but relevant simulation. We can also simulate with the "solver" the limit thresholds according to what is wanted as a result. For example, the threshold is 83%, so P3 and P4 are indifferent.

83%			
17%			
	M	m	
P 1	60	25	54.05
P 2	55	20	49.05
P 3	60	35	55.75
P 4	65	10	55.65
P 5	55	15	48.2

Otherwise, it is enough to equalize the functions:

$P = P3$ if $65\alpha + 10(1+\alpha) = 60\alpha + 35(1-\alpha)$

$65\alpha + 10 - 10\alpha = 60\alpha + 35 - 35\alpha$

$30\alpha => 25 => \alpha = 83\%$

2.2.6.1.5. Savage mMR

Unlike the previous criteria, it is the shortfalls, called Regrets, that will induce the choice. The calculations are no longer done in lines, but in columns where for each economic situation, we will choose the investment that will provide the lowest of the maximum losses to be won, that is the minimum of the Maximum of mMR Regrets.

The approach consists of establishing a regression matrix or a loss of earnings, in which for each column, the highest income of each investment is retained. Then, we calculate the shortfalls, if for each state, we made the wrong investment choice. For E1, the maximum gain is 60 of I3. Therefore, if we had chosen

I1 we would have lost 60-50 = 10

I2 we would have lost 60-30 = 20

I3 we would have lost 60-60 = 0, etc.

For E2, the maximum gain is 65 corresponding to I2, so if we had chosen I1, we would lose 65-40 = 25

I2, we would lose 65-55 = 10

etc.

Matrix of Regrets or loss of profit if:

	E1	E2	E3	E4
I1	60-50 = 10	65-40 = 25	40-25 = 15	60-60 = 0
I2	60-30 = 20	65-55 = 10	40-20 = 20	60-35 = 25
I3	60-60 = 0	65-35 = 30	40-40 = 0	60-45 = 15
I4	60-25 = 35	65-65 = 0	40-10 = 30	60-30 = 30
I5	60-55 = 15	65-45 = 20	40-20 = 20	60-15 = 45

Choice	Max	E1 MR	E2 MR	E3 MR	E4 MR	MMax
P 1	60	10	25	15	0	**25**
P 2	65	30	10	20	25	30
P 3	40	0	30	0	15	30
P 4	60	35	0	30	30	35
P 5		5	20	20	45	45

The minimum of Maximum Regrets = 25 therefore Project P1 could be selected according to this criterion.

We note that, initially, we had no information about the investment to remember in case of projection in an opaque future, but according to these criteria, we would be spoiled for choice. As part of the strategy, the behavior of the external environment is integrated into a model and we try to foresee possible responses according to the adverse strategies.

In fact, it seems unlikely, but is that not how we proceed when we have the choice between going to three different places the same evening; we decide on the choice we would regret the least.

Without discount	Calculation	Advantages	Limitations
Return in investment (ROI)	Reports, in % the average annual income stream generated by the investment to the average amount of capital invested.	Simple to use. Suitable for low value and short life investments.	Ignores: -the cost of time -the flow deadline -the variation of "offsets". Requires the setting of a threshold of acceptability.

With discount	Calculation	Advantages	Limitations
Current Value Net NPV Net income or net discounted CF Net Present Value NPV Net Present Worth (NPW) Discounted Cash Flow (DCF)	The NPV > 0 would be the monetary surplus that the investment would generate from future discounted revenues. It is the contribution of the project to the enrichment of the company (or the project company). Expressed in monetary unit.	Suitable for executives and financial investors seeking the most attractive investments. Ensures possible consistency of view between shareholders and executives.	Depends on the discount rate and how the profit is determined
Profitability index (PI)	Calculates the discounted income from invested monetary unit. Ratio to compare to 1.	Suitable when there are investments of very different amounts.	Sometimes leads to rejecting good projects, requiring a higher amount that would have been retained with the NPV
Internal Rate of Return (IRR) Internal rate of return (IRR) Discounted Cash Flow Rate (DCF rate)	This is the discount rate that cancels the NPV of the investment project.	Reflects only the characteristics of the project.	Suppose that the project flows are reinvested at a rate equal to the IRR (unrealistic assumption when the IRR is very different from the market interest rates). Has economic significance if the NPV is a decreasing function of the discount rate.

3

Analysis of the Financial Structure: IFRS vs. US GAAP

Functional analysis of financial statements focuses on the structure of the balance sheet and the operating cash flows of the income statement. The French Accounting Plan's balance sheet is structured by major functions and international standards according to the order of increasing liquidity (assets) and the liabilities by increasing order (liabilities).

3.1. Major functions of the French Accounting Plan

The financial analysis of the balance sheet is based on the following four functions: financing, investment, exploitation and distribution. IFRS do not follow this structural analysis, but the financial statements of publicly traded companies are often referred to.

Structural analysis studies their proportions in relation to what we are normally entitled to comply with.

Asset and liability are therefore studied by major functions in which the order of payment and liquidity is possible (financing, exploitation).

3.1.1. *Assets*

Wealth items generating resources that a company disposes of for its activity are registered in the French Accounting Plan as either long-term or consumable goods:

– *Goods whose duration exceeds the accounting year* are called immobilized or fixed assets because they are intended to stay permanently in the company. This duration can be either unlimited without these goods depreciating (land on which the buildings are built) or shortened because these goods depreciate in several ways:

- provisions, when the depreciation is reversible (equity securities and other fixed financial assets),

- amortizations, when the depreciation is irreversible. In this case, the depreciable property is intended to be consumed (destroyed) due to multiple reasons:

- their use (consumption entering as an expense in the cost of the activity);

- technological obsolescence (computer equipment);

- time (disutility);

- any other reason.

This destruction of the value of fixed assets by annual depreciation (allocation) is a task that enters the cost price of the products manufactured. Thus, the more the company invests in production assets, the more it amortizes them, the more it has amortization expenses, plus it increases its cost.

But an expense added to the income statement each year (endowment) without being disbursed in the year is tantamount to additional income. Moreover, it diminishes the profit, all the corresponding tax and so on. Thus, each year, the allocations recognized as expenses in the profit and loss account make up a large part of the endogenous resources called "self-financing capacity (CAF)".

– *Consumable goods* that cannot be used without destroying them immediately are therefore consumed by their first use and the company records them in its inventory. This is in the balance sheet of:

- short-term financial investments called "investment securities" and very short-term financial investments or even liquid ones that represent a portion of its cash flow and

- specific assets: claims and fictitious assets.

– The debts are constituted by what the customers owe to the company. It therefore holds a claim on them, which will be turned into cash flow but with a deferred payment.

– Intangible assets are capitalized because the current activity cannot support their very high amount without seriously affecting the result of the year. They are placed with the non-current assets, to be able to sell them little by little in the routine operation. This is why they are considered as fictitious values of the asset. They cannot be said to be of the same nature as other assets.

• *For example, start-up costs are only accrued expenses, but their high amount is spread over several accounting periods, otherwise they would be too high on the income statement if they were deducted at one time.*

Financial study is always carried out from the balance sheet after distribution of the result, which sometimes requires prior work to find the balance sheet before distribution for financial analysis.

3.1.2. *Current liabilities*

Current liabilities only show debts and "obligations toward third parties, for external liabilities and toward shareholders for internal liabilities". All company debts are found there as means of financing assets.

"Net financial debt represents the portion of net interest-bearing debt. It is calculated on the basis of current and non-current borrowings, after the exclusion of non-controlling interest option debt and net of non-controlling interests, availability, short-term investments and derivative instruments – assets"[1].

3.1.2.1. *Certain, Probable and Possible Debts*

Debts can be certain, probable or possible:

– Certain in the short term, because they are established in comparison with:

- operating or non-operating suppliers (capital providers);

- personal and social organizations;

- banks and financial institutions.

– Probable if their amount and maturity are not precisely determined. These are generally provisions for reserves placed in the balance sheet.

– Possible in the medium and long term. They originate from the contributions of successive capital by the shareholders since the creation of the company. They constitute the "net position" of the enterprise composed of share capital; legal, statutory, contractual, and regulated reserves; other reserves; retained earnings; profit for the year and so on. The company must grow these assets and ultimately make them available to all shareholders.

---

1 Danone financial report.

As the mature payment amounts of these debts are known, the company will pay mainly via a cash outflow. In case of difficulty, the company is in cessation of payment. The risk of failure will then have reached its maximum level.

- This is why IFRS prefer cash flow as a risk indicator; it is better than income, which is a performance criterion more subject to manipulation.

3.1.2.2. *Provisions and differences in translation of liabilities*

– Provisions:

- are regulated and recorded directly under non-current liabilities and relate to the so-called derogatory depreciation because they are accelerated. This excess is to be reintegrated during the depreciation period but allows us to override the first years and to release a significant self-financing capacity close to the year of investment;

- concern risks and expenses that remain at the disposal of the company and increase shareholders' equity. However, they have a high share of latent taxes that are difficult to accurately account for in financial investigation.

– Translation differences arise from foreign exchange risk on receivables or debts in foreign currencies.

3.1.2.3. *Sinking funds*

Own resources consist of shareholders' equity and the depreciation and provisions funds. The latter comes from the fact that assets are taken into account for their gross values in financial analysis, which in fact increases the assets reported in the French chart of accounts, in net value. In order to regain active equality = liabilities, we add all these provisions and amortization of assets, in a sinking fund on the liabilities side.

3.1.2.4. *External financing*

These are loans and other external resources whose schedule is detailed in a table with loans. The rigid classification between the different categories of loans and interest rates is becoming less and less easy to operate because of the great variety of financing and the possibility of exchange rates (swap).

Financial investigation starts from the static analysis of the four main functions and provides a simple analytical framework adapted to most industrial and commercial companies.

The differential to be observed between financing of equity and investment must be in favor of financing and constitutes the working capital fund.

3.1.2.5. *Working capital (overall net)*

Working capital is the excess of long-term financing (non-current liabilities) over fixed asset investment (non-current assets). In the General Chart of Accounts, working capital or overall net working capital is calculated from the functional balance sheet after income distribution is divided into three main parts: non-current assets, non-current liabilities and current non-current assets.

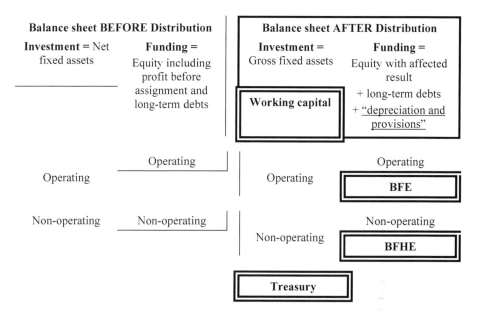

3.1.3. Sustainable resources

3.1.3.1. *Equity (I)*

Also referred to as net book assets, equity is composed of the net position, subsidies and contingent liabilities.

Shareholders' equity differs from equity capital and own resources, which include provisions for liabilities, which are therefore reserve-type liabilities.

Shareholders' equity is remunerated by dividends from current or past results, as a result of the decisions of shareholders' general meetings.

	LIABILITIES of the balance sheet before distribution of the result		
SHAREHOLDERS' EQUITY (I) ⇅	NET POSITION ⇅	+Share capital (of which pays)	STABLE FINANCING (IV) ⇅
		+Premiums for issue, merger, contribution,	
		+Re-evaluation differences	
		+Legal reserve	
		+Statutory or contractual reserves	OWN FUNDS (III) ⇅
		+Regulated reserves	
		+Other reserves	
		± Retained earnings	
		± RESULT OF THE FINANCIAL YEAR (± profit or loss)	
		+Investment grants	
		+Regulated provisions	
+ OTHER **OWN FUNDS** (II)		*+Equity issue product*	
		+Conditional advances	
+ LIABILITIES		*+Provisions for risks*	
		+Provisions for expenses	
+ **FINANCIAL DEBTS**		*+ Bonds convertible into shares (hybrids)*	
		+ Other obligatory bonds	
		+ Loans from credit institutions	
		+ Loans and other financial debts	

The ratio of earnings to equity excluding income, equity, is called "return on equity" [LEV 10].

3.1.3.2. *Own funds (III)*

Equity includes hybrid financing products entered on a separate line called "other equity" in the French Accounting Plan. They have the particularity of not possessing own funds or full loans at the time of their issue. They become *in fine* by either the delivery of shares of the company studied or a refund.

– IFRS no longer make this distinction and the line "other equity" no longer appears as it is up to the company to allocate them from the beginning according to their supposed final destination.

3.1.3.3. *Quasi-equity or hybrid capital, principles*

These are interesting in case of financial crises. If indices fall, it is unwise to call on the market to increase equity. Investors may be reluctant to engage in a capital increase. The company may favor a capital increase rather than resort to indebtedness. The issue of convertible bonds or stock warrants is then interesting in a sluggish financial climate to both obtain equity and assume increase in the long term its equity.

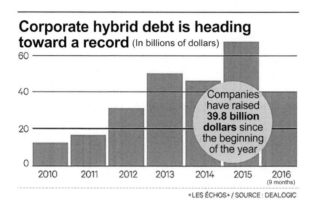

Figure 3.1. *Corporate hybrid debt is heading toward a record*[2]

When the market reverses its downward trend, the investor of a convertible bond, for example, will convert it into shares and participate in the group's capital. Long-term debt will decline in favor of its equity. However, the investor in convertible bonds will have a lower return than with a conventional bond.

3.1.3.4. *Quasi-funds used*

Quasi-funds have financial advantages but also limits for the issuing company.

Convertible Bonds (CB)

These are unique securities unlike subscription warrants that are likely to be converted into shares;

– *Advantages*:

- CBs also provide a cheaper loan.

---

2 See Benoit G., "Volumes records pour la dette hybride dans le monde", *Les Echos* 19/09/2016. To find out more, please visit: http://www.lesechos.fr/19/09/2016/LesEchos/22279-125-ECH_volumes-records-pour-la-dette-hybride-dans-le-monde.htm#ZcGyuEqQxS16p5hI.99

- CBs by nature are less speculative products than subscription warrants.

– *Disadvantages*:

- The conversion of bonds into equities converts debt into equity but does not provide any additional financing to the company.

- They "play" on the upward price and the market gravely sanctions the less favorable results than expected.

Warrants for Equity Warrants

This is a bond issue to which is attached one or more share warrants that allow us to subscribe to a future capital increase at a predetermined price.

– *Advantages*:

- The issue of the loan is generally at a lower rate than in a bond issue, so the cost of capital is lower for the company.

- In the event that the company's share price is low, OBSA can refinance itself without the risk of losing power by diluting its capital.

- If the share price improves, the company can rely on a conventional bond with a possible capital increase.

- The oppositions of interests between the shareholders with unlimited profit expectations and the creditors limited to financial expenses are blurred by this opportunity to become a shareholder.

- It protects against public takeover bids because the increase in the number of shares adds to the unfriendly takeover bid.

– *Disadvantages*:

If the stock price does not reach the exercise price of the warrants, then the capital increase cannot take place and this kind of information is analyzed as a bad sign by the market that will punish the company;

Callable bonds in shares (Ora)

This is an obligation that is repaid by the allocation of one share (usually from the issuer). This issue therefore leads to a capital increase in the long term.

Current accounts of partners

– Advantages:

Unlike contributions to capital, current account contributions are repayable at any time to the shareholder and may be remunerated by interest.

Thus, if the company does not generate a profit, then the contributors will receive the interest contrary to the dividends.

Associate current account use is less restrictive than a capital increase that requires a heavier formalism.

– Disadvantages:

Financial institutions often require blocking of current accounts to provide financing.

When the company generates profits and distributes them to shareholders, the current account provider will receive a lower dividend, as it is allocated based on the percentage of capital held.

Participatory borrowing

This is a loan where remuneration is indexed to a level of performance of the company or project: turnover, operating profit, net profit, etc. This is currently called crowdfunding: equity crowdfunding, crowdlending, etc.

Simple or bond loans

– Simple borrowing

The cost of borrowing can be incorporated at the acquisition cost of intangible assets, property, tangible fixed assets and inventories, but not financially.

– Bonds

A bond is a loan in the form of so-called bond units that are purchased by investors. They are generally negotiable and are worth between €500 and €100,000. They give rise to the payment of an interest, usually annual, and a repayment of the loan after several years.

Compared to a simple bank loan, the bond loan makes it possible to self-finance when the banks have difficulties in lending and it is a better appeal to the market.

Issuances have never been so high (€292 billion in 2016)

140 Financial Management

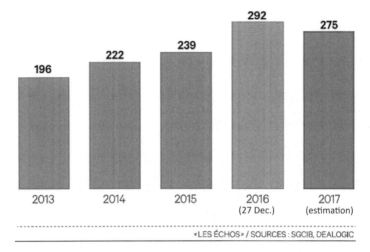

Figure 3.2. *"Bond issues in Europe in billions €³" and the financing costs so low*

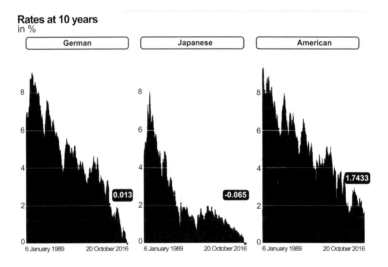

Figure 3.3. *"This is due to the collapse of 10-year rates between 1989 and the end of 2016"* (see footnote 3 below)

---

3 Benoit G., "la BCE pousse les géants européens vers les marchés obligataires", *Les Echos* 28/12/2016, http://www.lesechos.fr/finance-marches/marches-financiers/0211636333983-la-bce-pousse-les-geants-europeens-vers-les-marches-obligataires-2053133.php#Pze00zfp4Sqg Lvbi.99

However, in the event of a fall in low interest rates, bond financing may become difficult[4].

The following graph shows an anomaly in the corporate debt market that could cause a recession.

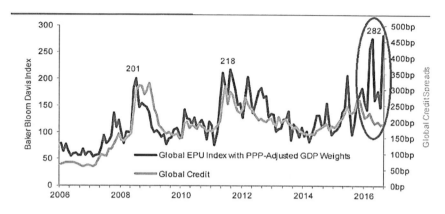

Figure 3.4. *"The uncertainty of global economic policies are at historic highs. Why are there no margins?"*[5]

3.1.4. *Fixed assets*

Fixed assets consist of identifiable and non-current assets and are a resource generator.

In functional financial analysis in the French Accounting Plan, fixed assets are taken for their gross value, the one that is recorded on the date of entry in the balance sheet. This is why a "depreciation and provisions fund" is created in the equity capital of an equal amount to balance the balance sheet.

---

4 Couet I., "Les marchés obligataires redoutent la fin de trente-cinq ans de hausse", *Les Echos*, 21/10/2016, http://www.lesechos.fr/21/10/2016/LesEchos/22303-126-ECH_les-marches-obligataires-redoutent-la-fin-de-trente-cinq-ans-de-hausse.htm#6LlX0hwBsaYTCPuW.99
5 Benoit G., "Le graphique boursier le plus effrayant du monde", *Les Echos*, 02/01/2017 http://www.lesechos.fr/finance-marches/marches-financiers/0211651107511-le-graphique-boursier-le-plus-effrayant-du-monde-2053919.php#MBugTaLjyZ67xBiS.99

			Gross
IMMOBILIZED ASSETS	**Intangible assets**	Subscribed uncalled capital (**I**)	
		Administration fees	
		Research and development costs	
		Concessions, patents and similar rights	
		Commercial fund including right to lease	
		Other intangible assets	
		Advances and down payments on fixed assets	
		= TOTAL	
	Fixed assets	Grounds	
		Constructions	
		Industrial installations, equipment and tools	
		Other intangible fixed assets	
		Assets in progress	
		Advances and deposits	
		= TOTAL	
	Financial Assets	Investments (equity method)	
		Other participations	
		Receivables related to equity investments	
		Other fixed securities	
		Loans	
		Other financial assets	
		= TOTAL	
		= **TOTAL fixed asset** (**II**)	

3.1.5. *Calculation of global net revolving fund*

The sinking fund and provision recorded with own resources could:

– have been voluntarily reduced by a policy of systematic linear amortization of fixed assets (as required by IFRS) and low provisions;

– have been voluntarily increased by accelerated depreciation or degressive tax or by comparison with recovery value (IFRS) and justified but with high provisions;

– include provisions for depreciation of current assets. They may want to hedge recurring (current) operating assets. However, the French Order of Chartered Accountants has recommended not to incorporate them to retain the balance sheet specificity.

Some French Accounting Plan analysts have recommended making restatements that change the balance sheet:

– Passively:

- Provisions for risks, which have the character of irreversible and assignable provisioned debts, must remain in equity.

- In regard to current accounts, if the exigibility can be immediate, then they must be in accordance with the current debts, even passive cash flow.

- Interest accrued on loans: they must be removed from the financial debts if they are included in the long-term debts and added to the current debts.

– Assets:

- Bonded bonds (notes payable to the State) must be invested with passive cash flow.

- Employee stock ownership plan. This must be placed in non-current liabilities of the balance sheet.

- Marketable securities: if they are risk-free and quickly liquidable, they must be included in the active cash flow.

- Provisions for depreciation of inventories and customers. These must be placed in non-current resources;

- Discounted and unmatured effects: when the company has a negative cash flow, it can offer the bank bills regarding customers (commercial bill) before maturity. The company discounts them and the bank gives them the corresponding money after deduction of the financial expenses it has taken. Thus, it is necessary to increase the customer item and reduce the cash discounted effects and other debt mobilization credits to regain the risk related to cash.

– Assets and liabilities:

- "Unclaimed shareholders": this asset account is to be eliminated as non-value and to be deducted from equity.

- "Adjustment accounts" in assets include the costs of issuing loans. They must be eliminated from current assets and deducted from equity.

• They no longer exist under IFRS because the account is charged directly to the account that generated them.

- Bond repayment premiums: this is the difference between the repayment price and the bond issue price. They offset the difference between the nominal amount recorded in long-term debt and what it received as cash. These premiums must be deducted from the assets and liabilities.

- Current banking competitions: they are to deduct financial debts and either add to the passive cash or deduct cash from assets.

- Conversion differences between assets and liabilities: They are to be eliminated and the claims and debts relating to these deviations must return to their original value.

– Property taken out of leasing: The functional analysis of the balance sheet calculates the overall net working capital and should integrate all the elements of the durable assets and liabilities. So:

- the original value of the leased property not recorded as an asset must be added to the fixed assets;

- the depreciation that would have been made must be added to the resources and

- the unamortized portion must be added to the financial debts.

Non-current assets		Non-current liabilities
Current operating assets	Global net working capital	
		Current operating liabilities
Current assets excluding current operations (PCG)		Liabilities circulating outside current operations (PCG)

- Working capital = Non-current liabilities − Non-current assets

3.2. The need for working capital requirement (WCR)

The analysis of the WCR is done in a static way over a year, or dynamically, that is to say, over several years. It focuses on the analysis of:

– a structural balance sheet;

– normative WCR calculated in days of HVAC, whose aim is to determine the relationship between the level of working capital requirement and the activity.

EXAMPLE.– The WCR consists of a current operating portion (WCRE) and a non-current operating portion, known as the current operating portion (WCREE).

- $\boxed{WCR = WCRE + WCREE}$

3.2.1. *WCRE (or WCE)*

What the company owes to its creditors is current liabilities, trade payables and receivables and, in prepaid income, *deferred revenue*.

What the debtors owe the company is in the accounts receivable and other receivables, prepaid expenses and PCG investment securities. In addition to these gaps, there is the need to finance stocks. So:

$\boxed{WCE = \text{stocks} + \text{current customers} - \text{current suppliers}}$

It therefore corresponds to the financial needs of the operating cycle.

The policy followed by the company to manage its WCE has an influence on cash flow because:

$\boxed{T = GNWC - (WCE + WCREE)}$

The only organizations that generate working capital resources (working capital requirement <0) by the mere fact of their current activity are the financial entities or similar. They may belong not only to the banking sector, insurance, etc., but also to the tertiary sector of distribution. Indeed, the first two categories have no stock to finance and live from the investment of funds generated by their activity. Mass distribution generates large funds by charging its customers to access the fund but regulates its suppliers with important deadlines. Therefore, although they sell, whatever the type of products they offer, the commercial outstanding is financially very favorable to them. They then grow these "working capital resources" as do financial institutions, hence the financial similarity.

3.2.2. *WCREE*

The WCREE or Working Capital Requirements Except Exploitation includes receivables from assets and debts related to financing and investment transactions and, therefore, not related to current operations.

EXAMPLE.– Profit tax for a business that would rarely be a beneficiary could be part of the non-recurring need, same for capital providers, etc.

CIRCULATING ASSETS	**Stocks**	Raw materials and supplies	
		In the process of producing goods	
		In production of services	
		Intermediate and finished products	
		Merchandise	
			= *Total*
		Advances and down payments	
	Receivables	Clients and related accounts (± 1 year detail)	
		Other receivables (± 1 year detail)	
		Subscribed and called capital, unpaid	
			= *Total*
		Investment securities	
			= *Total*
REGULARIZATION ACCOUNTS		Prepaid expenses (± 1 year detail)	
		TOTAL	**(III)**
		Expenses to be spread over several years **(IV)**	
		Bond repayment premiums **(V)**	
		Active conversion gap **(VI)**	

Linked accounts are receivables and related prepaid income.

Operating liabilities:

Exploitation DEBT	Advances and down payments received on orders in progress
	Trade payables and related accounts
	Social and tax debts
	Debts on fixed assets and accounts receivable
	Other debts
Regularization accounts	Products noted in advance

Accounts linked to payable accounts are accrued liabilities and prepaid expenses related to these current operating cash flows.

3.2.3. Recommendations on the need for working capital

Favorable trade receivables are generally not sufficient to finance stocks.

We understand then that the search for minimum stocks (zero stock policy) is always a priority. It is enough to have stocks of materials and goods held by the suppliers who then deliver just in time what is necessary, so it is just-in-time inventory management. It is necessary that the company can have a certain dimension to put pressure on its suppliers to be delivered without risk of running out of stock and does not solve the problem of the suppliers which, to loosen their commercial stock, oppress their own suppliers and the domino effect multiplies the risk of failures.

– The stock level changes with changing stock turnover rates.

– Accounts receivable and payable levels change as the business changes the timeframes for:

- settlement of claims;

- settlement of current operating debts and

- billing (more efficient internal organization).

Thus, the WCR expressed in turnover days undergoes variations according to the variation of these delays due to the variation of the activity.

The Days Sales Outstanding (DSO) is the time that elapses between delivery and the date of payment by the customer. DSO is a widely recognized indicator of business health. It testifies to the improvement or the degradation of the customers' risk.

"In Western Europe, the average payment time is slightly down: after 62 days in 2014, and 60 days in 2015, the DSO of European companies will reach 59 days in 2016. Despite this overall improvement, payment practices remain heterogeneous, and European countries are divided into two groups: Northern European countries (Scandinavia, the Netherlands, Germany, Austria, etc.), where the average payment time is around 50 days. Payment behavior is comparable: 46% of companies are paid within 30 to 60 days, and only 7% of them have to wait more than 90 days. On the other hand, in Mediterranean countries (Spain, Portugal, Greece, Italy, France, etc.), where DSO is greater than 60 days and the payment practices are more heterogeneous, 30% of the suppliers must wait more than 90 days to obtain the payment of their debt obligation, and only 28% of them are paid within 30 to 60 days. In 2015, the average time of French companies recorded a significant decrease of −2 days to 72 days. In 2016, this trend is expected to continue. French companies will have to wait 70 days before being paid (2 days).

There is a close relationship between the real economy and DSOs: ordinarily, the harder the economic context, the higher the average payment time of companies, but the DSOs are also a major indicator of the confidence that prevails between companies and their customers, so they can be drastically reduced in times of mistrust, resulting in cash shortages for wholesalers and importers" [6].

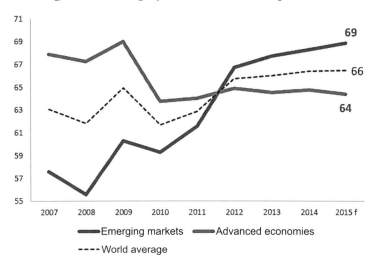

Figure 3.5. *Evolution of DSO in advanced economies and emerging markets in days*

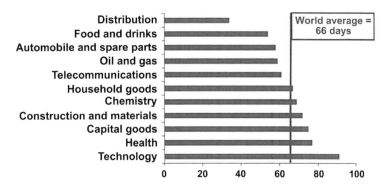

Figure 3.6. *Average customer time in the world by sector (2015)*

---

6 http://www.eulerhermes.fr/mediacenter/actualites/Pages/etude-DSO-2016.aspx

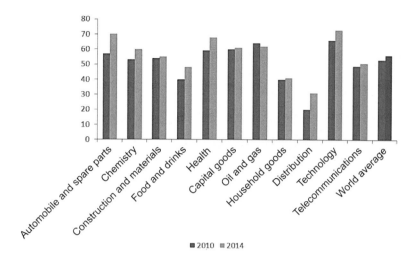

Figure 3.7. *Evolution of the DSO in GB between 2010 and 2014*

This helps to change the level of WCR and cash flow, with consequences for the risk of default.

3.2.4. *WCR in days of HVAC*

According to the Observatory's annual report on payment deadlines[7], the following are the statistical indicators:

– Customer turnaround time, expressed in days of turnover, including VAT, is a ratio that reports the receivables, including discounted bills that are not yet due, to the turnover all charges included (TTC), multiplied by 360. The receivables are calculated after deduction of advances and installments paid upon order (recorded on the liabilities side of the balance sheet).

– Supplier's delay, expressed in days of purchases, is a ratio that brings the supplier's debts to purchases and other external expenses, including VAT, multiplied by 360. The supplier's debts are calculated after deduction of the advances and installments paid to the suppliers (registered to the balance sheet asset).

---

7 http://www.economie.gouv.fr/files/files/PDF/observatoire_delais_paiement_rapport_annuel_2015.pdf

– Trade balance (or balance of the inter-company credit), which corresponds to the balance of the receivables of the company and its supplier debts (net of advances and down payments), is expressed in days of turnover. It can also be defined as the difference between the customer delay and the supplier's time adjusted for the ratio of purchases to sales. The commercial balance of a company reflects its lending or borrowing position vis-à-vis trading partners. When it is positive, the company finances its partners.

– The average customer lead time is 44 days of turnover.

– The average supplier times are 50 days of purchases.

– The average commercial balance was 12 days of turnover in 2014.

– The levels of payment periods and the balance of the inter-company credit are very heterogeneous from one sector to another.

– In 2014, 32% of companies had an average customer time above the 60-day sales threshold, and 29% paid their suppliers 60 days from purchase.

– In 2016, average payment delays were estimated between 22 and 25 days of turnover.

– In 2014, the persistence of many lagging behaviors put the whole economy at risk of increasing delays and failures. In fact, companies experiencing late payments from their customers were encouraged to defer payments to their own suppliers, thereby transferring their difficulties to other companies, resulting in late chain payment behavior. The entrepreneur can mobilize other forms of financing, rather than burdening customers with late payments. However, the presence of risky customers in the company's portfolio can also lead lenders to restrict their credit offer. The lack of liquidity due to collection delays leads the company to a risk of default and bankruptcy, so its suppliers waiting for a settlement suffer a loss that can lead them to a high risk of default. Based on being 30 days late, the probability of customer failure is multiplied by 6.

– The situation in Europe is characterized by a lack of a clear trend. The overall average delay is almost stable, at 15 days in 2016. Portugal and Italy remain the worst, being 30 and 20 days late, respectively. Germany continues to set the example, with an average delay of close to 6 days. In Europe, nearly one out of two companies has been asked to provide longer payment terms. This practice is observed more in southern countries: 83% of Spanish companies have received such a request, compared to 20% of companies in the United Kingdom.

Example Calculation of the Normative Working Capital Requirement:

For a growing trading company, the data are determined for the year N.	
100 u.	the quantity of goods purchased per day
€60	unit purchase price
35 days	average storage time
€96	unit selling price
20%	VAT rate
45 days	average time to customer settlements
65 days	average time to supplier settlements

	Settlement time			Structural ratio	Need or resources
Stock		Tax included purchases	No tax included sale		
	35 days	€50	€80	0.63	21.88 days
Customers		Sales taxes included	Sale no taxes included		
	45 days	€96	€80	1.20	54 days
Providers		Purchases tax included	Sale no tax included		
	65 days	€60	€80	0.75	48.8 days
			Normative working capital requirement		27.13 days

Financing growth

If the company forecasts a turnover for N1 of 36,000 u. = WCE = 36,000 u. × €80 × 27.125 days/360 days = € 217,000 to be financed by working capital.

If the company predicts a figure for N1 of 54,000 u. => Its WCE = 54,000 u. × €80 × 27.125 days/360 days = €325,500 to be financed by working capital, etc.

It is a simulation and forecasting tool before the cash is defective.

Variable part of working capital requirement

Merchandise stock (M) 40 days of turnover excluding tax

Finished goods inventory (F) 60 days of turnover excluding tax

Cost of purchase of goods sold as % of sales price = 60%

Raw materials 30%, consumables 50%, direct labor 20%

Sales price of F = 120%

The manufacturing time of M = about 10 days (materials incorporated at the beginning of production)

M customers pay after 50 days from the end of month

F customers pay after 80 days

Sales of M are equal to 40 % of sales

F sales are equal to 60% of sales

Export sales percentage = 30%

VAT at 20% is paid the following month on the 20th after the end of the month

The raw material suppliers are paid at 30 and 15 days after

Suppliers of consumables are paid after 30 days

Goods suppliers are paid in cash

Personnel expenses amount to 35% of turnover

Employer's contributions as % of gross salary are 20%

Salary costs as % of gross salary are 45%

Employees are paid at the end of the 30-day period

Social charges paid the month following the 15th

Calculation of the variable part of the WCE

The rent payable every month in advance is €240,000 excluding taxes.

The other fixed costs are €10,000 per month without tax (they are paid in 35 days).

Management's net salary is €14,000 monthly.

WCE	Deadlines	Structure	WCE
Stock of M	40 days	× 18%	**7.2 days**
Stock of F	60 days	× 50%	**30 days**
Outstanding F	10 days	× 33%	**3.25 days**
Customers M	65 days	× 46%	**29.64 days**
Customers F	80 days	× 68%	**54.72 days**
Deductible VAT	35 days	× 12%	**4.06 days**
VAT collected	35 days	× 14%	**−4.9 days**
M suppliers 1st	60 days	× 18%	**−10.8 days**
Suppliers of M Cons.	30 days	× 30%	**−9 days**
Net wages	15 days	× 19%	**−2.9 days**
Social Charges	30 days	× 16%	**−4.71 days**
		Variable need of the WCE	**+ 97 days**

Calculation of the fixed part of the WCE

Rents	€240,000 / 12 months × 15 days / 30 days × 120%				€12,000
Other expenses	€5,000	€5,000 × 120%	35 days	30 days	− €12,833
Social charges	€14,000	/ 80%	× (45%	+ 20%)	− €11,375
Net wages	€14,000	× 15 days	/ 30 days		− €7,000
VAT	€240,000 / 12 months + € 5 000		× 20% × 35 days	/ 30 days	€5,833
				Working capital resource =	− €13,375

Function of the WCR	Y =	97 ×	− € 13,375

In other words, the WCR will be variable with growth but not proportional.

If turnover = €500,000,	then the need for working capital to be financed by the FR will be				
If the turnover = €400,000	× 97	/ 360	− €13, 375, then the	BFE =	€93,921
If the turnover = €500,000	× 97	/ 360	− €13, 375, then the	BFE =	€120,745
If the turnover = €600,000	× 97	/ 360	− €13, 375, then the	BFE =	€147,569
If the turnover = €700,000	× 97	/ 360	− €13, 375, then the	BFE =	€174,393
etc.					

The fixed charges increase in stages and you have to know from what level of turnover they change.

3.3. Net cash

For the French Chart of Accounts, marketable securities are included in working capital requirements.

Therefore, the treasury is composed only of cash and cash equivalents:

− Cash is made up of immediate cash balances + cash balances + demand deposits.

− Cash equivalents consist of highly liquid short-term investments that are easily convertible into cash and whose risk of a change in value is negligible, their term not exceeding 3 months.

− Passive cash is written over liabilities with financing.

• For IFRS, investments that can be liquidated immediately at the convenience of the company (marketable securities) should be entered in the cash position. The cash flow recorded in current liabilities is therefore to be deducted from net cash.

It is often believed that a company that increases its turnover will have less liquidity problems, but the company is made to generate profit and not cash. In fact, the need for working capital shows that the more the activity develops, the more the operating cycle purchase → stock → production → stock → sales, which will be done with cash offsets, will generate cash requirements. So, you have to increase financial liabilities. This is why a large company has a high debt and high equity that it will not pay without risk, but it will have to pay the costs: dividends and financial expenses.

3.3.1. *Cash flow and the result are linked without being correlated*

On the one hand, cash flow and the result are finally linked but not correlated and, on the other hand, all cash flow does not come from activity.

– They are linked:

EXAMPLE.– If a company pays €10,000 to buy goods, has a fee of €1,000 and sells the goods by cashing €14,000, it makes a profit of turnover – cost price = €14,000 – (€10,000 + €1,000) = €3,000, which is found in its cash flow or business assets. In this case, the variation in cash is well linked and correlated to the result of €3,000.

– They are not correlated because there are gaps and uncertainties:

- *Time differences* between the registration dates of transactions and those of their regulations. Therefore, all payments that are not made immediately (cash, such as at the barber's or baker's) generate cash offsets and give rise to deferred settlements, receivables and operating debts.

- Uncertainties about:

– *Obligations* that will have to be fulfilled while the amount and the deadline are imprecise. These uncertainties lead to the creation of reserves:

- liabilities in the form of a provision for risks and expenses, which reduce the profit on the balance sheet by the same amount;

- in expenses in the form of provisions, which decrease the result of the income statement.

– *The value of certain assets*, which give rise to a probable loss (inventory, receivables, etc.). The company recognizes these depreciations:

- as a deduction from the asset, a provision for depreciation which reduces the profit on the balance sheet by the same amount (decrease in assets);

- in expenses in the form of provisions (decrease in profit or loss in the income statement);

– *The spread over time* of the consumption of fixed assets whose lifetime is programmed. The company recognizes these depreciations:

- a provision for depreciation which reduces the profit on the balance sheet by the same amount (decrease in assets);

- in expenses in the form of amortization expense (decrease in income statement profit).

– Business assets do not come from the result because the activity generates:

- receipts of receivables and debts already on the balance sheet;

– receivables already capitalized;

– new debts due to capital increases, new loans, etc.

- disbursements of debts already on the balance sheet;

– suppliers already on the liabilities side;

– old loans that the company repays;

– dividends to shareholders, etc.

It will be noted about debts that:

– increases or decreases in capital have no impact on the result but rather on cash flow;

– the cost of the debt (financial expenses) or the proceeds of the investments (financial income) modify the cash flow and the result. These transactions therefore involve both balance sheet and income statement accounts.

Thus, because it is impossible to rely on the balance sheet and the profit and loss account to reflect all the cash flows, a financing table has been provided in the Glossary of Economic and Financial Concepts.

3.3.2. *Analysis and recommendations*

If the cash is insufficient, it is because:

– the working capital is too low;

– and/or the working capital requirement is too high.

But, taking T = [GNWC] − [WCR], and by developing we get:

T = [non-current liabilities − non-current assets] − [WCR].

By developing the components, we have:

+ (non-current funds − non-current assets)
− [(stocks + receivables − accounts payable)]
= Cash

Or

+ equity
+ non-current financial debts
− fixed assets (tangible, intangible and financial)
− stocks
− claims
+ accounts payable
= Cash flow

Or

+ Capital
+ reservations
+ benefit
+ long-term loans
+ similar debts
− tangible, intangible and financial
− stocks
− claims
+ suppliers
= Cash

The company has a multitude of positions over which it can act, but not all policies are equivalent because they conflict with the different stakeholders as depicted by the following table:

Policy	ElEment	STAKEHOLDERS	RISK OF CONFLICT
Increase	Capital	Institutional	☺ risk decreases
		Shareholders	☹ *profitability decreases*
		Staff	☺ Increased security
Increase	Stocks	Institutional	☺ risk decreases
		Shareholders	☹ *lower dividends*
		Staff	☺ security increases
Increase	Profit	Shareholders	☺ profitability increases
		Institutional	☺ profitability increases
		Staff	☺ wages could increase
Increase	Non-current debts	Shareholders	☺ increased leverage
		Institutional	☹ *prefer that the shareholder take the risks*
		Staff	☺ financial security increases
Decrease	Stocks	Shareholders	☺ less working capital requirements
		Managers	☹ *risk of shortage increases*
		Staff	☹ *rates increase*
Decrease	Current claims	Shareholders	☺ lower working capital requirement
		Managers	☹ *tenser relations with clients*
		Staff	☹ *tenser relations with clients*
Increase	Current suppliers	Shareholders	☺ resources increase
		Managers	☹ *tenser relations with suppliers*
		Staff	☹ *tenser relations with suppliers*

Thus, the company can:

– increase own funds, which means paying the shareholders a risk premium of loss of power, due to the arrival of new shareholders and additional dividends payable;

– increase the result, but this is not easy. Companies are systematically reducing costs (outsourcing, offshoring, downsizing, creating mergers, etc.) as a priority to increase profit margins. In this case, the result increases and with it the reserves. They increase the GNWC and with it the net cash;

– increase debts, which implies:

- remunerating lenders with higher financial expenses, which increases the average cost of capital,

- risking seeing shareholders and managers abandon some of their sovereignty,

- but also having a favorable leverage effect that will increase the financial profitability of the company, provided of course that it still has a debt capacity in the long term,

– decrease operating or non-current assets, which implies reducing the value of items,

- intangible assets, thus reducing the policy of developing quality, skills and innovation,

- tangible fixed assets and equipment at risk of the company not renewing its amortized or dilapidated assets. In any case, this situation is only conceivable if the company is too large. That is why many companies sell investments that are no longer part of their core business,

- financial fixed assets and it will be necessary for the company to sell its fixed and participating securities, which correspond to its external growth strategy,

– increase provisions or obtain subsidies, but:

– on the one hand, it is a short-term policy and therefore inappropriate,

– on the other hand, it risks improperly provisioning the company and having to reintegrate these operations:

• the cash flow expresses the difference between:

– (long-term) financing and investment strategies measured by working capital;

– the policy (short-term) measured by the working capital requirement.

Daily overdraft is a day-to-day tactic that compares the allowed overdraft rate with the short-term investment rate.

Because of this, tactic = strategy − policy or:

tactics (cash flow) = strategy (of financing − investment) − policy (BFR).

EXAMPLE: RECOMMENDATION.–

"Which period should be chosen to close accounts in?"

The closing of accounts in France on 31 December coincides with the financial year and tax and social commitments. However, it is not always relevant. A trader will be interested in closing his accounts after January, the month of sales and prosperity. By closing in the middle of a production season for Christmas, a chocolate manufacturer will not show its business in the best light, because it will have supplied raw material and stocked up, in order to be able to deliver to its customers. "We have to identify the time when the company has the lowest needs and where it is easier for it to conduct inventory and closing operations", advises Laurent Prost. The first accounting year of companies subject to corporation tax may be extended to 23 months, instead of 12. "To avoid accounting costs, the manager may be tempted to postpone the closing date of his first year", observes Laurent Prost. It is conceivable if he is able to give intermediate information. A start-up that needs to raise funds will have to provide monthly or quarterly reporting elements, as the financial partner is rarely satisfied with approximate information and a long deadline for financial communication. "The choice of the date depends on the information desired by the partners involved in funding", insists Laurent Prost. A true communication tool, the company's accounts, deserves to be stopped at the time of the year when it shows the best of itself. If the need for working capital and indebtedness are at their lowest, and cash is at its maximum, the financial independence of the company will appear in its best light. On the other hand, accounts showing a large number of customer and inventory outstandings, but few supplier outstandings, and therefore a large need for working capital, will result in a depressed cash position compared to the average of its exercise. "The accounts are an instrument of communication". It may be wise to change the date of closing, to enhance the image of the company, so business cycles must be taken into account.[8]

3.3.3. *Financial analysis in market value*

Financial market value analysis of financial wealth allows analysts of financing organizations to better guard against the risk of bankruptcy. It is therefore necessary to restate the social accounts, to appreciate:

– *solvency*, that is, its ability to settle its debts;

– *the exigibility*, that is to say, the propensity of the company to honor these deadlines;

---

8 Dauvergne G., "Quelle période choisir pour clôturer ses comptes ?", *Les Echos*, 23 February 2017, https://business.lesechos.fr/entrepreneurs/gestion-finance/quelle-periode-choisir-pour-cloturer-ses-comptes-306435.php?LUyCLPsjGLZqFZqH.99

– *liquidity*, that is, the rapid transformation of assets into cash.

This financial market analysis seeks to assess the risks that affect payment capacity and seeks an assessment of the company at fair value at market price.

This analysis will therefore reclassify the following elements:

– assets in decreasing order of liquidity (from the least to the most liquid) to determine the company's very short-term solvency. Do current receivables cover current debts? To respond to this question, the analyst:

- values the non-current asset at its market value, therefore very close to the sale value at the market price;

- excludes assets with a market value of zero. These assets are here non-securities (start-up costs, development costs, etc.);

– liabilities in an increasing order of due date, as the term of the debt term prevails over the nature of the sources of financing.

This financial market analysis is very close to that of IFRS at total fair value.

However, an important aspect of the company lies in its technicality, its network of customers, the competence of its human resources, etc. These are not possible to report in the PCG balance sheet or in IFRS.

Oddly enough, these elements of intangible capital will only appear in the case of a purchase (merger, acquisition, etc.) of the company by another entity. It is the latter that will be able to value its assets, in the form of goodwill, the difference between the estimated value and the value that the buyer wishes to pay.

In this financial market analysis, the search for company failure has a precise meaning. Indeed:

– there is probable bankruptcy or default when (Basel Committee):

- an analyst considers that it is improbable that the company fully repays its credit without taking appropriate measures such as the provision of a guarantee (if it exists),

- the arrears of the company on a large credit exceeds 90 days,

– a company that generates excessive cash is solvent, even infallible, that is to say:

- able to self-finance its growth,

- likely to negotiate well with its lenders,

- has a "war chest".

However, its financial health makes it at the mercy of any company that lacks liquidity to finance its growth and no longer has debt capacity. It is likely to be absorbed by competitors, often helped by lenders who see their risks reduced by this guarantee of new liquidity.

To change the functional balance sheet and make it venal with a solvency indicator, reclassifications and restatements are carried out.

3.3.4. *Presentation of the balance sheet in net asset values*

3.3.4.1. *Principles*

This is the presentation that allows the financier to determine the financial risk in the short term. It is the spirit of IFRS.

Assets classified from top to bottom in order of increasing liquidity and increasing due liabilities make it possible to obtain a financial balance sheet composed of large amounts classified as a sort of schedule.

Assets at + 1 year *Close to non-current in IFRS total fair value*	Fixed assets in net values therefore after deduction of depreciation and provisions	Equity (without total depreciation and provisions)	*close to non-current under IFRS and total fair value*	Non-current liabilities
		Provisions for risks and expenses (PCG)		
Assets at - 1 year *Close to current in IFRS total fair value*	Current assets in net values therefore after subtracting provisions	Non-current debts	*close to current in IFRS and total fair value*	Current liabilities
		Short-term debts		
	Net cash			

3.3.4.2. *Reclassifications*

Fixed assets are taken for their accounting value and are therefore closer to their financial value. Indeed, if the managers had thought that they could have lost more value (test of depreciation), they would have passed a complementary depreciation.

EXAMPLE.– IMPAIRMENT TEST

As a result, the accounting value is often reduced and the value of the property can offer capital gains.

IFRS have chosen a similar method because any goodwill is taken into account each year by the impairment test to bring the assets back to their value of use, which may not be the market value, and it therefore remains subjective.

– The maturity of more or less than 1 year is chosen because it is more consistent with the accounting and budgetary period. It should be noted that the schedule provides a table of debt and debt maturities according to their maturities. Therefore, reclassification work is needed to identify items in the balance sheet that relate to current (short term) and non-current (long term).

– Transaction instruments are included in cash flow, unlike the functional analysis of the PCG, which, in its cash flow statement, leaves the assets, SICAV, FCP Mutual Fund, derivative short term, etc.

– Because the company cannot withdraw money from the sale of a property taken out of a finance lease, it is not planned here to restate this item by including it in the balance sheet as recommended by IFRS.

– The processing of the financial balance sheet is done only from a balance sheet after the distribution of the result (the only possibility under IFRS). Therefore, the dividends to pay are necessarily short term and are to be withdrawn from equity to place them with current debts.

– As for dividends, the provisions for risks and expenses are here permanent capital, and could be broken down into:

- equity for the reserve portion;

- non-current debts at more than 1 year when they cover expenses payable at more than 1 year and

- short-term current liabilities when they cover expenses payable within 1 year.

– Unrealized tax debts must be updated and added to the relevant items in the spirit of IFRS.

PROGNOSIS AND RECOMMENDATIONS.– The analyst must respond in his report to specific risk questions.

3.3.5. *Structural risks*

– Who are the main creditors, lenders or shareholders and for what reasons?

– Does the company have sufficient equity to maintain the long-term debt capacity necessary to use other loans to finance its growth?

– What is the degree of independence of the company vis-à-vis each lender?

– Is the level of indebtedness of the company bearable?

– Do long-term resources help cover long-term jobs?

– Does the company have the capacity to repay all its debts?

– Can the burden of financial expenses jeopardize future results?

– Is the financing structure – long-term resources/long-term jobs, short-term/long-term assets and liabilities, internal/external – consistent with its activity?

3.3.6. *The risk of imminent failure*

– Is the company solvent?

– At what date could it be out of cash, or even bankrupt?

– Is there a shortage or excess of own funds (i.e. a debt capacity and a calculable risk rate)?

– Is there an excessive, insufficient or adequate level of debt?

– Is the cash position tense or comfortable, etc.?

– Is the risk of bankruptcy high or low or non-existent?

– Is the profitability (profit/capital) correct or insufficient?

3.3.7. *Recommendations*

These are the same policies to recommend as for the functional analysis except that it is now cash flow available expressed by the difference between a permanent working capital fund (and a working capital requirement).

3.4 Balance sheet analysis: US GAAP

Four major financial statements are required for every listed company: the balance sheet, the income statement, the cash flows statement and the statement of shareholders' equity. These financial statements are indicators of the firm's performance.

3.4.1. *Balance sheet features*

The balance sheet in an indicator of the financial position of the company and it reports total assets (economic resources), total liabilities (outside claims) and shareholders' equity (inside claims).

The balance sheet is a convenient means of organizing and summarizing what a firm owns – economic resources – (its assets), what a firm owes – outside claims – (its liabilities), and the difference between total assets and total liabilities is the inside claims (the firm's equity) at a given point in time.

Figure 3.8 illustrates how the balance sheet is constructed. As shown, the left-hand side lists the assets of the firm, and the right-hand side lists the liabilities and equity.

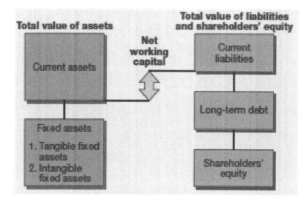

Figure 3.8. *The balance sheet*

Assets: the left-hand side

Assets are classified as either current (short-term) or fixed (long-term). A fixed asset is one that has a relatively long life. Fixed assets can be either tangible, such as land or a computer, or intangible, such as a trademark or patent. A current asset has a life of less than 1 year. This means that the asset will convert to cash within 12 months. For example, inventory would normally be purchased and sold within a year and is thus classified as a current asset. Obviously, cash itself is a current asset. Accounts receivable (money owed to the firm by its customers) are also current assets.

Liabilities and owners' equity: the right-hand side

The firm's liabilities are the first thing listed on the right-hand side of the balance sheet. These are classified into current and long-term liabilities. Current liabilities, like current assets, have a life of less than 1 year (meaning they must be paid within the year) and are listed before long-term liabilities. Accounts payable (money the firm owes to its suppliers) are one example of a current liability.

A debt that is not due in the coming year is classified as a long-term liability. A loan that the firm will pay off in 5 years is one such long-term debt. Firms borrow in the long term from a variety of sources. We will tend to use the terms bonds and bondholders generically to refer to long-term debt and long-term creditors, respectively.

By definition, the difference between the total value of the assets (current and fixed) and the total value of the liabilities (current and long-term) is the shareholders' equity, also called common equity or owners' equity or stockholders' equity. This feature of the balance sheet is intended to reflect the fact that, if the firm were to sell all its assets and use the money to pay off its debts, then whatever residual value remained would belong to the shareholders.

Therefore, the balance sheet "balances" because the value of the left-hand side always equals the value of the right-hand side. Thus, the value of the firm's assets is equal to the sum of its liabilities and shareholders' equity.

The accounting equation or the balance sheet identity is the following:

Assets = Liabilities + Shareholders' equity

Example

Building the balance sheet

Suppose a firm has current assets of $200, net fixed assets of $800, short-term debt of $90, and long-term debt of $500. What does the balance sheet look like? What is shareholders' equity? What is net working capital?

Solution

In this case, total assets = current assets + fixed assets = $200 + 800 = $1,000

Total liabilities = current liabilities + long-term liabilities = $90 +500 = $590, thus, shareholders' equity is the difference between total assets and total liabilities = $1,000 - 590 = $410.

Table 3.1 shows simplified balance sheets for a fictitious U.S. corporation. The assets on the balance sheet are listed in order of the length of time it takes for them to convert to cash in the normal course of business. Similarly, the liabilities are listed in the order in which they would normally be paid. The structure of the assets for a particular firm reflects the line of business the firm is in and also managerial decisions about how much cash and inventory to have and about credit policy, fixed asset acquisition and so on.

The liabilities side of the balance sheet primarily reflects managerial decisions about capital structure and the use of short-term debt. For example, in 2012, the total long-term debt for U.S. Corporation was $454 and total equity was $640 + 1,629 = $2,269.

U.S. CORPORATION
2011 and 2012 Balance Sheets
($ in millions)

Assets	2011	2012	Liabilities and Owners' Equity	2011	2012
Current assets			Current liabilities		
Cash	$ 104	$ 160	Accounts payable	$ 232	$ 266
Accounts receivable	455	688	Notes payable	196	123
Inventory	553	555	Total	$ 428	$ 389
Total	$1,112	$1,403			
Fixed assets					
Net plant and equipment	$1,644	$1,709	Long-term debt	$ 408	$ 454
			Owners' equity		
			Common stock and paid-in surplus	600	640
			Retained earnings	1,320	1,629
			Total	$1,920	$2,269
Total assets	$2,756	$3,112	Total liabilities and owners' equity	$2,756	$3,112

Table 3.1. Balance sheet U.S. Corporation (source: Ross, Westerfield and Jordan [ROS 14])

The assets on the left-hand side show how the firm uses its capital (its investments), and the right-hand side summarizes the sources of capital, or how a firm raises the money it needs. Because of the way stockholders' equity is calculated, the left- and right-hand sides must balance:

In Table 3.1, total assets for 2012 ($3,112 million) are equal to total liabilities ($389 + $454) plus stockholders' equity ($2,269 million).

Let us examine assets, liabilities and stockholders' equity in more detail.

Assets

In Table 3.1, total assets are divided into current assets (short-term) and fixed assets (long-term assets).

Current Assets. Current assets are either cash or assets that could be converted into cash within 1 year. This category includes the following:

– cash and other marketable securities, which are short-term, low-risk investments that can be easily sold and converted to cash (such as money market investments like government debt that matures within a year);

– accounts receivable, which are amounts owed to the firm by customers who have purchased goods or services on credit;

– inventories, which are composed of raw materials as well as work-in-progress and finished goods.

Long-Term Assets. The first category of long-term assets is net property, plant and equipment. These include assets such as real estate or machinery that produce tangible benefits for more than 1 year. If the U.S. corporation spends $1,709 million on new equipment, this value will be included with property, plant and equipment on the balance sheet. Because equipment tends to wear out or become obsolete over time, the company will reduce the value recorded for this equipment each year by deducting a depreciation expense. An asset's accumulated depreciation is the total amount deducted over its life. The firm reduces the value of fixed assets (other than land) over time according to a depreciation schedule that depends on the asset's lifespan. Depreciation is not an actual cash expense that the firm pays; it is a way of recognizing that buildings and equipment wear out and thus become less valuable the older they get. The book value of an asset, which is the value shown in the firm's financial statements, is equal to its acquisition cost minus accumulated depreciation.

Liabilities

We now examine the liabilities shown on the right-hand side of the balance sheet, which are divided into current and long-term liabilities.

Current Liabilities. Liabilities that will be satisfied within 1 year are known as current liabilities. They include the following:

– accounts payable, the amounts owed to suppliers for products or services purchased with credit;

– short-term debt or notes payable, and current maturities of long-term debt, which are all repayments of debt that will occur within the next year.

Long-Term Liabilities. Long-term liabilities are liabilities that extend beyond 1 year. We describe the main types as follows:

– Long-term debt is any loan or debt obligation with a maturity of more than a year. When a firm needs to raise funds to purchase an asset or make an investment, it may borrow those funds through a long-term loan.

– Capital leases are long-term lease contracts that obligate the firm to make regular lease payments in exchange for use of an asset. They allow a firm to gain use of an asset by leasing it from the asset's owner. For example, a firm may lease a building to serve as its corporate headquarters.

– Deferred taxes are taxes that are owed but have not yet been paid. Firms generally keep two sets of financial statements: one for financial reporting and one for tax purposes. Occasionally, the rules for the two types of statements differ. Deferred tax liabilities generally arise when the firm's financial income exceeds its income for tax purposes. Since deferred taxes will eventually be paid, they appear as a liability on the balance sheet

Stockholders' Equity

The sum of the current liabilities and long-term liabilities is total liabilities. The difference between the firm's assets and liabilities is the stockholders' equity; it is also called the book value of equity. As we stated earlier, it is an accounting measure of the net worth of the firm.

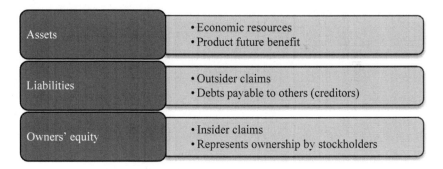

Figure 3.9. *Balance sheet parts*

3.4.2. *Balance Sheet Diagnosis*

Market value versus book value

The values shown on the balance sheet for the firm's assets are book values and generally are not what the assets are actually worth. Under Generally Accepted Accounting Principles (GAAP), audited financial statements in the United States generally show assets at historical cost. In other words, assets are "carried on the books" at what the firm paid for them, no matter how long ago they were purchased or how much they are worth today.

For current assets, market value and book value might be somewhat similar because current assets are bought and converted into cash over a relatively short span of time. In other circumstances, the two values might differ quite a bit. Moreover, for fixed assets, it would be purely a coincidence if the actual market value of an asset (what the asset could be sold for) were equal to its book value. For example, a railroad might own enormous tracts of land purchased a century or more ago. What the railroad paid for that land could be hundreds or thousands of times less than what the land is worth today. The balance sheet would nonetheless show the historical cost.

The difference between market value and book value is important for understanding the impact of reported gains and losses. For example, to open the chapter, we discussed the huge expenses against earnings taken by Bank of America. What actually happened is that these expenses were the result of accounting rule changes that led to reductions in the book value of certain types of assets. However, a change in accounting rules all by itself has no effect on what the assets in question are really worth. Instead, the market value of an asset depends on things like its riskiness and cash flows, neither of which have an impact on accounting.

The balance sheet is potentially useful to many different parties. A supplier might look at the size of accounts payable to see how promptly the firm pays its bills. A potential creditor would examine the liquidity and degree of financial leverage. Managers within the firm can track things like the amount of cash and the amount of inventory the firm keeps on hand.

Managers and investors will frequently be interested in knowing the value of the firm.

This information is not on the balance sheet. The fact that balance sheet assets are listed at cost means that there is no necessary connection between the total assets shown and the value of the firm. Indeed, many of the most valuable assets a firm might have – good management, a good reputation, talented employees – do not appear on the balance sheet at all. Similarly, the shareholders' equity figure on the balance sheet and the true value of the stock need not be related. For financial managers, then, the accounting value of the stock is not an especially important concern; it is the market value that matters. Henceforth, whenever we speak of the value of an asset or the value of the firm, we will normally mean its market value. Hence, for example, when we say that the goal of the financial manager is to increase the value of the stock, we mean the market value of the stock.

Successful firms are often able to borrow in excess of the book value of their assets because creditors recognize that the market value of the assets is far higher than the book value. Thus, it is not surprising that the book value of equity will often differ substantially from the amount investors are willing to pay for the equity. The total market value of a firm's equity equals the number of shares outstanding times the firm's market price per share:

Market Value of Equity = Shares outstanding × Market price per share

The market value of equity is often referred to as the company's market capitalization (or "market cap"). The market value of a stock does not depend on the historical cost of the firm's assets; instead, it depends on what investors expect those assets to produce in the future.

Market-to-Book Ratio (or Price-to-book ratio) = Market Value of Equity/ Book Value of Equity

The market-to-book ratio for most successful firms substantially exceeds 1, indicating that the value of the firm's assets when put to use exceeds their historical cost. Variations in this ratio reflect differences in fundamental firm characteristics as well as the value added by management. In July 2012, Citigroup (C) had a market-to-book ratio of 0.43, a reflection of investors' assessment that many of Citigroup's assets (such as mortgage securities) were worth far less than their book value. At the same time, the average market-to-book ratio for major U.S. banks and financial firms was 1.2, and for all large U.S. firms, it was 2.3. In contrast, Pepsico (PEP) had a market-to-book ratio of 4.8, and IBM had a market-to-book ratio of 10.7. Analysts often classify firms with *low market-to-book ratios as value stocks* and those with *high market-to-book ratios as growth stocks*.

Enterprise value

A firm's market capitalization measures the market value of the firm's equity or the value that remains after the firm has paid its debts. But what is the value of the business itself?

The enterprise value of a firm (also called the total enterprise value or TEV) assesses the value of the underlying business assets, unencumbered by debt and separate from any cash and marketable securities. We compute it as follows:

Enterprise Value = Market Value of Equity + Debt − Cash

Example 2

Global's market capitalization in 2012 is $50.4 million. Its debt is $116.7 million ($3.5 million of notes payable, $13.3 million of current maturities of long-term debt and remaining long-term debt of $99.9 million). Therefore, given its cash balance of $21.2 million, Global's enterprise value is 50.4 + 116.7 − 21.2 = $145.9 million. The enterprise value can be interpreted as the cost to take over the business. That is, it would cost 50.4 + 116.7 = $167.1 million to buy all of Global's equity and pay off its debts, but because we would acquire Global's $21.2 million in cash, the net cost of the business is only 167.1 − 21.2 = $145.9 million.

GLOBAL CONGLOMERATE CORPORATION
Consolidated Balance Sheet
Year Ended December 31 (in $ million)

Assets	2012	2011	Liabilities and Stockholders' Equity	2012	2011
Current Assets			**Current Liabilities**		
Cash	21.2	19.5	Accounts payable	29.2	24.5
Accounts receivable	18.5	13.2	Notes payable/short-term debt	3.5	3.2
Inventories	15.3	14.3	Current maturities of long-term debt	13.3	12.3
Other current assets	2.0	1.0	Other current liabilities	2.0	4.0
Total current assets	57.0	48.0	Total current liabilities	48.0	44.0
Long-Term Assets			**Long-Term Liabilities**		
Land	22.2	20.7	Long-term debt	99.9	76.3
Buildings	36.5	30.5	Capital lease obligations	—	—
Equipment	39.7	33.2	Total debt	99.9	76.3
Less accumulated depreciation	(18.7)	(17.5)	Deferred taxes	7.6	7.4
Net property, plant, and equipment	79.7	66.9	Other long-term liabilities	—	—
Goodwill and intangible assets	20.0	20.0	Total long-term liabilities	107.5	83.7
Other long-term assets	21.0	14.0	Total Liabilities	155.5	127.7
Total long-term assets	120.7	100.9	Stockholders' Equity	22.2	21.2
Total Assets	177.7	148.9	Total Liabilities and Stockholders' Equity	177.7	148.9

Table 3.2. *Global's balance sheet (source: Berk and DeMarzo [BER 14])*

Example 3

General Electric case

Suppose in 2014, General Electric (GE) had a total equity of $290 billion, 15 billion shares outstanding, and a market price of $13 per share. GE also had cash of $60 billion, and total debt of $600 billion. Three years later, in early 2017, GE had a total equity of $340 billion, 18 billion shares with a market price of $20 per share, cash of $90 billion, and total debt of $780 billion. Over this period, what was the change in GE's:

1) market capitalization?

2) market-to-book ratio?

3) enterprise value?

Solution

1) 2014 Market Capitalization: 15 billion shares × $13/share = $195 billion.

   2017 Market Capitalization: 18 billion shares × $20/share = $360 billion.

   The change over the period is $360 – $195 = $165 billion.

2) 2014 Market-to-Book ratio = 195/290 = 0.672

   2017 Market-to-Book ratio = 360/340 = 1.058.

   The change over the period is: 1.058 – 0.672 = 0.386.

3) 2014 Enterprise Value = $195 – 60 + 600 = $735 billion.

   2017 Enterprise Value = $360 – 90 + 780 = $1,050 billion.

   The change over the period is: $1,050 – $735 = –$315 billion

Example 4

ANF versus GPS

Suppose in 2016, a company ANF had a book equity of $2,000 million, a price per share of $40, and 90 million shares outstanding. At the same time, a company

GPS had a book equity of $4,600 million, a share price of $32, and 600 million shares outstanding.

1) What is the market-to-book ratio of each of these companies?

2) What conclusions can you draw by comparing the two ratios?

Solution

1) ANF's market-to-book ratio = (40× 90)/2,000 = 1.8.

GPS's market-to-book ratio = (32× 600)/4,600 = 4.174.

2) For the market, the outlook of ANF is less favorable than that of GPS. For every dollar of equity invested in ANF, the market values that dollar today at $1.8 versus $4.174 for a dollar invested in GPS. Equity investors are willing to pay relatively less today for shares of ANF than for GPS because they expect GPS to produce superior performance in the future.

Net working capital

The difference between current assets and current liabilities is the firm's *net working capital*, the capital available in the short term to run the business. For example, in Table 3.1, in 2012, U.S. Corporation's net working capital totaled $1,014 million ($1,403 million in current assets − $389 million in current liabilities). Firms with low (or negative) net working capital may face a shortage of funds unless they generate sufficient cash from their ongoing activities.

Net working capital is positive when current assets exceed current liabilities. Based on the definitions of current assets and current liabilities, this means the cash that will become available over the next 12 months exceeds the cash that must be paid over the same period. For this reason, net working capital is usually positive in a healthy firm.

Liquidity

Liquidity refers to the speed and ease with which an asset can be converted to cash. Liquidity actually has two dimensions: ease of conversion and loss of value. Any asset can be converted to cash quickly if we cut the price enough. A highly liquid asset is therefore the one that can be quickly sold without significant loss of value. An illiquid asset is the one that cannot be quickly converted to cash without a substantial price reduction.

Assets are normally listed on the balance sheet in order of decreasing liquidity, meaning that the most liquid assets are listed first. Current assets are relatively liquid and include cash and assets we expect to convert to cash over the next 12 months. Accounts receivable, for example, represent amounts not yet collected from customers on sales already made. Naturally, we hope these will convert to cash in the near future. Inventory is probably the least liquid of the current assets, at least for many businesses.

Fixed assets are, for the most part, relatively illiquid. These consist of tangible things such as buildings and equipment that do not convert to cash at all in normal business activity (they are, of course, used in the business to generate cash). Intangible assets, such as a trademark, have no physical existence but can be very valuable. Like tangible fixed assets, they won't ordinarily convert to cash and are generally considered illiquid. Liquidity is valuable. The more liquid a business is, the less likely it is to experience financial distress (i.e. difficulty in paying debts or buying needed assets). Unfortunately, liquid assets are generally less profitable to hold. For example, cash holdings are the most liquid of all investments, but they sometimes earn no return at all – they just sit there. There is therefore a trade-off between the advantages of liquidity and forgone potential profits.

Financial analysts often use the information in the firm's balance sheet to assess its financial solvency or liquidity. Specifically, creditors often compare a firm's current assets and current liabilities to assess whether the firm has sufficient working capital to meet its short-term needs. This comparison can be summarized in the firm's current ratio, the ratio of current assets to current liabilities:

Current Ratio = Current Assets/Current Liabilities

Note that U.S. Corporation's current ratio increased from $1,112/428 = 2.6$ in 2011 to $1,403/389 = 3.6$ in 2012.

A more stringent test of the firm's liquidity is the quick ratio, which compares only cash and "near cash" assets, such as short-term investments and accounts receivable, to current liabilities.

Quick Ratio = (Current Assets − Inventories)/Current Liabilities

In 2012, U.S. Corporation's quick ratio was $(1,403 − 555)/389 = 2.18$. A higher current or quick ratio implies less risk of the firm experiencing a cash shortfall in the near future. A reason to exclude inventory is that it may not be that liquid; indeed, an increase in the current ratio that results from an unusual increase in inventory could be an indicator that the firm is having difficulty selling its products.

Ultimately, firms need cash to pay employees and meet other obligations. Running out of cash can be very costly for a firm, so firms often gauge their cash position by calculating the cash ratio, which is the most stringent liquidity ratio:

Cash Ratio = Cash/Current Liabilities

Of course, all of these liquidity ratios are limited in that they only consider the firm's current assets. If the firm is able to generate significant cash quickly from its ongoing activities, it might be highly liquid even if these ratios are poor. In 2012, U.S. Corporation's cash ratio was $160/389 = 0.41$.

Leverage ratios

An important piece of information that we can obtain from a firm's balance sheet is the firm's leverage, or the extent to which it relies on debt as a source of financing. The debt-equity ratio is a common ratio used to assess a firm's leverage. We calculate this ratio by dividing the total amount of short- and long-term debt (including current maturities) by the total stockholders' equity:

Debt-Equity Ratio = Total Debt/Total Equity

We can calculate the debt-equity ratio using either book or market values for equity and debt. Recall that total debt includes both short-term borrowings and long-term borrowings. From Table 3.1, U.S. Corporation's debt in 2012 includes only long-term debt ($454 million). Therefore, its book debt-equity ratio is $454/2,269 = 0.20$, using the book value of equity. Note the slight decline from 2011 when the book debt-equity ratio was $408/1,920 = 0.21$.

In addition, from Table 3.2, Global's debt in 2012 includes notes payable ($3.5 million), current maturities of long-term debt ($13.3 million) and long-term debt ($99.9 million), for a total of $116.7 million. Therefore, its book debt-equity ratio is $116.7/22.2 = 5.3$, using the book value of equity. Note the increase from 2011, when the book debt-equity ratio was only $(3.2 + 12.3 + 76.3)/21.2 = 91.8/21.2 = 4.3$.

Because of the difficulty interpreting the book value of equity, the book debt-equity ratio is not especially useful. Indeed, the book value of equity might even be negative, making the ratio meaningless. For example, Domino's Pizza (DPZ) has, based on the strength of its cash flow, consistently borrowed in excess of the book value of its assets. In 2012, it had a debt of $1.6 billion, with a total book value of assets of only $600 million and an equity book value of −$1.4 billion! It is therefore most informative to compare the firm's debt to the market value of its equity (see [BER 14]).

Recall from example 2 that, in 2012, the total market value of Global's equity, its market capitalization, is 3.6 million shares * $14/share = $50.4 million. Therefore, Global's market debt-equity ratio in 2012 is 116.7/50.4 = 2.3, which means that Global's debt is a bit more than double the market value of its equity. As we show later in the text, a firm's market debt-equity ratio has important consequences for the risk and return of its stock.

We can also calculate the fraction of the firm financed by debt in terms of its debt-to-capital ratio:

Debt-to-Capital Ratio = Total Debt/(Total Equity + Total Debt)

Again, this ratio can be computed using book or market values. While leverage increases the risk to the firm's equity holders, firms may also hold cash reserves in order to reduce risk. Thus, another useful measure to consider is the firm's net debt, or debt in excess of its cash reserves:

Net Debt = Total Debt − Excess Cash & Short-term Investments

To understand why net debt may be a more relevant measure of leverage, consider a firm with more cash than debt outstanding: because such a firm could pay off its debts immediately using its available cash, it has not increased its risk and has no effective leverage.

Analogous to the debt-to-capital ratio, we can use the concept of net debt to compute the firm's debt-to-enterprise value ratio:

Debt-to-Enterprise Value Ratio = Net Debt/Market Value of Equity + Net Debt

= Net Debt/Enterprise Value

Given Global's 2012 cash balance of $21.2 million, and total long- and short-term debts of $116.7 million, its net debt is 116.7 − 21.2 = $95.5 million. Given its market value of equity of $50.4 million, Global's enterprise value in 2012 is 50.4 + 95.5 = $145.9 million, and thus its debt-to-enterprise value ratio is 95.5/145.9 = 65.5%. That is, 65.5% of Global's underlying business activity is financed via debt.

A final measure of leverage is a firm's equity multiplier, measured in book value terms as *Total Assets/Book Value of Equity*. As we will see shortly, this measure captures the amplification of the firm's accounting returns resulting from leverage. The market value equity multiplier, which is generally measured as Enterprise Value/Market Value of Equity, indicates the amplification of shareholders' financial risk that results from leverage.

4

Analysis of Activity: Analysis of Profit and Loss Account: IFRS vs. US GAAP

The *analysis of the company's activity* is the starting point for any diagnosis. It is based on the short term, and it allows us to assess the *growth* of the company and *measure its profitability, that is, its ability to generate profits*. Efficiency and profitability should not be confused. In fact:

– the profitability reports the result on invested capital; it concerns a balance sheet analysis (balance sheet profit and balance sheet capital), which interests the investors;

– the profitability is the propensity to produce a result (profit margin). Profitability does not only relate to the net accounting result but also to all the other performance indicators such as the interim management balances of the PCG or even the few indicators under IFRS.

4.1. Profitability and management performance

Intermediate management balances are management indicators, representing the partial results obtained by the entity and which are available down to the net result. This stratigraphy is important for the year studied and especially in terms of evolutions. These are internal performance indicators, which are very relevant indicators of profitability. They have their advantages and limits.

Current operating income *corresponds to Danone's operating profit before taking into account other operating income and expenses. Pursuant to the ANC's recommendation 2013-03 "relating to the format of consolidated accounts of* companies established in accordance with international accounting standards", other operating income and expenses include significant items that, due to their nature and their unusual character, cannot be considered as inherent to its current activity. They mainly include capital gains and losses on the sale of consolidated businesses and investments, goodwill impairment, significant costs related to strategic restructuring and major acquisitions and costs (incurred or estimates) related to major crises and litigation. In addition, in accordance with IFRS 3 and IAS 27 Revised on Business Combinations, the Company also reports in the Other Operating Income and Expenses section: (i) the acquisition costs of the companies it controls (ii) remeasurement differences recognized as a result of a loss of control and (iii) changes in purchase price adjustments subsequent to a takeover.

The "*current operating margin*" is the ratio of current operating income to net sales.

> "**The net current result – Group share** measures the recurring performance of the Company and excludes significant items which, due to their nature and unusual character, cannot be considered as inherent to Danone's current performance. Non-current items mainly include other operating income and expenses, capital gains or losses on disposals and impairment of investments accounted for using the equity method or non-consolidated companies, as well as income and tax costs relating to non-current items. These items that are excluded from the net current result – Group share represent Net Profit or Loss – Group Share".[1]

4.1.1. *Intermediate Management Balances*

Many analysts have reprocessed the indicators of the French Chart of Accounts, but they remain the norm (the PCG has defined them).

• Those that appear under IFRS have no official reference or obligation of consistency in their calculation from one year to another:

INTERMEDIATE MANAGEMENT REBATE	N0	N1
+ Sale of goods		
− Cost of purchase of goods sold		
➔ 1. COMMERCIAL MARGIN		

---

1 Rapport financier Danone 2016

+ Sold production		
+ Stored production		
+ Capitalized production		
➔ 2. PRODUCTION OF THE EXERCISE		

+ Purchase of materials and other supplies		
± Change in stock of materials, goods and supplies		
+ Purchase and external expenses (including rent-to-lease)		
+ Leasing rents		
= Intermediate consumption		
+ 2. PRODUCTION		
− Intermediate consumption		
➔ 3. VALUE ADDED		
+ Current Operating Grant		
− Levies, taxes and payments		
− Interim external staff (for reprocessing for comparison)		
− Wages, salaries, staff benefits and social charges		
➔ 4. GROSS OPERATING SURPLUS[2]		
+ Other operating income		
+ Reversal of depreciation and provisions and transfer of expenses		
+ Other expenses (including share of joint operation N1 and N0)		
± Share of common operation		
− Depreciation, provisions (possibly leasing)		
➔ 5. OPERATING RESULT		

+ Financial products		
− Financial expenses		
− Financial burden of leasing (if restated for comparison)		
FINANCIAL RESULT*		

---

[2] According to IFRS, this is *EBITDA*, Earning Before Interest Taxes Depreciation & Amortization.

+ 5. OPERATING RESULT		
± Share of common operation		
+ Financial result		
➔ 6. CURRENT RESULT³		

+ Exceptional products		
− Extraordinary expenses		
➔ 7. EXCEPTIONAL RESULT		

− Employee participation		
− Income tax		
+ 6. CURRENT RESULT		
+ 7. EXCEPTIONAL RESULT		
➔ 8. RESULT OF THE EXERCISE		

+ Proceeds from sale of assets		
− Net book value of assets sold		
➔ 9. RESULT OF DISPOSALS OF ASSETS		

Although the financial result does not appear in IFRS, it is possible to calculate it.

Saint Gobain example – financial result:

The financial result includes the cost of the gross financial debt, the cash income, the net financial cost of the pension after taking into account the yield of the funds and the other financial expenses and income (notably the foreign exchange losses and profit and the bank commissions).

---

3 According to IFRS, this is the operating profit. It is an indicator of operating profitability. It considers expenses before financials (financial income and expenses) and depreciations. It is therefore the balance of the current activity, before investment and financial policy.

(In millions of euros)	2016 financial year	2015 financial year
Cost of gross financial debt	**(376)**	**(444)**
Income from cash and cash equivalents	27	25
Cost of net financial debt	(349)	(419)
Financial cost of pensions	**(387)**	**(393)**
Return on funds	278	297
Financial cost of net pensions	(109)	(96)
Other financial expenses	**(111)**	**(131)**
Other financial products	28	17
Other financial income and expenses	(83)	(114)
Financial result	(541)	(629)

4.1.2. Current exploitation

4.1.2.1. The commercial margin

Commercial margin is an essential indicator for the financial analysis of commercial enterprises. We must be wary when it is calculated for industrial companies that tend to relocate their production in countries at lower costs. They therefore receive finished products on which they add only their brand or services to the customer. In this case, it is difficult to know whether this balance corresponds to all production or only part of the goods, which it resells as commodities.

EXAMPLE.– If a company manufactures 55% of its products and buys 45% of its range, the commercial margin will only be calculated for the 45% of "goods" that it sells as is. Thus, the margin rate, which usually makes most of the profitability of a commercial enterprise, no longer has probative value with which to judge an industrial enterprise. If it makes extensive use of outsourcing, then it actually sells products that it has manufactured and is receiving after completion or at a very advanced stage of completion. Even if it conditions them, the products already finished remain as goods as repackaging is not part of the production process in a strict sense.

Therefore, the commercial margin should cover a greater share of products, which are made elsewhere and which are only elements resold in their current state. Thus:

+ Sales of goods and subcontracting
− Sales reductions already deducted in the income statement
− Cost of purchase of goods sold
= Market Margin

With:

± Stocks of goods [initial stock of m / s − final stock of m / s]
+ Purchase of goods and subcontracting (607)
− Incidental expenses on purchases of goods (6087)
+ Discounts, rebates, rebates granted on purchases of goods (6097)
= Cost of purchase of goods sold

No specific margin is foreseen for industrial companies. They often use the concept of "gross margin", which is rather confusing because it is not standardized by the French Accounting Plan but by the Banque de France. When an indicator is presented as "gross" or "net" (cash flows, sales, etc.), we do not know what they are net of: tax, commercial expenses, etc. However, we can consider calculating an industrial and commercial margin as:

+ Turnover of goods, services, products and merchandise
− Cost of goods, services products and goods
= Margin on cost of goods, services produced and goods

+ Margin on cost of goods, services produced and merchandise
− Marketing cost
= Net margin of goods, services produced and goods

As a result, the analyst's share of the company's total business activity is not part of the reduced turnover of goods.

4.1.2.2. Production

Production is not to be confused with the production cycle, which goes back far upstream (feasibility, studies, research, etc.), nor with the cost of production of a product that remains so much that the product exists on the market (packaging surveillance, recovery, etc.). Here, the production of an exercise is composed of the following four elements:

1) *Production sold*, excluding sales of products assimilated with goods, already included in the commercial margin. This sold production is not to be confused with turnover, because it takes into account all activity: commercial, goods, services.

2) *Stored production* is equal to final stock − initial stock. Any strong amplitude must alert the analyst. Thus, speculative stocks must be invested in financial fixed assets and not in the need for financing.

3) *Capitalized production* is the immobilization by the company of part of its own production. Workflows (purchases, labor, costs, etc.) gradually increase the level of an asset under construction, which, once completed, will be emptied to a capital account. Only then will depreciation begin with depreciation flows.

4) *Self-consumed production* includes production items that are in the process of being finished and are used in the manufacture of finished products.

For example, waste and scrap production that would be used as raw materials or consumables.

COMMENTS.– This year's production is a more comprehensive measure of activity than turnover. However, there remains a great heterogeneity. In fact:

– *Stored production* is valued by management accounting. The full cost assessment should only include expenses, thus neutralizing (as for IFRS) the sub-activity. This implies that there is management accounting that determines them.

– *Financial expenses* that form part of a full cost of production should be rejected along with other financial expenses (IFRS recommend directly allocating financial expenses to their generating account).

– *The sold production* is valued at the selling price, which takes into account:

- marketing costs, therefore out of production and

- profit margin on sales.

RECOMMENDATIONS ON MARGIN AND PRODUCTION.– To make the connection with the "Production of the exercise", we can calculate the "Industrial margin" as:

+ Production of the financial year
− Stored purchases
+ Inventory change
= Industrial margin

To make all elements of this production homogeneous, a production can be calculated at its cost of production.

+ Production of the year at the cost of rational allocation activity
+ Production stored at cost of rational allocation activity
+ Production capitalized at the cost of rational allocation activity
+ Self-consumed production and outstanding values
= **Production at the cost of production charged to the activity**

In addition, the production is carried out by subcontractors, while an increase in the offshored production increases the production but not the economic growth of the client company. It is the subcontractor that grows. For the PCG, subcontracting costs are included in the "other purchases and external expenses" account.

4.1.2.3. *Added value*

This balance is an economic and social reference, which is calculated as follows:

+ Commercial margin (intermediate management balances 1)

+ Production (intermediate management balances 2):

− exercise consumption from third parties =
   + purchases
   + change in inventories
   + other purchases and external expenses

= **Added value created**

Value added expresses the surplus that the company has produced over what it has destroyed. It is an added value created. It expresses the contribution of the company to the economy; it is a macroeconomic concept transposed to the company.

Added value is a significant indicator of company growth, even of its survival, because if the added value is negative, nothing can be allocated to human resources or capital. The Banque de France also considers that the company will disappear within three years if its added value is negative. It can be seen from the preceding diagram that without growth in value added, there is no possible growth in wages or capital financing.

COMMENTS.–

– The *operating subsidies received* compensate for a lost turnover and they must be included in the value added as additional turnover.

– *Taxes, duties and similar payments* do not actually benefit the state, but often a public service consumption. The attitude of reintegrating the account of taxes, duties and assimilated payments into internal consumption is acceptable, especially for the small amount that it generally represents in relation to total expenses.

– The *operating subsidy* and *taxes, duties and similar payments* could be offset to give added value that only remunerates labor and capital.

– We can determine an *added value created for the production* that starts with an added cost calculation from management accounting:

+ Production calculated at cost of production
– Cost of purchasing supplies consumed =

+ *purchases of consumed supplies*
     – *outsourcing purchases*
     + *purchases of external services*
     + *change in inventories*

+ Net Margin of Stored Goods Sold
= **Value added for production**

Expenses

The Banque de France, as in IFRS, proposes an approach that gives a cross-sectoral vision of added value. It removes the added value for comparison:

– External staff, entered into account 621 "other management expenses" to add them to account 64 or "salary expenses";

– The leasing fees, initially entered in account 612 and reintegrated into account 68 "depreciation allowances" and account 66 "financial expenses".

The comparative value added is then the following:

+ Added value created (intermediate management balances 3)
+ Operating subsidies
+ Outside staff
+ Leasing fee
= **Comparative value added at factor cost**

Each analyst starts with standardized intermediate balances and then refines them according to the firm's context and the degree of analysis required.

– To take into account the total cost of Human Resources in all its components, the following should be included:

+ Personal and employee benefits (64) including stock options
+ Temporary staff (621)
+ Outsourced paid external staff (622)
+ Director's fees (65)
+ Benefits (golden parachutes, golden retirements, etc.)
+ Participation (691)

Thus, accounts 621 and 622 are no longer considered as intermediate consumption and their withdrawals increase the value added. The cost of human resources thus determined makes it possible to better compare companies with each other, regardless of how they are paid.

4.1.2.4. *Gross Operating Surplus*

If the added value is the flow that "remunerates" the labor and capital factors, then the gross operating surplus "remunerates" the sources of finance.

+ Added value (intermediate management balances 3)
+ Operating grants received
− Taxes, duties and similar payments (under certain conditions)
− Staff costs
= **Gross operating surplus**

This gross excess of exploitation or in IFRS, Ebit (Earnings Before Interest and Taxes), is separated from the financing and depreciation policies and from the exceptional items. This gross excess of exploitation is used to calculate the Excess operating cash flow (operating cash flow from the cash flow statement) or the Free cash flow.

It also allows us to determine by a ratio:

– the *risk of default*: financial burden/gross operating surplus;

– a *profitability*: EBITDA/turnover.

This balance is a necessary step between the economic flows of the profit and loss account and purely financial flows.

COMMENTS.– The Banque de France presents a modified EBITDA derived from the calculation of a corrected value added.

The Banque de France, like IFRS, includes the Exceptional or Excluded items in the current activity, to determine a Gross Global Surplus. The idea of integrating as many elements as possible into the business (current and non-current) is in line with IFRS, which reduces the off-load only to extreme cases.

This homogeneity of all these indicators is fundamental for inter-company financial analysis.

The gross operating surplus schematically remunerates the capital:

+ borrowed by the flow of financial expenses
+ invested by the depreciation stream
+ provided by the flow of dividends
+ of the State by the flow of taxes
+ of the company by the flow of self-financing reserves

The operating result:

In the PCG, operating profit is calculated by reducing the gross operating surplus of the remuneration of the interior elements, namely:

Gross Operating Surplus (EBITDA)
+ Other operating income (account 75 except 755)
− Other operating expenses (account 65 except 655)
+ Transfer of expenses (791)
− Depreciation (consumption of capital) (681)
= Operating result

COMMENTS.– The operating result is in fact, after the financing of capital consumption (depreciation), available to distribute to the rest of the capital.

This operating result depends on the depreciation flow. The more the company invests, the more it is favorable to its development and the lower the operating profit will be (which might seem unfavorable). These depreciation allowances favorably contribute to increase self-financing, which is then favorable for financial analysis.

We must not be indifferent to the decline in operating income, because when the financial situation deteriorates, it also drops and becomes premonitory of this degradation.

Finally, the operating result has the clearest denomination, yet the fuzziest content. It had all of its significance when the current and the outflow were about two-thirds of the income statement. With the trend of the Central Balance Sheet Office and IFRS to include a maximum of non-exceptional operations in the exploitation, the probative value of this intermediate management balance is less strong. Its similarity to operating profit is illusory if the contents differ greatly.

Saint Gobain example:

"The operating result measures the performance of the business lines of the divisions and is the main management indicator used internally and externally for many years. Foreign exchange gains and losses and changes in fair value of non-qualified hedging instruments related to income from operating activities are recognized in operating income, and the share of earnings of companies accounted for by the equity method whose activity is in line with that of the Group..."

4.1.2.5. Current result

This result is more satisfactory and tends to replace the operating result for two reasons:

– It is calculated by integrating the net financial burden and therefore part of the cost of capital required for the current.

– IFRS performance indicators tend to bring into the mainstream everything that is long-lasting, recurrent, repetitive, persistent, etc.

Operating income (balance 5)
+ financial products
+ Reversal of depreciation and provisions of a financial nature
– Financial expenses
– Depreciation and provisions of a financial nature
+ Transfer of financial expenses
+ the share of the operating results in common (755–655)
= **Current result**

COMMENTS.– In order for a financial expense to be current, it was necessary for its share in the income statement to be relatively constant: for example, 3% of turnover and 12% of the gross operating surplus. However, the international trend is to reduce the financial expenses of the current result by withdrawing them directly from the posts concerned, leaving in the financial expenses only the cost of the general loans.

Example of the Saint Gobain company in 2017, 2016 and 2015

Turnover and accessory products	(3)	39 093	39 623
Cost of products sold	(3)	(29 106)	(29 694)
General and research expenses	(3)	(7 200)	(7 336)
Share in results of companies accounted for by the equity method	(6)	31	43
Operating profit		2 818	2 636
Other operational products	(3)	61	49
Other operating expenses	(3)	(575)	(1 391)
Operating income		2 304	1 294
Cost of gross financial debt		(376)	(444)
Income from cash and cash equivalents		27	25
Cost of net financial debt		(349)	(419)
Other financial income and expenses		(192)	(210)
Financial result	(8)	(541)	(629)
Share in results of non-operating companies	(6)	5	0
Taxes on results	(10)	(416)	(248)
Net income from continuing operations		1 352	417
Net income from discontinued operations		0	929
Net income of the consolidated group		1 352	1 346
Net income from continuing operations, Group share		1 311	374
Net income from discontinued operations, Group share		0	921
Net income Group share		1 311	1 295
Net income from continuing operations, attributable to minority interests		41	43
Net income from discontinued operations, attributable to minority interests		0	8
Share of minority interests		41	51

4.1.3. *Non-operating current*

4.1.3.1. *The exceptional result*

+ Exceptional products
− Exceptional shares
+ Reversal of depreciation and exceptional provisions
+ Depreciation, amortization and exceptional provisions
+ Exceptional share transfer
= **Exceptional result**

COMMENTS.– This balance cannot be deduced from the previous ones. It is an entity in its own right. As we have said previously, the tendency is to reduce it to exceptional cases, but not to the simple running current.

The net accounting result:

The balance of the income statement (and the balance sheet) will be used to calculate the profitability of invested capital. It is determined on a cascading basis from the current result after deducting the employee contribution (if it has not already been deducted with staff costs) and the corporation tax (the State), to obtain:

+ Current result (intermediate management balances 6)
+ Exceptional result (intermediate management balances 7)
− Employee participation
− Corporate Income Taxes
= **Net accounting result (therefore also that of the Balance Sheet)**

COMMENTS.– Some analysts believe that employee participation is an expense that compensates for the labor factor and suggests including it in staffing costs as a mandatory operating expense.

4.1.3.2. *Result of asset disposals*

The interest of this balance contains essential data for the financial analysis because it indicates the results of the operations in capital, that is to say, the exits of the wealth of assets.

+ Proceeds from asset sales (capital transactions)
− Net book value of the assets sold
= **Profit or loss on disposal of fixed assets**

COMMENTS.– This result mainly concerns disposals of fixed assets. It can either reinforce the impression of a beneficial reinvestment policy or reveal the liquidation of the company's assets to finance a difficult management.

4.2. Management indicators of the Banque de France

For nearly 40 years, the Banque de France has been studying the behavior of companies grouped into different business sectors.

Its economic orientation is therefore more marked than that of the PCG by its necessary comparison between companies. Banque de France analysis is therefore closer to the IFRS logic.

The advantage of the Banque de France's method of analysis is that its studies focus on a database of 50,000 companies analyzed with:

– a consistent method of analyzing the company accounts;

– a reconciliation of the accounts of individual companies with those of similar populations.

The analysis of the Central Balance Sheet Office of the Banque de France identifies the four main functions of the company, which can be found at the level of the balance sheet and the income statement or the financing table: financing, investment, exploitation and distribution. Its functions include:

– Exploitation, which evaluates the business in its vital role of creating more value than it consumes and rewarding the factors it implements.

– Breakdown, which includes income distribution operations to factors that are personal (salaries and social charges, employee participation, etc.), of the State (income tax, taxes, duties and assimilated payments), of shareholders (dividends) and self-financing.

– Investment, which includes acquisitions, creations and disposals of fixed assets on the plan:

- internal growth by premises, capital goods and intangible items recorded as fixed assets;

- external growth through participation in the businesses of other companies over which it exercises control.

– Financing that controls liquidity and solvency and thus its survival.

To carry out its financial analysis, the Central Balance Sheet Office of the Banque de France recomposed some accounting packages. This analysis requires:

– isolating:

- trade accounts receivable and related accounts and accounts payable and related operating accounts;

– productive fixed assets, which together with the balance of "trade receivables and rat-run operating accounts" and "accounts payable and related operating accounts", determine operating capital.

– retreating for comparison purposes:

- equipment acquired under finance leases for inclusion in the balance sheet (as in IFRS);

- trade receivables mobilized or sold to attach them to trade receivables and related operating accounts;

- by adding:

+ the staff made available to the company (temporary, etc.) with the number of employees;

+ expenses related to these external personnel (whose expenses are billed as part of cost, in turnover), with personnel costs.

– correcting balance sheet items by taking all items of assets in gross values and by placing the depreciation and provisions of these asset items with the liability's own funds (as in the functional analysis). These depreciations are considered to be self-financing.

4.2.1. *Partial or current indicators*

The former Central Balance Sheet Office of the Banque de France has been transformed into OPALE[4] Analyse, which uses analyses and proposes the "diagnosis of your structured business" around the following major themes:

– *Activity and results.* "OPALE Analyse" highlights the evolution of your business and the margin levels. At a glance, you can obtain the main changes in your company over the past two years, thanks in particular to the intermediate management balances and the ratios calculated by the tool.

– *Operating means.* "OPALE Analyse" allows you to analyze the components of the working capital requirements that your business generates and to measure the impact of your investment effort.

– *Financial structure.* This theme highlights the balance and the financial structure of your company. Is the capital sufficient? Is the level of indebtedness comparable to that in your sector of activity? Can this level of indebtedness be justified by the level of investments put in place?

---

4 Outil de Positionnement et d'Analyse en Ligne des Entreprises. This is a French tool that is only available to French businesses that have a turnover of at least €750,000.

– *A sector study*. OPALE provides you with information on your sector of activity: outstanding bank loans, unpaid balances and distribution of Banque de France quotes via a graphic presentation of this information.

– *A complete financial analysis report*. Finally, a detailed report in PDF format (presenting results, ratios, summaries and graphs) is at your disposal at the end of the diagnosis.

The study of intermediate management balances is done for:

– the current operation;

– all operations of the company in a global approach (total would have been a more appropriate term).

There are specific indicators such as own production, margin on own production, gross operating margin, value added and gross operating income.

4.2.1.1. *Own production*

This expresses the company's contribution to its economic growth, without outsourcing.

4.2.1.2. *Industrial margin on own production*

A margin is the difference between a product and a cost.

In the case of a commercial enterprise, the margin on marketing cost is the difference between the turnover and the marketing cost.

Similarly, the own cost of production margin is the difference between own production and the cost of resources consumed for that production.

4.2.1.3. *Gross operating margin or current*

This is a total margin combining the two activities of the company: production and commercial.

DIAGNOSIS.– With this trend that companies have to outsource their production at lower costs, these two margins are interesting and their relative share over time is significant to the company's growth strategy.

4.2.1.4. Added value

-Intermediate consumption	+ production made, stored and sold
= added value	+ goods stored and sold

DIAGNOSIS.– It expresses the contribution of the company to the creation of value and the diffusion of goods and services. It shows that the company has created more than it has destroyed and therefore measures the economic weight of the company. It measures the specific contribution of the company in the process of production and distribution of a good. This contribution is closely linked to the importance and qualification of the human resources and capital goods resources. Value added is therefore, at the same time, an indicator measuring the development of the company and its contribution to overall development. The Banque de France has corrected the added value of the PCG, taking into account:

– finance lease: fees that are usually classified as external expenses; the Banque de France considers them a mode of financing;

– expenditure of external staff who are here considered as staff costs and

– operating subsidies received for a deficiency in turnover.

Thus, this added value has a comparative purpose and constitutes both a criterion of:

– size, relevant for the classification of companies and

– development or regression of the activity.

PROGNOSIS.– For the Banque de France, a company with an added value of < 0 disappears within three years.

4.2.1.5. Operating profit

This is the first balance obtained after production and marketing processes. This is what the company extracts as its own resource of its branch.

It is larger than the gross operating surplus as it includes patent royalties and credit losses.

ANALYSIS.– This operating result is not influenced by the breakdown of the result: financial expenses, dividends, taxation, etc. The higher this operating profit, the more the company has a financial autonomy to ensure the consumption (depreciation) of invested capital:

+ Other income and expenses (see note)
+ Other financial income and expenses (see note)
−Taxes other and payments
= **Gross BDF Exploitation Result**

DIAGNOSIS.–

– They are removed from the account "other income and other expenses":

   - *operating subsidies received (excluding compensatory compensations for insufficient sales price already taken into account for the calculation of value added);*

   - *royalties received and paid. These are products or expenses of industrial property and intangible items that come under operating capital;*

   - recurring bad debt losses;

   - income from buildings not allocated to operations.

– They are removed from the accounts "financial income and expenses" of the PCG:

   - *income on trade receivables*

   - *interest on commercial debts*

– They are added to staff costs:

   + wages and social expenses;

   + expenses of external staff, temporary employment, fees, etc.;

   + provisions for social and tax expenses for paid leave.

PROGNOSIS.– This gross operating profit must be higher as the company is highly capital-intensive because it is from the gross operating result that the depreciation expenses will be deducted. This will induce the renewal rate of equipment. Gross operating income is independent of decisions regarding own or borrowed financing, tax policy, dividend distribution or self-financing.

4.2.1.6. *Net operating profit: self-financing*

This is a margin that is net of factor cost. This net operating profit is a measure of the company's industrial and commercial performance. It is independent of the two factors of production: capital and labor.

Net operating income measures net profitability of operating capital after adjusting gross operating income as follows:

+ added expense transfers

– deduct the calculated expenses composed of:

- amortization and operating provisions net of reversals;

- depreciation for the portion included in finance lease rents and

- changes in provisions for current risks and expenses.

4.2.2. Global indicators

In addition to the current portion of the current operations, the overall indicators include the non-current income-generating part, which is not directly related to current operations. This corresponds to IFRS analysis, which does not differentiate current operations from the rest.

Global indicators measure the entire profitability of the company, which ultimately amounts to equity.

DIAGNOSIS.– When these overall results are related to financial capital (equity – unless uncalled for – and debt), the ratios define indicators of the company's global profitability.

4.2.2.1. *Overall gross profit*

This is the total but gross remuneration (before depreciation, provision and taxes) of financing, both own and foreign. Moreover, to determine the cost of capital and more explicitly the interest on the debt, it is of course in relation to the overall gross result that it must be done.

The result on non-operating operation includes:

– the share of profit on operations carried out jointly and

– financial income, except interest expense and amortization and provisions net of reversals.

Overall net income measures the company's ability to make a profit. It is the gross remuneration (before amortization, provision and taxes) of equity and financial debts.

4.2.2.2. Result of the exercise

This is calculated after taking all income and expenses into account but before non-current items such as capital gains or losses on disposals of fixed assets or contributions.

Data banks such as OPALE of the Banque de France offer as a prognosis, a simulation regarding the following six themes:

1) Management. "You introduce your assumptions about the level of activity you are promoting, the variation in your payroll, the level of your external expenses or the desired margin".

2) Investment. "You formulate your assumptions regarding future investments (real estate, machinery purchases, etc.); OPALE makes it possible to immediately measure their impact on your balance sheet".

3) Financing. "How will your company's business be financed? Your simulations allow you to measure the impact of an increase in your capital and/or loans or leasing commitments on your business and the overall financial balance of your business".

4) Cash. "With the theme 'cash flow', your simulation on the components of the working capital requirement highlights their impact on cash flow and highlights the overall financial closure: equity, long-term financial debt, fixed assets, overall net working capital, overall working capital requirements, net cash flow".

5) Results. "OPALE highlights the overall balance of the financial statements (balance sheet and income statement)".

6) Final report. "The final report recalls the hypotheses of simulations that you have entered and takes the strengths and points of improvement of your company. This report can be used at will with your main partners (banks, customers, suppliers, etc.)".

It is possible to follow the OPALE financial investigation at a less-modeled level.

4.3. Correspondences of FCA indicators – Banque de France

French Chart of Accounts	Central Balance Sheet B. de F.	
Merchandise sales − Cost of purchase of merchandise sold		
= **Market margin**		
+ Sold production + Stored production + Fixed production		
= **Production of the exercise**		
	− Manufacturing outsourcing	
	= **Own production**	
	− Cost of material consumed	
	= **Industrial margin**	
+ Market margin		
+ Production of the exercise	+ Industrial margin	
− Consumption of the exercise from third parties (including subcontracting manufacturing, rental, external staff)	= **Gross operating margin**	
= **Added value**	− Purchases and external expenses (excluding manufacturing outsourcing, lease rent, outside staff)	**CURRENT operation**
+ Operating Grant (even if not in addition to price)	+ Operating Grant (if additional price)	
	= **Value added B of F**	
− Taxes and other payments	− Taxes and other payments (under certain conditions)	
− Staff costs		
	+ Operating subsidy received (excluding price supplement)	
	+ Income from operating receivables	
	+ Discounts obtained	
	+ Fees collected on patents, licensees, concessions	
	+ Income from buildings not allocated to the branch	
	− Interest of the commercial debt	
	− Discounts granted	
	− Fees paid on patents, licenses, concessions	
	− Losses/bad debts	

= Gross Operating Profit (EBITDA)		
+ Gross Operating Income		
+ Other income net of expenses (including royalties collected, income from non-current assets, capital gains on ordinary disposals)	+ Transfer of operating expenses	
− Depreciation and amortization	− Net allocation of reversals to depreciation and amortization	
+ Reversals on calculated expenses and transfer of expenses	− Depreciation and amortization from finance lease	
+ Gross Operating Income	= **Net Operating Result**	
	+ Gross Operating Income	

+ Share of results on operations made jointly			
+ Financial income (including discounts obtained, income from trade receivables, recoveries on calculated expenses and transfer of expenses.)	+ Financial transactions excluding interest and discounts		
− Interest expense (including interest on debt, interest on commercial debts, discounts granted, depreciation and financial provisions)	+ Exceptional operations excluding capital gains and disposals		
= **Current result before tax**			
+ Exceptional products (including capital gains on disposals and contributions, recovery on calculated expenses and transfer of expenses, investment subsidy transferred to the CR)	+ Transfers between operating expense accounts, financial and exceptional accounts		GLOBAL
− Exceptional expenses (including capital losses on disposals and contributions, amortization expenses and exceptional provisions)	= **Gross Global Result**		
= **Exceptional result**	+ Gross result of operation		
+ Current result before tax	+ Investment grants transferred to the profit and loss account		

+ Exceptional result	+ Transfer of expenses to assets in expenses to be distributed
	= Global Net Result
	− Interest on debt
	−Interest on borrowings extracted from lease financing rents
− Employee participation (under certain conditions for BdF)*	
− Income tax	
	= Result of the exercise
	± capital gains and contributions
= Reported net income	

* The Banque de France complies with the analysis of the FCA for the allocation of accounts, taxes, similar payments and participation, which are no longer considered systematically as State compensation in the first case or staff compensation in the second.

4.4. CAF cash flow

4.4.1. *Principles*

The income statement records the expenses and revenues of the year. It is assumed that all proceeds have been, or will be, recorded and all expenses have or will be disbursed. In this case, the profit is equal to the variation in immediate and deferred cash (working capital requirement).

If we add to these expenses and products, items that are not disbursable or cashable but simply calculated, then the income statement consists of two types of flows, namely:

– having an influence on cash flow in the year and

– having no influence on cash flow in the year:

Analysis of Activity: Analysis of Profit and Loss Account: IFRS vs. US GAAP

Income statement	
Expenses	**Products**
(Cash costs deducted from the Treasury)	Cash costs cashed in **the Treasury**
Expenses for disbursement of **working capital requirement**	Cash proceeds from **working capital requirements**

+ +

Calculated expenses (FR):	*Calculated products (FR):*
N provisions and provisions for allowances	*Reversals of depreciation and provisions*
Depreciation and amortization	*Sale price of disposed assets*
Net book value of assets sold	
Accounting net income	*Share of investment grants transferred to the profit and loss account*

It can be seen that these calculated costs will decrease the profit by the same amount and that the calculated products will increase it.

EXAMPLES.–

Income statement			
Charges		**Products**	
Cash costs (cash flow)	200	*Cashed products (cash flow)*	400
Expenses to be disbursed (working capital requirement)	100	*Cash products (BFR)*	50
Result before calculated items	150		
Calculated Charges (FR):		**Calculated Products (Rollover Fund):**	
Depreciation and amortization	60	*Depreciation reversals and provisions*	10
Carrying amount of transferred assets	35	*Sale price of disposed assets*	20
etc.		*Resumption of investment grants*	
Accounting net income	85	*etc.*	

We see that the result that was 150 is now only 85 because of the mandatory inventory entries. Thus, there are two ways to find it:

– deduct cashed or cashable products, disbursed and disbursable expenses

- 450 − 300 = 150

– add the calculated expenses and subtract the sum of the calculated products

- 60 + 35 + 85 − 10 − 20 = 150

The self-financing capacity of 150 is precisely the algebraic sum of the items calculated as well as the net potential cash flow.

Self-financing is what remains of the CAF when we paid the shareholders

$$\boxed{\text{Self-financing} = \text{CAF dividends distributed}}$$

4.4.2. *FCA approach*

The FCA presents two ways of calculating the self-financing capacity: through the gross operating surplus by the potential cash flows or through the result by the elements without influence in the year on the treasury;

Through the Gross Operating Surplus

+ Gross operating surplus
+ Other products
− Other expenses
+ Transfer of operating expenses
+ Financial products
− Financial expenses
+ Exceptional products
− Extraordinary expenses
− Employee participation
− Income tax
= FCA self-financing capacity

This second approach is the most logical and is the one recommended in the cash flow table.

4.4.3. *Analysis of the Order of Chartered Accountants*

Through the fastest net book result:

FCA		Chartered Accountants
± Net income	⇔	± Net income
+ Depreciation and amortization		+ Depreciation, amortization and operating provisions **EXCEPT those on current assets** *(provisions for risks with the nature of provisioned debts as well as provisions for depreciation of inventories and receivables)*
+ Extraordinary expense regarding capital transaction = net book value of assets sold	⇔	+ Extraordinary expense on capital transaction = net book value of assets sold
+ Investment grants transferred to the income statement	⇔	+ Investment grants transferred to the income statement
− Reversals on provisions		− Reversals of depreciation and operating provisions **EXCEPT those on current assets** *(provisions for risks with the nature of provisioned debts as well as provisions for depreciation of inventories and receivables)*
− Net exceptional proceeds on capital transactions (proceeds from asset sales)	⇔	− Net exceptional proceeds on capital transactions (proceeds from asset sales)
		− **Transfer of expenses to the account of expenses to be distributed**
= FCA self-financing capacity		= Cash flow OEC

4.5. Renewed indicators (IFRS) of management

Management balances were renewed owing to the rise of IFRS. Former indicators have added new ones without standardization; hence, distrust is created.

Danone communicates about the financial indicators not defined by the following IFRS as follows:

– like-for-like changes in sales, current operating income, current operating margin, net current result – Group share and net current result – Group share per diluted share;

– current operating income;

– current operating margin;

– net current result – Group share;

– diluted net current earnings per share or net current result – Group share per diluted share;

– free cash flow;

– free cash flow excluding exceptional items;

– net financial debt.

4.5.1. EBITDA

Earnings Before Interest Tax Depreciation and Amortization is equal to the Gross Operating Profit deducting all personnel costs, participation, profit sharing, etc.

EBIDTA = GOP − staff costs

4.5.2. ROA

Return On Assets is an expression of the profitability of the activity: ROA = activity result / assets.

4.5.3. ROE

Return On Equity is the return on equity ratio (financial profitability). It depends on how the net income is broken down into GAAP or IFRS and differences are apparent in the explanation of the performance: ROE = net income / equity.

4.5.4. NOPAT

Net Operating Profit After Taxes is an expression of operational profitability: NOPAT = result of the activity − corresponding tax.

4.5.5. ROCE

Return On Capital Employed is an expression of economic profitability: ROCE = NOPAT / economic assets, with economic assets = fixed assets + working capital.

4.5.6. COFROI

Cash Flow Return On Investment is an improved measure of ROCE: COFROI = EBIDTA / economic assets.

4.5.7. Free cash flow

"Free cash flow represents the cash balance from operating activities after taking into account net industrial investments of disposal and, in the context of IFRS 3, Revised on Business Combinations, before taking into account (i) the acquisition costs of the companies over which Danone acquires control and (ii) cash flows related to acquisition price supplements paid subsequently to a takeover"[5].

Free cash flow excluding exceptional items corresponds to free cash flow before taking into account the cash flows relating to the initiatives implemented as part of the Danone organization's savings and adaptation plan in Europe.

Free cash flow = EBIDTA − ΔBFR − Δ operating investments of the period − taxes.

4.5.8. EVA MVA

4.5.8.1. EVA (Economic Value Added)

This is an approximation of the creation of shareholder value. EVA = RON − (CMC × CE), with:

− *OR = Operating result*

− *NOI* = net operating income = OR − corresponding tax

− *WACC* = average cost of capital = (financial expenses + dividends) / (equity + financial debt) weighted by the weight of capital in the total

− *CE* = cost of capital employed = equity + financial debt + provisions + hybrid capitals and quasi-equity.

4.5.8.2. MVA (Market Value Added)

This is the added value of the market and the discounted value of future EVA flows. The discount cost retained is the WACC.

There is no standardization or certification of these indicators.

4.6. Income statement analysis: US GAAP

In this section, we will present the income statement (or P&L) according to US GAAP and the different indicators or ratios to be calculated using this financial statement.

---

5 Danone financial Report (Rapport financier Danone)

Income statement features

When you want somebody to get to the point, you might ask him or her for the "bottom line". This expression comes from the income statement. The income statement or statement of financial performance lists the firm's revenues and expenses over a period of time. The last, or "bottom", line of the income statement shows the firm's net income, which is a measure of its profitability during the period. The income statement is sometimes called a profit and loss, or "P&L", statement, and the net income is also referred to as the firm's earnings. In this section, we examine the components of the income statement in detail and introduce ratios we can use to analyze these data. The income statement equation is:

Revenues − Expenses = Net Income if Revenues > Expenses

= Net Loss if Revenues < Expenses

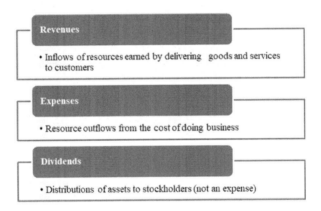

Figure 4.1. *Income statement picture*

Example 1.

ABC Company had the following accounts and balances at the end of 2015:

Accounts payable	$12,000	Equipment	$50,000
Cash	74,000	Inventory	25,000
Common stock	21,000	Long-term debt	33,000
Cost of goods sold	85,000	Revenues	200,000
Dividends	8,000	Salaries expense	24,000

Refer to example 1:

1) What were the ring total assets for ABC Company at the end of the year?
2) What were the ring total liabilities for ABC Company at the end of the year?
3) What was the ring net income for ABC Company for the year?

Solution

1) Total assets = cash + equipment + equipment

   $= 74{,}000 + 50{,}000 + 25{,}000 = \$149{,}000$

2) Total liabilities = accounts payable + long-term debt

   $= 12{,}000 + 33{,}000 = \$45{,}000$

3) Net income = revenues − cost of goods sold − salaries expense

   $= 200{,}000 - 85{,}000 - 24{,}000 = \$91{,}000$

Although the balance sheet shows the firm's assets and liabilities at a given point in time, the income statement shows the flow of revenues and expenses generated by those assets and liabilities between two dates. Table 4.1 shows Global's income statement for 2012.

We will examine each category on the statement.

GLOBAL CONGLOMERATE CORPORATION
Income Statement
Year Ended December 31 (in $ million)

	2012	2011
Total sales	186.7	176.1
Cost of sales	(153.4)	(147.3)
Gross Profit	33.3	28.8
Selling, general, and administrative expenses	(13.5)	(13.0)
Research and development	(8.2)	(7.6)
Depreciation and amortization	(1.2)	(1.1)
Operating Income	10.4	7.1
Other income	—	—
Earnings Before Interest and Taxes (EBIT)	10.4	7.1
Interest income (expense)	(7.7)	(4.6)
Pretax Income	2.7	2.5
Taxes	(0.7)	(0.6)
Net Income	2.0	1.9
Earnings per share:	$0.556	$0.528
Diluted earnings per share:	$0.526	$0.500

Table 4.1. Global's income statement (source: Berk and DeMarzo [BER 14])

Gross Profit. The first two lines of the income statement list the revenues from sales of products and the costs incurred to make and sell the products. Cost of sales shows costs directly related to producing the goods or services being sold, such as manufacturing costs. Other costs such as administrative expenses, research and development and interest expenses are not included in the cost of sales. The third line is gross profit, which is the difference between sales revenues and the costs.

Operating Expenses. The next group of items is operating expenses. These are expenses from the ordinary course of running the business that are not directly related to producing the goods or services being sold. They include administrative expenses and overhead, salaries, marketing costs and research and development expenses. The third type of operating expense, depreciation and amortization, is not an actual cash expense but represents an estimate of the costs that arise from wear and tear or obsolescence of the firm's assets. The firm's gross profit net of operating expenses is called operating income.

Earnings before Interest and Taxes. We next include other sources of income or expenses that arise from activities that are not the central part of a company's business. Income from the firm's financial investments is one example of other income that would be listed here. After we have adjusted for other sources of income or expenses, we have the firm's earnings before interest and taxes, or EBIT.

Pretax and Net Income. From EBIT, we deduct the interest expense related to outstanding debt to compute Global's pretax income, and then we deduct corporate taxes to determine the firm's net income.

Net income represents the total earnings of the firm's equity holders. It is often reported on a per-share basis as the firm's earnings per share (EPS), which we compute by dividing net income by the total number of shares outstanding:

EPS = Net Income / Shares Outstanding = $2.0 Million / 3.6 Million Shares = $0.556 per Share

Although Global has only 3.6 million shares outstanding as of the end of 2012, the number of shares outstanding may grow if Global compensates its employees or executives with stock options that give the holder the right to buy a certain number of shares by a specific date at a specific price. If the options are "exercised", the company issues new stock and the number of shares outstanding will grow. The number of shares may also grow if the firm issues convertible bonds, a form of debt that can be converted to shares. Because there will be more total shares to divide the same earnings, this growth in the number of shares is referred to as dilution. Firms disclose the potential for dilution by reporting diluted EPS, which represents earnings per share for the company calculated as though, for example, in-the-money stock options or other stock-based compensation had been exercised or dilutive convertible debt had been converted. For example, in 2011, Global awarded 200,000 shares of restricted stock to its key executives.

While these are currently unvested, they will ultimately increase the number of shares outstanding, so Global's diluted EPS is:

$2 million / 3.8 million shares = $0.526.6.

The adjustment for options is usually done based on the treasury stock method, in which the number of shares added has the same value as the profit from exercising the option. For example, given Global's share price of $14 per share, an option giving an employee the right to purchase a share for $7 would add ($14 − $7) / $14 = 0.5 shares to the diluted share count.

If you think of the balance sheet as a snapshot, then you can think of the income statement as a video recording covering the period between before and after pictures [ROS 14]. Table 4.2 gives a simplified income statement for U.S. Corporation.

U.S. CORPORATION 2012 Income Statement ($ in millions)	
Net sales	$1,509
Cost of goods sold	750
Depreciation	65
Earnings before interest and taxes	$ 694
Interest paid	70
Taxable income	$ 624
Taxes (34%)	212
Net income	$ 412
Dividends	$103
Addition to retained earnings	309

Table 4.2. *U.S. Corporation Income statement (source: Ross, Westerfield and Jordan [ROS 14])*

As indicated, U.S. Corporation paid cash dividends of $103. The difference between net income and cash dividends, $309, is the addition to retained earnings for the year. This amount is added to the cumulative retained earnings account on the balance sheet. If you look back at the two balance sheets for U.S. Corporation, you will see that retained earnings went up by this amount: $1,320 + 309 = $1,629.

Recall that retained earnings means exactly what the term implies, that a portion of net income the company is kept over a period of years. If, historically, revenue exceeds expenses, then the result will be a positive balance in retained earnings. On the contrary, if, historically, expenses have exceeded sales revenues, then the accumulation of these losses will result in an accumulated deficit in retained earnings (usually shown in parentheses). Net income or net loss flows from the income statement to the statement of retained earnings. Net income increases retained earnings, and net losses and dividends decrease retained earnings.

The statement of retained earnings: (a) opens with the beginning retained earnings balance; (b) adds net income (or subtracts net loss; net income comes directly from the income statement; (c) subtracts dividends and (d) reports the retained earnings balance at the end of the year. The retained earnings statement is the following:

Ending retained earnings = Beginning retained earnings + Net income − Dividends.

Example 2.

Suppose the Candy Company had beginning retained earnings of $5,000, net income of $3,000 and paid dividends of $1,000 to their stockholders. Therefore, what is the ending retained earnings?

Solution

Ending retained earnings = Beginning retained earnings + Net income − Dividends

$$= 5{,}000 + 3{,}000 - 1{,}000 = 7{,}000.$$

Example 3.

Suppose a company had revenues for $210,000, expenses for $140,000 and cash dividends for $45,000. What is the net income and the change in retained earnings for the period?

Solution

Net income = Revenues − Expenses = 210,000 − 140,000 = $70,000

Retained earnings = Net income − Dividends = 70,000 − 45,000 = $25,000

Retained earnings increased by 70,000 and decreased by 45,000 for dividends for a change of 25,000.

Example 4.

Suppose a company had the following activity during the year:

Revenue	$139,500
Cost of goods sold	68,000
Salaries expense	21,000
Utilities expense	12,100
Dividends	7,000

At the beginning of 2015, the balance in retained earnings was $51,000. In addition, the company had assets at the end of the year of $205,000 and common stock of $85,000.

1) Compute the amount of the net income or loss for the year.

2) Compute the ending retained earnings balance.

3) Compute the amount of the liabilities at the end of 2015.

Solution

1) Calculations: revenues − cost of goods sold − salaries expense − utilities expense = 139,500 − 68,000 − 21,000 − 12,100 = $38,400 net income.

2) Calculations: beginning balance + net income − dividends = ending retained earnings = 51,000 + 38,400 − 7,000 = $82,400 ending retained earnings

3) Calculations: Assets = Liabilities + Stockholders' Equity

Assets = Liabilities + Paid-in-Capital + Retained Earnings

205,000 = Liabilities + 85,000 + 82,400

205,000 = Liabilities + 167,400

205,000 − 167,400 = Liabilities

37,600 = Liabilities

Income statement Diagnosis

Non-cash items

A primary reason that accounting income differs from cash flow is that an income statement contains non-cash items. The most important of these is depreciation. Suppose that a firm purchases an asset for $5,000 and pays in cash. Obviously, the firm has a $5,000 cash outflow at the time of purchase. However, instead of deducting the $5,000 as an expense, an accountant might depreciate the asset over a five-year period. If the depreciation is straight line and the asset is written down to zero over that period, then $5,000 / 5 = $1,000 will be deducted each year as an expense. The important thing to recognize is that this $1,000 deduction is not cash – it is an accounting number. The actual cash outflow occurred when the asset was purchased.

The depreciation deduction is simply another application of the matching principle in accounting. The revenues associated with an asset would generally occur over some length of time. Therefore, the accountant seeks to match the expense of purchasing the asset with the benefits produced from owning it. As we will see, for the financial manager, the actual timing of cash inflows and outflows is critical in coming up with a reasonable estimate of market value, so we need to learn how to separate the cash flows from the non-cash accounting entries. In reality, the difference between cash flow and accounting income can be dramatic. For example, consider the case of automaker Chrysler. For the third quarter of 2010, Chrysler reported a net loss of $84 million. Sounds bad, but Chrysler also reported positive cash flow of $419 million, a difference of about $503 million [ROS 14].

Working capital ratios

We can use the combined information in the firm's income statement and balance sheet to gauge how efficiently the firm is utilizing its net working capital. To evaluate the speed at which a company turns sales into cash, firms often compute the number of accounts receivable days. Accounts receivable days can also be calculated based on the average accounts receivable at the end of the current and prior year. The accounts receivables days are the number of days' worth of sales that accounts receivable represents:

Accounts Receivable Days = Accounts Receivable / Average Daily Sales.

According to Table 1, average daily sales of $186.7 million / 365 = $0.51 million in 2012, Global's receivables of $18.5 million represent 18.5 / 0.51 = 36 days' worth of sales. In other words, on average, Global takes a little over one month to collect payment from its customers. In 2011, Global's accounts receivable represented only 27 days' worth of sales. Although the number of receivable days can fluctuate seasonally, a significant unexplained increase could be a cause for concern (perhaps indicating that the firm is doing a poor job of collecting from its customers or is trying to boost sales by offering generous credit terms). There are similar ratios for accounts payable and inventory. For these items, it is natural to compare them to the firm's cost of sales, which should reflect the total amount paid to suppliers and inventory sold. Therefore, accounts payable days is defined as:

Accounts Payable Days = Accounts Payable / Average Daily Cost of Sales.

Similarly, inventory days = (inventory / average daily cost of sales). Turnover ratios are an alternative way to measure working capital. We compute turnover ratios by expressing annual revenues or costs as a multiple of the corresponding working capital account. For example:

Inventory Turnover = Annual Cost of Sales / Inventory.

Global's inventory turnover in 2012 is 153.4 / 15.3 = 10.0*, indicating that Global sold roughly 10 times its current stock of inventory during the year. Similarly, accounts receivable turnover = (annual sales / accounts receivable) and accounts payable turnover = (annual cost of sales / accounts payable). We note that higher turnover corresponds to shorter days and thus a more efficient use of working capital. While working capital ratios can be meaningfully compared over time or within an industry, there are wide differences across industries. While the average large U.S. firm had about 45 days' worth of receivables and 65 days' worth of inventory in 2012, airlines tend to have minimal accounts receivable or inventory, as their customers pay in advance and they sell a transportation service as opposed to a physical commodity. On the contrary, distillers and wine producers tend to have very large inventory (over 300 days on average), as their products are often aged prior to sale.

Profitability ratios

The income statement provides very useful information regarding the profitability of a firm's business and how it relates to the value of the firm's shares. The gross margin of a firm is the ratio of gross profit to revenues (sales):

Gross Margin = Gross Profit / Sales.

A firm's gross margin reflects its ability to sell a product for more than the cost of producing it. For example, in 2012, Global had a gross margin of 33.3 / 186.7 = 17.8%.

Because there are additional expenses of operating a business beyond the direct costs of goods sold, another important profitability ratio is the operating margin, the ratio of operating income to revenues:

Operating Margin = Operating Income / Sales.

The operating margin reveals how much a company earns from each dollar of sales before interest and taxes. In 2012, Global's operating margin was 10.4 / 186.7 = 5.57%, an increase from its 2011 operating margin of 7.1 / 176.1 = 4.03%. We can similarly compute a firm's EBIT margin = (EBIT / Sales). By comparing operating or EBIT margins across firms within an industry, we can assess the relative efficiency of the firms' operations.

In addition to the efficiency of operations, differences in operating margins can result from corporate strategy. For example, in December 2011, high-end retailer Nordstrom (JWN) had an operating margin of 11.5% over the past year; Wal-Mart Stores (WMT) had an operating margin of only 5.9%. In this case, Wal-Mart's lower operating margin was not a result of its inefficiency. Rather, the low operating margin is part of Wal-Mart's strategy of offering low prices to sell common products in high volume. Indeed, Wal-Mart's sales were over 41 times higher than those of Nordstrom [BER 14].

Finally, a firm's net profit margin is the ratio of net income to revenues:

Net Profit Margin = Net Income / Sales.

The net profit margin shows the fraction of each dollar in revenues that is available to equity holders after the firm pays interest and taxes. In 2012, Global's net profit margin was 2.0 / 186.7 = 1.07%.

We must be cautious when comparing net profit margins; while differences in net profit margins can be due to differences in efficiency, they can also result from differences in leverage, which determines the amount of interest expense, as well as differences in accounting assumptions.

Valuation ratios

Analysts use a number of ratios to gauge the market value of the firm. The most common is the firm's price–earnings ratio (P/E):

P/E Ratio = Market Capitalization / Net Income

= Share Price / Earnings per Share

That is, the P/E ratio is the ratio of the value of equity to the firm's earnings, either on a total basis or on a per-share basis. For example, Global's P/E ratio in 2012 was 50.4 / 2.0 = 14 / 0.556 = 25.2. In other words, investors are willing to pay over 25 times Global's earnings in order to purchase a share.

The P/E ratio is a simple measure that is used to assess whether a stock is over- or under-valued based on the idea that the value of a stock should be proportional to the level of earnings it can generate for its shareholders. P/E ratios can vary widely across industries and tend to be highest for industries with high expected growth rates. The risk of the firm will also affect this ratio – all else equal, riskier firms have lower P/E ratios. Because the P/E ratio considers the value of the firm's equity, it is sensitive to the firm's choice of leverage. The P/E ratio is therefore of limited usefulness when comparing firms with markedly different leverage. We can avoid this limitation by instead assessing the market value of the underlying business using valuation ratios based on the firm's enterprise value. Common ratios include the ratio of enterprise value to revenue, or enterprise value to operating income, EBIT, or EBITDA. These ratios compare the value of the business to its sales, operating profits or cash flow. Like the P/E ratio, these ratios are used to make intra-industry comparisons of how firms are priced in the market.

Operating returns

Analysts often evaluate the firm's return on investment by comparing its income to its investment using ratios such as the firm's return on equity (ROE):

Return on Equity (ROE) = Net Income / Book Value of Equity

Global's ROE in 2012 was 2.0 / 22.2 = 9.0%. The ROE provides a measure of the return that the firm has earned on its past investments. A high ROE may indicate that the firm is able to find investment opportunities that are very profitable. The ROE is an indicator of financial return.

The specialty literature allots important studies to this indicator, considered one of the most characteristic barometers of some commercial enterprise performances. In the bank's situation, a normal margin of this indicator is appreciated to be situated between the significant thresholds of 10% and 30% [BEN 16].

Another common measure is return on assets (ROA). For the banking industry, this indicator is an expression of profitability for the entire activity. It measures the effect of management capacity to use the financial and real resources of an institution in order to generate profit. It is appreciated that the return of assets indicator is the most exact measure of banking activity due the fact that it directly expresses the result, accordingly to the specific management of intermediate banking, of active operations optimization, related to a volume of resources considered [BEN 16]. It is calculated as:

Return on Assets (ROA) = (Net Income + Interest Expense) / Book Value of Assets.

The ROA calculation includes interest expense in the numerator because the assets in the denominator have been funded by both debt and equity investors. As a performance measure, ROA has the benefit of being less sensitive to leverage than ROE. However, it is sensitive to working capital: for example, an equal increase in the firm's receivables and payables will increase total assets and thus lower ROA. To avoid this problem, we can consider the firm's return on invested capital (ROIC):

Return on Invested Capital (ROIC) = EBIT (1 − tax rate) / (Book Value of Equity + Net Debt).

The return on invested capital measures the after-tax profit generated by the business itself, excluding any interest expenses (or interest income), and compares it to the capital raised from equity and debt holders that has already been deployed (i.e. is not held as cash). Of the three measures of operating returns, ROIC is the most useful in assessing the performance of the underlying business.

Example 5. Global's performance

Assess how Global's ability to use its assets effectively has changed by calculating the change in its return on assets and return on invested capital between 2011 and 2012.

Solution

In 2012, Global's ROA was (2.0 + 7.7) / 177.7 = 5.5%, compared to an ROA in 2011 of (1.9 + 4.6) / 148.9 = 4.4%.

To compute the return on invested capital, we need to calculate after-tax EBIT, which requires an estimate of Global's tax rate. Because net income = pretax income × (1 − tax rate), we can estimate (1 − Tax rate) = net income / pretax income. Thus, EBIT × (1 − tax rate) = 10.4 × (2.0 / 2.7) = 7.7 in 2012 and 7.1 × (1.9 / 2.5) = 5.4 in 2011.

To compute invested capital, note first that Global's net debt was 3.2 + 12.3 + 76.3 − 19.5 = 72.3 in 2011 and 3.5 + 13.3 + 99.9 − 21.2 = 95.5 in 2012. Thus, ROIC in 2012 was 7.7 / (22.2 + 95.5) = 6.5%, compared with 5.4 / (21.2 + 72.3) = 5.8% in 2011. The improvement in Global's ROA and ROIC from 2011 to 2012 suggests that Global was able to use its assets more effectively and increase its return over this period.

The DuPont Identity

We can gain further insight into a firm's ROE by using a tool called the DuPont Identity (named after the company that popularized its use), which expresses the ROE in terms of the firm's profitability, asset efficiency and leverage:

ROE = (Net Income / Sales) × (Sales / Total Assets) × (Total Assets / Book Value of Equity)

= ROA × (Total Assets / Book Value of Equity)

The first term in the DuPont Identity is the firm's net profit margin, which measures its overall profitability. The second term is the firm's asset turnover, which measures how efficiently the firm is utilizing its assets to generate sales. Together, these terms determine the firm's return on assets. We compute ROE by multiplying by a measure of leverage called the equity multiplier, which indicates the value of assets held per dollar of shareholder equity. The greater the firm's reliance on debt financing, the higher the equity multiplier will be.

Applying this identity to Global, we see that in 2012 its asset turnover was 186.7 / 177.7 = 1.05, with an equity multiplier of 177.7 / 22.2 = 8. Given its net profit margin of 1.07%, we can compute its ROE as 9.0% = 1.07% × 1.05 × 8.

Example 6

Suppose in 2016, the company A had revenue of $13.50 billion, gross profit of $9.80 billion, and net income of $2 billion. The company B had revenue of $400 million, gross profit of $80 million, and net income of $22 million.

1) Compare the gross margins for these two companies.

2) Compare the net profit margins for these two companies.

3) Which firm was more profitable in 2016?

Solution

1) Company A's gross margin = Gross profit / total sales = 9.8 / 13.50 = 72.6%

   Company B's gross margin = 80 / 400 = 20%.

2) Company A's net margin = Net income / total sales = 2 / 13.50 = 14.815%

   Company B's net margin = 22 / 400 = 5.5%.

3) Company A was more profitable in 2016 than the company B.

Example 7

Assume that in 2015, Apple had cash and cash equivalents of $80 billion, accounts receivable of $20 billion, current assets of $70 billion, and current liabilities of $40 billion.

1) What was Apple's current ratio?

2) What was Apple's quick ratio?

3) What is Apple's cash ratio?

4) In 2015, Dell had a cash ratio of 1.2, a quick ratio of 1.80 and a current ratio of 1.90. What can you say about the asset liquidity of Apple relative to Dell?

Solution

1) Apple's current ratio = current assets / current liabilities = 70 / 40 = 1.75.

2) Apple's quick ratio = (cash and cash equivalents + accounts receivable)/ current liabilities = (80 + 20) / 40 = 2.5.

3) Apple's cash ratio = cash and cash equivalents/current liabilities = 80 / 40 = 2.

4) Apple has significantly more liquid assets than Dell relative to current liabilities.

4.6.1. Case study 1: Mydeco Corporation

Table	2009–2013 Financial Statement Data and Stock Price Data for Mydeco Corp.				
Mydeco Corp. 2009–2013	(All data as of fiscal year end; $ in millions)				
Income statement	2009	2010	2011	2012	2013
Revenue	404.3	363.8	424.6	510.7	604.1
Cost of goods sold	−188.3	−173.8	−206.2	−246.8	−293.4
Gross profit	216	190	218.4	263.9	310.7
Sales and marketing	−66.7	−66.4	−82.8	−102.1	−120.8
Administration	−60.6	−59.1	−59.4	-66.4	-78.5
Depreciation & amortization	−27.3	-27	−34.3	−38.4	−38.6
EBIT	61.4	37.5	41.9	57	72.8
Interest income (expense)	−33.7	−32.9	−32.2	−37.4	−39.4
Pretax income	27.7	4.6	9.7	19.6	33.4
Income tax	−9.7	−1.6	−3.4	−6.9	−11.7
Net Income	**18**	**3**	**6.3**	**12.7**	**21.7**
Shares outstanding (millions)	55	55	55	55	55
Stock price	$7.92	$3.30	$5.25	$8.71	$10.89
Balance sheet	2009	2010	2011	2012	2013
Assets					
Cash	48.8	68.9	86.3	77.5	85
Accounts receivable	88.6	69.8	69.8	76.9	86.1
Inventory	33.7	30.9	28.4	31.7	35.3
Total current assets	171.1	169.6	184.5	186.1	206.4
Net property, plant & equip.	245.3	243.3	309	345.6	347
Goodwill & intangibles	361.7	361.7	361.7	361.7	361.7
	778.1	774.6	855.2	893.4	915.1
Liabilities & stockholders' equity					
Accounts payable	18.7	17.9	22	26.8	31.7
Accrued compensation	6.7	6.4	7	8.1	9.7
Current liabilities	25.4	24.3	29	34.9	41.4
Long-term debt	500	500	575	600	600
Total liabilities	525.4	524.3	604	634.9	641.4
Stockholders' equity	252.7	250.3	251.2	258.5	273.7
Total liabilities & stockholders' equity	778.1	774.6	855.2	893.4	915.1

Questions

1) Return on asset (ROA)
2) Return on equity (ROE)
3) Mydeco's enterprise value
4) Current ratio
5) Quick ratio
6) Debt-to-equity ratio
7) Net working capital
8) Mydeco's earnings per share at the end of each year
9) Mydeco's market-to-book ratio at the end of each year
10) Mydeco's enterprise value at the end of each year
11) By what percentage did Mydeco's revenues grow each year from 2010 to 2013?
12) By what percentage did the net income grow each year?
13) Suppose Mydeco repurchases two million shares each year from 2010 to 2013. What would its earnings per share be in 2013?

Solution

		2009	2010	2011	2012	2013
1)	ROA	0.023133273	0.003872967	0.007366698	0.014215357	0.023713255
2)	ROE	0.071230708	0.011985617	0.025079618	0.049129594	0.079283887
3)	Market cap	$435.60	$181.50	$288.75	$479.05	$598.95
	EV	$886.80	$612.60	$777,45	$1001.55	$1,113.95
4)	Current ratio	6.736220472	6.979423868	6.362068966	5.332378223	$4,985507246
5)	Quick ratio	5.409448819	5.70781893	5.382758621	4.424068768	4.132850242
6)	Debt/equity	1.978630787	1.997602877	2.289012739	2.321083172	2.19218122
7)	NWC	145.7	145.3	155.5	151.2	165

8) EPS = net income / shares outstanding

Net Income	18.0	3.0	6.3	12.7	21.7
Shares outstanding (millions)	55.0	55.0	55.0	55.0	55.0
Earnings per share	$0.33	$0.05	$0.11	$0.23	$0.39

9) and 10) Market to book ratio = market cap / total equity

Enterprise value = Market cap + debt − cash

Year	2009	2010	2011	2012	2013
Market Capitalization (millions)	$435.60	$181.50	$288.75	$479.05	$598.95
Stockholders' Equity	252.7	250.3	251.2	258.5	273.7
Market-to-book	1.72	0.73	1.15	1.85	2.19

Year	2009	2010	2011	2012	2013
Market Capitalization (millions)	$435.60	$181.50	$288.75	$479.05	$598.95
Cash	48.8	68.9	86.3	77.5	85.0
Long-term Debt	500.0	500.0	575.0	600.0	600.0
Enterprise Value	886.80	612.60	777.45	1,1001.55	1,113.95

11) and 12) % change = Yt − (Yt − 1) / (Yt − 1)

Year	2009	2010	2011	2012	2013
Revenue	404.3	363.8	424.6	510.7	604.1
Revenue Growth		−10.02%	16.71%	20.28%	18.29%

Year	2009	2010	2011	2012	2013
Net Income	18.0	3.0	6.3	12.7	21.7
Net Income Growth		−83.33%	110.00%	101.59%	70.87%

13) A repurchase does not impact earnings directly, so any change to EPS will come from a reduction in shares outstanding. 2013 shares outstanding = 55 − 4 × 2 = 47 million, EPS = 21.7 / 47 = $0.46.

4.6.2. Case study 2: Atlas

Atlas, Inc. has the following assets, liabilities, revenues and expenses for the current year. The accounts are listed below in alphabetical order. The company has a December 31, 2014 year end.

Accounts receivable	$28,000	Office equipment	$59,500
Accounts payable	37,000	Office supplies	5,000
Building	45,000	Service revenue	130,000
Cash	80,000	Supplies expense	8,000
Commission expense	20,500	Utilities expense	8,500
Common stock	22,000	Wage expense	11,500
Interest payable	1,500		
Land	40,000		

Beginning retained earnings was $120,000 and dividends were $5,000 for the year. Prepare the income statement, statement of retained earnings and balance sheet for Atlas, Inc. for the current year.

Solution

Atlas financial statements:

Income Statement

For the year ending December 31, 2014

Service revenue	$130,000
Expenses:	
Wage expense	11,500
Utilities expense	8,000
Supplies expense	8,000
Total expenses	48,000
Net income	**$82,000**

Statement of Retained Earnings

For the year ending December 31, 2014

Beginning balance	$120,000
Net income	82,000
Dividends	(5,000)
Ending balance	**$197,000**

Balance Sheet

December 31, 2014

Assets

Cash	$80,000
Accounts receivable	28,000
Office supplies	5,000
Building	45,000
Land	40,000
Office equipment	59,500
Total assets	$257,500

Liabilities

Accounts payable	$37,000
Interest payable	1,500
Total liabilities	$38,500

Stockholders' Equity

Common stock	22,000
Retained earnings	197,000
Total stockholders' equity	219,000
Total liabilities and Stockholders' equity	$257,500

5

Analysis of Operational Profitability and Risk: IFRS

Cost-effectiveness, profitability, cash flow, etc. depend on the financial accounting result (balance sheet and income statement). However, these come from the elements of social accounts, which themselves are composed of items that do not all have an invoice origin.

These items are calculated (inventories, depreciation, etc.) according to the assumptions of the cost models. Therefore, depending on the calculation, the items have a variable value, which inexorably implies a repercussion on the amount of the result.

It is therefore not possible to determine the value of TIR, NPV, etc. with a result function of the assumptions of calculation of their cost.

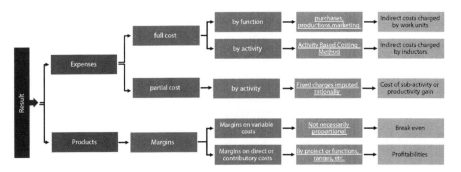

Figure 5.1. *Tree of cost calculation models*

5.1. Profitability according to the chosen full cost model

The performance of the business is the difference between the sales of the products and the expenses they need. Expenses are the components of costs. The way in which costs are calculated therefore affects the performance.

5.1.1. *Results Achieved in Full Cost by Analysis Centers and Unit Cost of Indirect Costs*

The director of an ABC Business Unit announces its results at the end of the period. He considers that the profitability demanded by the management of 5% is reached but according to his calculations of complete costs he asks to abandon or to externalize the product P1 which is too expensive for him and not profitable, and investments to increase the production and sales of P2 products on which it makes a margin on.

You must check your full cost calculations according to your calculation method

ABC manufactures two product lines P1 and P2 on order. ABC applies management analytics based on the functional method with homogeneous sections, from which the following data are extracted for the period:

Main centers	Purchase	Production	Distribution	Executive	
Indirect expenses	€24,209	€232,260	€29,625	€77,209	=€363,303
Work units imputed according to:	Kilos purchased	Machine hours	Sold products	Production cost	

Consumption	P1	P2
Material M	2,700 kg	
Material N		390 kg
Consumable materials	5% of CM*	
Time in machine hours	540 h.	195 h.
* Consumption of materials in euros		

Purchase	Quantity	Amount
Material M	2,680 kg	€144,720
Material N	400 kg	118,800 €

Initial stock	Quantities	Amount
Material M	350 kg	€21,373
Material N	80 kg	€24,264

Sold production	
P1	1,200 P1
P2	1,300 P2

Sales	Price
P1	€325
P2	€217

Confirmation of the distribution of the current result of €33,160 between P1 and P2

Main centers	Purchase	Production	Distribution	Executive	
Indirect expenses	€24,209	€232,260	€29,625	€77,209	= €363,303
Work units and expense base	Kilos purchased	Machine hours	Sold products	Production cost	
Number of units	3,080 kg	735 h.	2,500 u.	€532,107	This sum is calculated after since it is the cost of production
Cost of unit of work	€7.86/kg	€316 per MH	€11.85 /P Sold	+14.51%	

Cost of purchase		Material M			Material N			
	Quantities	Cost	Amount	Quantities	Cost	Amount		
Direct	2,680 kg	€54	= €144,720	400 kg	€297.00	= €118,800		
Indirect	2,680 kg	€7.86 €/kg	= €21,065	400 kg	€7.86	= €3,144		
Total	2,680 kg	€61.86	= €165,785	400 kg	€304.86	= €121,944	€287,729
Distribution of the cost of purchase:			58%			42%	100%

Material stocks		Material M			Material N			
	Quantities	Cost	Amount	Quantities	Cost	Amount		
Initial stock	350 kg	€61.07	= €21,373	80 kg	€303.30	= €24,264		
Cost of purchase	2,680 kg	€61.86	= €165,785	400 kg	€304.86	= €121,944		
Input	3,030 kg	€61.77	= €187,158	480 kg	€304.60	= €146,208		
Consumption	2,700 kg	€61.77	= €166,774	390 kg	€304.60	= €118,794	€285,568
Final stock	330 kg	€61.77	= €20,384	90 kg	€304.60	= €27,414	€47,798

Production cost		P1			P2			
	Quantities	Cost	Amount	Quantities	Cost	Amount		
M and N consumption	2,700 kg	€61.77	= €166,774	390 kg	€304.60	= €118,794		
Consumable material CM	5%		= €8,339	MC	5%	= €5,940		
Manufacturing CI	540 h.	€316.00	= €170,640	195 h.	€316.00	= €61,620		
Total	1,200 u.	€288.13	= €345,753	1,300 u.	€143.35	= €186,354	€532,107
Distribution of the production cost:			65%			35%	100%

Cost price		P1 produced and sold			P2 produced and sold			
	Quantities	Cost	Amount	Quantities	Cost	Amount		
Production PV	1,200 u.	€288.13	= €345,753	1,300 u.	€143.35	= €186,354		
Distribution	1,200 u.	€11.85	= €14,220	1,300 u.	€11.85	= €15,405		
Administrative	€345,753	14.51%	= €50,169	€186,354	14.51%	= €27,040		
Total	1,200 u.	€341.78	= €410,142	1,300 u.	€176.00	= €228,799	€638,941
Cost breakdown:			64%			36%	100%

Financial Management

Analytical results	P1 produced and sold			P2 produced and sold			
	Quantities	Price/Cost	Amount	Quantities	Cost	Amount	
Sales	1,200 u.	€325	= €390,000	1,300 u.	€217	= €282,100	€672,100
Cost price	1,200 u.	€341.78	= €410,142	1,300 u.	€176.00	= €228,799	5%
Results	1,200 u.	€16.78	€20,142	1,300 u.	€41.00	€53,301	€33,159

ANALYSIS.– We confirm the profitability of 5% of turnover and that the product P1 is in deficit.

DIAGNOSIS.– One should think of abandoning it or outsourcing it because the P2 product has a profit of €53,301, which would make 8% turnover.

It is also questionable whether the allocation keys for indirect charges between the P1 and P2 ranges do not overload one and benefit the other.

PROGNOSIS.– A stronger correlation analysis showed that the indirect costs depend more closely on other keys as indicated below (units of work that no longer represent real activity). This risk of subsidization must be eliminated from one range to another.

Calculation of unit costs and expense rates						
		Production:				
Main centers	Purchase	Machining	Finish	Administrative		
Indirect expenses	€24,209	€125,420	€106,840	€106,834	=€363,303	
Work units and plates of expenses	For 100 € of purchases	Machine hours	Hour man power	Production cost		
Number of units	€2,635	735 h.m	700 h.	€531,466	Calculated after (cost of production	
Cost of units of work	€9.19	€170.64/HM	€152.63/hMOD	20.10%		

Cost of purchase	Material M			Material N				
	Quantities	Cost	Amount	Quantities	Cost	Amount		
Direct	2,680 kg	× €54.00	= €144,720	400 kg	× €297.00	= €118,800		
Indirect	€1,447.20	× €9.19	= €13,295 €	€1,188.00	× €9.19	= €10,914		
Total	2,680 kg	= €58.96	€158,015	400 kg	= €324.28	€129,714	€287,729	
Cost allocation:		Instead of 58%	55%		Instead of 42%	45%	100%	

Material stocks	Material M			Material N			
	Quantities	Cost	Amount	Quantities	Cost	Amount	
Initial stock	350 kg	× €61.07	= €21,373	80 kg	× €303.30	= €24,264	
Cost of purchase	2,680 kg	× €58.96	= €158,015	400 kg	× €324.28	= €129,714	
Input	3,030 kg	CM €59.20	€179,388	480 kg	CM €320.79	= €153,978	
Consumption	2,700 kg	€59.20	€159,851	390 kg	€320.79	= €125,107	€284,958
Final stock	330 kg	€59.20	€19,537	90 kg	€ 320.79	= €28,871	€48,408

Production cost	P1			P2			
	Quantities	Cost	Amount	Quantities	Cost	Amount	
Consumption M and N	2,700 kg	× €59.20	= €159,851	390 kg	× €320.79	= €125,107	
CM	€159,851	5%	= €7,993	€125,107	5%	= €6,255	
Machining	540 h. Mac.	× €170.64	= €92,146	195 h. Mac.	× €170.64	= €33,275	
Finishing stage	185 h. Mod	× €152.63	= €28,236	515 h. Mod	× €152.63	= €78,603	
Total	1,200 u.	€240.19	€288,225	1,300 u.	€187.11	€243,241	€531,466
Distribution of costs		And not 65%	**54%**		Instead of 35%	**46%**	**100%**

Cost price	P1 produced and sold			P2 produced and sold			
	Quantities	Cost	Amount	Quantities	Cost	Amount	
Sold production	1,200 u.	× €240.19	= €288,225	1,300 u.	× €187.11	= €243,241	
Administrative	€288,225	20.10%	€57,938	€243,241	20.10%	€48,896	
Total	1,200 u.	€288.47	€346,163	1,300 u.	€224.72	€292,136	€638,300
Distribution of costs:		And not 64%	**65%**		Instead of 36%	**55%**	**100%**

Analytical results	P1 produced and sold			P2 produced and sold				
	Quantities	Price/Cost	Amount	Quantities	Cost	Amount		
Sales	1,200 u.	€325	€390,000	1,300 u.	€217	€282,100	= 672,100 €	
Cost price	1,200 u.	€288.47	€346,163	1,300 u.	€224.72	€292,136		5% profitability
Results	1,200 u.	€36.53	€43,837	1,300 u.	−7.72	−10,036.20	€33,800	Difference in stocks

5.1.2. Study

ANALYSIS.– For the same current result, this time we have the product P2, which is the loser, and the product P1, which is the winner.

DIAGNOSIS.– This proves that there was indeed a subsidization of P2 product by the product P1. Thus, we overloaded P1, so that, its costs being higher than sales, it appeared to be in deficit.

PROGNOSIS.– As we are in the presence of two contradictory solutions P1 and P2, we will choose a third to decide between.

RECOMMENDATION.– Before any calculation of cash flows or investment or even recovery of a product, it must be certain that the calculations of results are correctly established. An analysis of indirect costs is based on activities, not functions, purchasing, production, distribution and administrations.

5.1.3. Results obtained in full cost by activity (Activity by Costing)

To make a decision, and because cost dominance is a major element of the apparent profitability of the products, we decided to set up an activity-based analysis and the cost drivers that link the costs to the corresponding activity, which are as follows:

Activity centers	Activities	Cost drivers	Cost	
Purchases	Orders	Purchased batches	€6,200	
	Stock management	Amount of purchases in €	€15,649	
	Disposition	Manufactured batches	€2,360	=€24,209
Machining	Preparation	Manufactured batches	€34,595	
	Launching	H. machine	€76,020	
	Maintenance	Operating machine hours	€14,805	=€125,420
Finishing stage	Polishing	Polite. Unit	€24,800	
	Quality	Controlled unit	€66,400	
€106,840	Expedition	Shipped batch	€15,640	=€106,840
Administrative	Organization	Production cost	€106,834	=€106,834
We have of course always the same indirect expenses				=€363,303

Purchases	M	N
Batches	8 L.	4 L.
Of	300 kg	100 kg
At	350 kg	

Production	P1	P2
Batches of	200 U.	100 U.

Quality control	P1	Samples	20 U./batch
	P2		100%

Shall we check the unit cost of inductors?

Functions	Activities	Inductors	Cost	Number of inductors		Total	Cost of inductors
Purchases	Orders	Purchased batches	€6,200	8 C	+ 4 C	= 12 C	= €516.67
	Stock management	Purchases in €	€15,649	263,520 €		€263, 520	= 5.94%
	Disposition	Manufactured batches	€2,360	6 L.	+ 13 L.	= 19 C	= €124.21
Machining	Preparation	Manufactured batches	€34,595	6 L.	+ 13 L.	= 19 C	= €1,820.79
	Launching	H. machine	€76,020	735 h.		735 h.	= €103.43
	Maintenance	H. Function	€14,805	735 h.		735 h.	= €20.14
Finishing stage	Polishing	U. Polite	€24,800	1,200 u.p.	1,300 u.p.	2,500 u.p.	= €9.92
	Quality	Controlled units	€66,400	120 u.c.	1,300 u.c.	1,420 u.c.	= €46.76
	Expedition	Shipped batches	€15,640	6 L.	+ 13 L.	19 L.	= €823.16
Administrative	Organization	€	€106,834	€263,226	€252,899	516,126 €	20.70%

10 inductors = €363,303

Grouping by homogeneous families of inductors

The reduction in the number of inductors is not necessarily homogeneous; this is therefore an identical problem for analysis with homogeneous sections. We bring together the occurrences of kg (not kilos of lead and feathers), hours (machine hours and meeting) etc. This is a different problem…

Inductors	Cost of inductor families		
Purchased batches €			€516.67
Purchases in €			5.94%
Manufactured batches	€124.21	+€1,820.79	€1,945
Shipped batches			€823.16
H. machine	€103.43	+€20.14	€123.57
Units manufactured and polished			€9.92
Controlled units			€46.76

= 7 inducers only on 10 inductors at the beginning

How much do P1 and P2 come to in the end?

Cost of purchases	Material M			Material N			
	Quantity	Cost	Amount	Quantities	Cost	Amount	
Direct	2,680 kg	€54.00	= €144,720	400 kg	€297.00	= €118,800	
Orders	8 C	€516.67	€4,133	4 C	€516.67	€2,067	
Stock management	€144,720	5.94%	€8,594	€118,800	5.94%	€7,055	
Total	2,680 kg	CMP €58.75	€157,447	400 kg	CMP €319.80	€27,922	=€285,369
			Before it was 55% **Idem 55%**			Before it was 45% **Idem 45%**	**100%**

Stock materials	Material M			Material N			
	Quantities	Cost	Amount	Quantities	Cost	Amount	
Initial stock	350 kg	€61.07	= €21,373	80 kg	€303.30	=€24,264	
Cost of purchase	2,680 kg	€58.75	€157,447	400 kg	€319.80	= €127,922	
Enter	3,030 kg	WAC €59.02	€178,820	480 kg	WAC 317.05	€152,186	
Consumption	2,700 kg	€59.02	€159,345	390 kg	€317.05	€123,651	= €282,996
Final stock	*330 kg*	*€59.02*	*€19,475*	*90 kg*	*€317.05*	*€28,535*	= €48,010

Production cost	P1			P2			
	Quantities	Cost	Amount	Quantities	Cost	Amount	
Consumption	2,700 kg	€59.02	€159,345	390 kg	€317.05	€123, 651	
Products batches	6 L.	€1,945.00	€11,670	13 L.	€1, 945.00	€25, 285	
H. Machine	540 h.	€123.57	€66,729	195 h.	€123.57	€24,096	
Manufacturing	1,200 u.	€9.92	€11,904	1,300 u.	€9.92	€12, 896	
Control	120 u.	€46.76	€5,611	1,300 u.	€46.76	€60, 789	
Consumable	€159,345	5%	€7,967	€123,651	5%	€6,183	
Total	1,200 u.	€219.36	€263,226	1,300 u.	€194.54	€252,899	€516,126
			Before it was 54% **Here 51%**			Before it was 46% **Here 49%**	**100%**

Cost of return	P1 products and sold			P2 products and sold			
	Quantities	Cost	Amount	Quantities	Cost	Amount	
Production PV	1,200 u.	€219.36	€263,226	1,300 u.	€194.54	€252,899	
Dispatch	6 u.	€823.16	€4,939	13 u.	€823.16	€10,701	
Administrative	€263,226	20.70%	€54,486	€252,899	20.70%	€52,348	
Total	1,200 u.	€268.88	€322,651	1,300 u.	€243.04	€315,949	€638,600
			Before it was 65% **Here 51%**			Before it was 55% **Here 49%**	**100%**

The results by products P1 and P2 are now

Analytical results	P1 products and sold			P2 products and sold			
	Quantities	Price/Cost	Amount	Quantities	Cost	Amount	
Sales	1,200 u.	€325	€390,000	1,300 u.	€217	€282,100	= €672,100
Cost of return	1,200 u.	€268.88	€322,651	1,300 u.	€243.04	€315,930	= €638,581
Results	1,200 u.	€56.12	€67,349	1,300 u.	−€26.02	−€33,830	= €33,519

ANALYSIS.– We confirm that the charge distribution was made at the expense of P1 because it is P2 that has a deficit result. Moreover, this one is much higher than before. The slight difference in the current result is as always partly in rounding and partly in the consideration of necessarily different indirect costs in the calculation of final stocks. Finally, we have in the stocks: €48,408 − €48,010 = €400 and in the current results €33,800 − €33,519 = €281 which is about 1% and therefore not significant.

DIAGNOSIS.– The distinction between the batches manufactured and sold is unclear as ABC works via outsourcing. Attempting to group inductors does not bring clarity.

PROGNOSIS.– Driver research such as value added to products, perceived or expected value, etc. is much better as a working hypothesis. In any case, we should no longer have subsidies and cost cascades.

RECOMMENDATION.– This analysis has improved the knowledge of income and profitability by product and financial calculations that will follow. However, to consider the indirect expenses as a group remains an analysis to refine. In fact, it should be clearer to separate in the indirect expenses those which come under the structure, generally fixed by the level of activity and those which are directly assignable according to the activity. This will bring out a concept of margin per product that is more complete than the only result.

5.2. Budget based on normal activity

A budget for which only certain expenses are taken into consideration is a budget in partial and not complete cost. The interest of this analysis is to calculate the performance related to the decision to be made or not without taking into account the structural costs.

5.2.1. *Activity*

The activity criteria are numerous in a company, but in this analysis, we generally use unifying criteria such as activity times, production levels of goods or services.

5.2.2. *Budget for which indirect costs are unbundled in terms of being variable and fixed*

A variable cost budget only consists of expenses that vary with the volume of activity but without any proportionality between the change in expenses and the variation in the volume of activity.

In financial budgets only calculated with partial costs, in principle, the direct expenses are mostly variable and the indirect ones have two parts: one variable with the activity and the other fixed for a given time.

Variable expenses generally vary with activity. Their evolution depends on the degree of use, intensity and efficiency in the use of available capacities and means.

Structural charges are related to the existence of the activity but without their level having a well-established causal relationship with the activity. Indeed, before the activity starts, the structure expenses appear. However, their level and their level of incompressibility despite everything related to the activity are the object of a search for permanent reduction; mergers, re-groupings, relocation, outsourcing, etc. are examples of this are downsizing. These structural charges therefore correspond to a determined level of activity.

Fixed costs are not necessarily structural (linear depreciation, rents, taxes, etc.). They correspond, for each budget period, to a certain level of activity. The evolution of these expenses with the activity is discontinuous. They are fixed when the level of activity changes little during the period.

5.2.3. *Cost-effectiveness*

Expenses are allocated on a budget for a target activity level, which is normally achievable. However, the observed, so-called real activity for the period is different from that foreseen. The variable, supposedly proportional expenses are therefore consumed by the actual activity, but the fixed charges have been too much or not well enough endowed. Therefore, you have to adjust them to actual activity to find out how much money you really needed.

To properly adjust the cost to the actual activity and not to assume it, we will therefore take into account the cost of the activity and admit it as a loss and not a cost element. The budgetary allocation of these fixed costs is then recalculated in relation to the activity level assumed to be normal. Any overactivity in relation to their level will be analyzed as a productivity gain, thus an internal financial resource on absorption of structural charges; however, in the case of under-absorption of structural charges, it will be the observation of a financial loss due to the underactiveness.

EXAMPLE.– A production unit for the next period normally provides for a level of activity of 10,000 units plus or minus 20%. The variable operating costs would be €10 per unit, and the fixed costs €40,000 in total.

The total budgets in these three occurrences are:

BUDGETS	Expected normal activity	Hypothesis 1 of real activity		Hypothesis 2 of real activity	
Elements	Results	Budget H1	Loss by sub activity	Budget H2	Productivity gain
Activity rate	100 %	80%	−20 %	120 %	+ 20 %
Objective in units	10,000 u.	8,000 u.	−2,000 u.	12,000 u.	+ 2,000 u.
Full cost analysis					
Cost price	€140,000	€120,000	−20.000 €	€160,000	+€16,000
Unit cost	€14/u.	€15/u.	+€1/u.	€13.33/u.	−€0.67/u.
Partial cost analysis					
Variable cost	€100,000	€80,000	−€20,000	€120,000	+€20,000
Fixed cost	€40,000	€32,000	€0	€48,000	+€20.000
Loss or gain due to Δ of activity	+8.000 €	Loss (over-head) of sub-activity	−€8.000	Gain (less expense) productivity	
Variable unit cost	€10/u.	€10/u.	€0	€10/u.	€0
Fixed unit cost	€4/u.	€5/u.	+€1/u.	€3.33/u.	−€0.67/u.

ANALYSIS.– We reach the following conclusion:

– In the full cost analysis model, unit costs are based on the following three assumptions: €14, €15 and €13.33.

– In the partial cost analysis model:

- the total variable cost is proportional to the activity = €100,000, €80,000, €120,000; and

- the total fixed cost remains the same as the expected one and therefore constant = €40,000.

– Because the forecast is a standard of activity equal to 100% of the achievable, any difference in activity (in this case ±20%) has the consequence of underabsorbing or absorbing fixed resources. By obtaining an allocation of €40,000, one was supposed to reach a forecast activity of 10,000 units. Therefore, this activity goal:

- is reached and the budget absorbs the fixed cost of €40,000;

- is exceeded by +2,000 units and the fixed charges are overabsorbed, which generates a resource in the form of increased productivity;

- is not reached and the financial allocation for fixed costs for 10.000u. is underabsorbed and causes a loss due to underactivity.

– The normal activity rate of 100% is either 80% or 120%. Therefore:

- activity rate = (actual or observed activity)/(normal activity).

IN THE EXAMPLE.–

Standard of activity = 10.000u./10.000u. = 100%

Hypothesis 1: 8.000u. /10.000u. = 80% of activity rate = financial cost = €40,000 × 80% = €32,000 consumed with €40,000 – €32,000 = + €8,000 of cost of sub-activity.

Hypothesis 2: 12.000u./10.000u.=120% of activity rate; therefore, productivity gain €40,000 × 120% = €48,000 with €40,000 – €48,000 = –€8,000 of productivity gain. The sign – shows in the same way that a productivity gain absorbs charges so is an internal resource.

There is a major interest for an organization to look for productivity gains as a source of funding.

This analysis is important because the evaluation of the costs contained in the stored items (in FCA and IFRS standards) does not have to take the costs of the sub-activity into account. However, it comes up against the evaluation of the norm, which in fact conditions the sub-activity.

IRCF case

The determination of the result of the enterprise depends on the level of activity in the calculation of costs.

Regardless of the actual activity

The director of a business unit sends you the following income statement:

Center's budget			
Raw material purchases	€81,000	Sales	€264,600
Inventory change	−€25,500	Stored production	€26,850
Indirect expenses	€172,500		
Specific expenses	€54,000		
Result	**€9,450**		
	€291,450		€291,450

The director indicates in a note that he has achieved his objectives as he displays a profitability, which is 3.6% higher than the initial target of 3.5%, which he called for.

We will first check how this result was calculated. For this, we asked the financial controller for the following information and he gave us:

The director's reports in note form

The business unit manufactures P1 and P2 products from two M1 and M2 materials and its production process is as follows:

Needs for	M1	M2	Machine time
P1	2 kg	1 kg	1 h
P2	3 kg	2 kg	1.5 h

Purchases of the period					
M1			M2		
4,500 kg	€10	€45,000	2,400 kg	€15	€36,000

Initial stocks are null	
Productions	
P1	P2
900 P1	600 P2

Sales for the period					
P1				P2	
810 P1	€160	€129,600	540 P2	€250	€135,000

Distribution of structural charges (fixed indirect)			
	Purchase	Production	Sale
Secondary distribution	€69,000	€90,000	€13,500
Unit of work	kg bought	H. Machine	Sold units
Number of work units	6,900 kg	1,800 H.M	1,350 produced
Blow of unity	€10 /kg	€50 /HM	€10 /U. Sold

Specific production expenses	
P1	P2
€30,000	€24,000

Not taking into account resource consumption rationally for the actual activity in relation to the objectives assigned to the business unit

Verification of the profitability announced by the director of the *business unit*

Purchase Price

	M1	M2	Total
Purchase	€45,000	€36,000	€81,000
Indirect expenses	4,500 kg × €10/kg = €45,000	2,400 kg × €10 /kg = €24,000	€69,000
Cost of purchase	**€90,000**	**€60,000**	**€150,000**

Consumption of stocks for P1

M1 (€90,000/4,500 kg) × 2 kg × 900 P1 = €36,000

M2 (€60,000/2,400 kg) × 1 kg × 900 P1 = €22,500

- Final stock of materials M1 and M2 for P1 = (€90,000 of cost of purchase) – (€58,500 of consumption) = €31,500

Consumption of stocks for P2

M1 (€90,000/4,500 kg) × 3 kg × 600 P2 = €36,000

M 2 (€60,000/2,400 kg) × 2 kg × 600 P2 = €30,000

- Final stock of materials M1 and M2 for P2 = €60,000 of cost of purchase – €66,000 of consumption = –€6,000.

Either change in stocks of materials = −initial stock + final stock = −€31,500 + €6,000 = −€25,500, which confirms the profit and loss account of the manager of the business unit.

Production cost

	P1	P2	Total
Materials used	€58,500	€66,000	€124,500
Specific expenses	€30,000	€24,000	€54,000
Indirect expenses	€50 /HM × 900 P1 × 1HM = €45,000	€50 /HM × 600 P2 × 1.5 HM = €45,000	€90,000
Production cost	**€133,500**	**€135,000**	**€268,500**

Production cost of sold P1: €133,500/810 P1 × 900 P1 = €120,150

Production cost of sold P2: €135,000/540 P2 × 600 P1 = €121,500

Stored production = final stock − initial stock =

P1: €133,500 − €120,150 = €13,350

P2: €135,000 − €121,500 = €13,500

The stored production of the profit and loss account is verified, and it is equal to 26,850

Cost price

	P1	P2	Total
Products sold	€120,150	€121,500	€241,650
Indirect expenses	€10/kg × 810 P1 = €8,100	€10/kg × 540 P2 = €5,400	€13,500
Cost price	**€128,250**	**€126,900**	**€255,150**

Analyzed result

	P1	P2	Total
Sale	€129,600	€135,000	€264,600
Cost price	−€128,250	−€126,900	−€255,150
Results	**€1,350**	**€8,100**	**€9,450**

We confirm the result and therefore the apparent profitability of 3.6% announced by the business unit.

Taking into account the consumption of resources rationally for real activity in relation to the objective

NOTE.– The following objectives were planned for this business unit:

Purchases	Machine hours	Sold production	
8,100 kg	2,050 HM	1,000 P1	700 P2

It is necessary to calculate the actual result and the real and not apparent profitability of this unit.

	Rational distribution of indirect fixed charges		
	Purchase	Production	Sale
2nd distribution	€69,000	€90,000	€13,500
Activity coefficient	6,900 kg/8,100 kg = **85.19%**	1,800 HM/2,050 HM = **87.80%**	1,350 P/(100 P1 + 700 P2) = **79.41%**
Indirect costs to be charged	€58,778	79,024 €	€10,721
Unit of work	kg bought	Machine hours	Units sold
Number of units of work	6,900 kg	1,800 MH	1,350 produced
Blow of unity	€8.52/kg	€43.90/MH	€7.94/U. sold
Cost of this sub-activity	€10,222	€10,976	€2,779

Let cost of this sub-activity be €23,977.

Cost of the sub-activity on specific direct fixed costs			
P1	€30,000	−€30,000 (900 P1/1,000 P1) = €27,000	€3,000
P2	€24,000	−€24,000 (600 P2/700 P2) = €20,571	€3,429
		Cost of this sub-activity	€6,429

Purchase cost rationally charged to the activity carried out

		M1	M2	Total
	Purchases	€45,000	€36,000	= €81,000
	Indirect costs to be charged rationally	€38,333	€20,444	= €58,778
	Cost of purchase charged rationally	€83,333	€56,444	**= €139,778**
	Instead of	*€90,000*	*€60,000*	*€150,000*

Therefore, we see a reduction in the cost of purchase compared to what was displayed without taking into account the actual activity.

Consumption of stocks of M1 and M2 for P1:

M1 (€83,333/4,500 kg) × 2 kg × 900 P1 = €33,333

M2 (€56,444/2,400 kg) × 1 kg × 900 P1 = €21,166

- Final stock of material M1 and M2 for P1 = (€83,333 of purchase cost) − (€54,500 of consumption) = €28,333.

Consumption of stocks of M1 and M2 for P2:

M1 (€83,333/4,500 kg) × 3 kg × 600 P2 = €33,333

M 2 (€56,444 /2,400 kg) × 2 kg × 600 P2 = €28,222

- Final stock of materials M1 and M2 for P2 = (€56,444 of purchase cost) − (€61,555 of consumption) = −€5,111

Stock variation M1, M2 −€23,722

and not −€25,500, as shown in the income statement. Therefore, we see a difference in the value of inventories in assets by the business unit, which increased the result of the liabilities to balance the balance sheet.

Cost of production rationally charged to the activity carried out

	P1	P2		Total
Consumed materials M1 and M2	€54,500	€61,556	=	€116,056
Specific expenses imputed rationally	€27,000	€20,571	=	€47,571
Indirect expenses imputed rationally	€39,512	€39,512	=	€79,024
Cost of production rationally charged	**€121,012**	**€121,639**	=	**€242,651**
Instead of	*€133,500*	*€135,000*	=	*€268,500*

Therefore, we see a reduction in the cost of production compared to what was displayed without taking into account the actual activity.

Cost price rationally imputed to the activity carried out

	P1	P2		Total
Products sold	€108,911	€109,475	=	€218,386
Distribution expenses imputed rationally	€6,432	€4,288	=	€10,721
Cost price	**€115,343**	**€113,763**		**=€229,107**
Instead of	*€128,250*	*€126,900*		***€255,150***

Therefore, we see a reduction in the cost price compared to what was displayed without taking into account the actual activity.

Production cost of P1 and P2 produced: €242,651.

Production cost of P1 and P2 sold: €218,386.

Final stock − initial stock = stored production €242,651 − €218,386 = €24,265 instead of €26,850 as presented in the income statement. Thus, there is a reduction in the value of inventories on the asset side, which has increased the result of the liabilities to balance the balance sheet.

Result analyzed rationally and attributed to the activity performed

	P1	P2	Total
Sales	€129,600	€135,000	= €264 600
Cost − price	−€115,343	−€113,763	- €229,107
Direct cost of sub-activity	€3,000	€3,429	= €6,429
Indirect cost of sub-activity	€14,386	€9,591	€23,977
Result with sub-activity	**−€3,130**	**€8,217**	**€5,087**
Instead of	*−€1,350*	*−€8,100*	*=€9,450*

Therefore, we see a reduction in the result compared to what was posted in the income statement without taking into account the actual activity.

Income statement adjusted rationally to the activity carried out

Income statement with rational allocation of fixed costs in inventories							
Material purchases invoiced	€81,000		sales invoiced	€264,600	Without IR	Δstocks P1 P2	
Stock variation M1 and M2	− €23,722		Stored production P1 P2	€24,265	− €26,850	− €2,585	
Indirect expenses invoiced	€172,500					− €4,363	
Specific expenses invoiced	€54,000					Δ in stocks	
Result with sub-activity	€5,087						
Total expenses	€288,865		Total products	€288,865			

ANALYSIS.– Expenses and income statement earnings must not include items that are not consumed or not sold. For example, if goods bought during the year have not been sold, then they must be removed from the expenses. These corrections influence the changes in stocks of materials, goods and inventoried products. This shows that items that are not consumed and that involve a cost of underactivity inflate stocks and the result unduly.

DIAGNOSIS.–

If we do not take into account the objectives assigned to the business unit, we confirm:

- its financial result of €9,450;
- the distribution of this result in 14.36% for P1 and 85.63% for P2;
- apparent profitability (result/turnover) €9,450/€264,600 = 3.6%;
- the value of the final stocks of M1 and M2 = €25,500;
- the value of final stocks of P1 and P2 = €26,850.

– If we take into account the objectives that have been assigned to the business unit, then we charge the structural costs rationally to the actual activity in relation to what has been allocated as forecast resources:

- income statement items from invoices must keep their un-quoted values on invoices and payment methods;
- only the calculated costs and products, including inventories, can be "adjusted";
- its financial result of €5,087, i.e. 46% less;
- the breakdown of this result shows a loss on P1 and €8,217 for P2;
- the apparent profitability (result/turnover) €5,087/€264,600 = 1.92%;
- the value of the final stocks of M1 and M2 = €23,722;
- the value of the final stocks of P1 and P2 = €24,265;
- the result for the calculation of the return on equity is actually down by 46%;
- the shortfall is €9,450 − €5,087 = €4,363.

PROGNOSIS.– This overvaluation of the €4,363 result is due solely to the overvaluation of stocks outside this analysis of:

- materials = €25,500 − €23,722 = €1,778
- products = €26,850 − €24,265 = €2,585

and therefore, the need for working capital. There will therefore be a need for increased funding that can induce a financial interest expense, the origin of which is inexplicable without this analysis.

RECOMMENDATION.–

– The French Accounting Plan and IFRS require the value of inventories to be deflated by the cost of the sub-activity.

– By having overevaluation, the stocks that have no account in the liabilities will abnormally inflate the result.

In the event of profit distribution, a portion is based on fictitious dividends.

In the case of productivity gains, however, it is not necessary to deflate the value of inventories and income as there is no consumption of expenses justified by overactivity.

Therefore, before any calculation of results, cash flows, return on investments, etc., it is necessary to analyze the way in which accruals have been calculated (calculated products and expenses).

5.2.4. Profitability

Decisions made regarding partial costs can make each activity profitable, but once the fixed costs have been deducted, the profitability can be negative.

The calculation of margins that are partial or intermediate results makes it possible to determine profitability by project.

5.2.4.1. Margins

A margin is:

– the difference between a sale price and a partial cost. In fact, in this calculation, one immediately integrates the price or turnover and not at the end by comparing it with the cost price. Thus, a margin is:

– an intermediate result, a step before the final result (see interim management balances);

– also equal to the difference between turnover and the title of this margin. Indeed:

- margin regarding purchase cost = turnover − purchase cost;

- margin regarding variable cost = turnover − variable cost; and
- margin regarding distribution cost = turnover − distribution cost.

Margins express a sequential declination of results.

Example of a general budget of a decision center	Real	Planned	Differences
0 Turnover excluding VAT			
1 + Net sales of products			
2 - Cost of manufactured products			
3 = Manufacturer margin			
4 - Net sales of services			
5 - Cost of services			
6 - Margin regarding cost of services offered			
3 + 6 = No. 7 Margin regarding cost of production of goods and services			
8 - Marketing costs			
9 - Cost of feasibility: studies, research, etc.			
10 - Administrative costs			
11 - Financial income			
12 - Financial expenses			
13 - Other operating items			
7-8-9-10-11-12-13 = **No. 12 Operating Cost Margin**			
13 - Income from movable capital			
14 - Expenses due to movable assets			
12 + 13-14 = **No. 15 Operating margin before cost of capital**			
16 - Depreciation of fixed assets			
17 - Operating profit (16 - 17)			
18 - Products – non-current expenses			
19 - Revenue – exceptional expenses			
17 ± 18 ± 19 = **No. 20 Result**			

All things being equal, it is assumed, for a given period and initially, that:

– the structural charges remain fixed during a range of activity;

– operating expenses vary proportionally; and

– the explanatory variable of the activity is the value of the production sold.

5.2.4.2. *Margin regarding variable cost*

A positive variable cost margin activity absorbs the expenses it generates. There is therefore no reason to abandon an activity or a product that covers the expenses it generates and some or all of the direct fixed charges. Any abandonment of margin activity on negative variable cost has the effect of absorbing the structural charges on other activities or products.

5.2.4.3. *Variable Cost Margin Rate VCMR*

This is the ratio of the variable cost margin VCM to the turnover T/O. This is the unit margin for one euro of sales. Therefore:

$$\boxed{\text{Rate VCMR} = \text{VCMR}/\text{T/O}}$$

5.2.4.4. *Margins regarding specific cost or direct costing*

We cannot make decisions to abandon activities on the criterion of a negative variable cost margin. To decide, we assign certain fixed costs to each activity and we obtain a margin on direct cost. The remaining fixed costs are part of the organization's structure. Thus, the decision to abandon an activity, or its revival, subcontracting or even the re-allocation of some of its costs to other older activities is part of the company's strategy.

Companies that do not have management accounts sell their products below cost by:

– "Breaking" the market prices and increasing their turnover. However, the more they sell, the more profitability collapses. Thus, the turnover is only a criterion of performance if:

- it generates profitability by sector of activity, product line, etc. (IFRS);

- the company finds resources to finance the working capital requirement generated by this growth.

– Eliminating competing companies from the market, which do not have the financial means to wait for the failure of this company.

5.2.4.5. Diagram

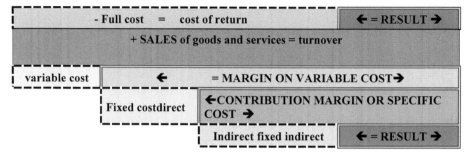

5.3. The breakeven point

Profitability is determined by the ratio of two items in the income statement.

We study the relationship between margin on variable cost MSCV/turnover T/O.

However, there is at least a moment, at the neutral point of equilibrium, where the activity makes no profit or loss. Therefore, at the breakeven point (profitability), when the operating result R is zero, at the same time:

1) VCMR = fixed charges (F);

2) turnover (sales) = total expenses (TE).

There is therefore a critical turnover or breakeven point S, for which the result = 0; thus, at the breakeven point, we have the equivalence of the profitability:

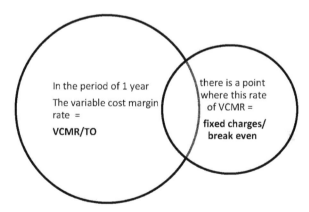

Figure 5.2. *Calculation of the profitability level*

Making: VCMR= F and T/O = S. or: VCMR/TO = F/S → $\frac{TO \times CF}{VCMR}$

EXAMPLE.– For a level of activity, a company has an operating budget of 800, 75% of which is variable. It considers itself beneficiary from a turnover of €800 k. The breakeven analysis shows that the €800 k coverage assumes a proportionality of all expenses, which is not necessarily the case. The breakeven point B/E for this activity can be determined in many ways. For a projected turnover of €1,000 k:

– Calculate the breakeven point S by the margin on variable cost:

VCMR = TO – VC =€1,000 k – (75% × €800 k) = €400 k

and fixed charges = €800 k – €600 k = €200 k.

So, the breakeven = $\frac{TO * FC}{VCM}$ is $\frac{€1,000 \text{ k} \times €200 \text{ k}}{€400 \text{ k}}$ = €500 k and not €800k as we tend to believe. All expenses are not proportional.

– Calculation of the threshold by variable cost margin rate (VCMR):

The VCMR is the ratio of the margin on variable cost to the turnover: VCMR = VCM/TO.

Therefore, the breakeven: S = $\frac{FC}{VCMR}$ is: ½ × €1,000 k = €500 k

It can be verified that, for this turnover of €500 k, the variable expenses are 75% of the €500 k, i.e. €375 k. Then, the fixed costs are equal, assuming the total cost minus the variable expenses, i.e. F = €500 k – €375 k = €125 k.

The result is therefore €500 k – €375 k – €125 k = €0 k.

5.3.1. *Representation*

At the breakeven point, there is equality between turnover and cost of returns (CR):

– Breakeven or profitability thresholds are located on the bisector. With (TO) = (CR) (or y = x).

– The breakeven point sought is that which, on this bisector, corresponds to the cost price = F + V.

– Fixed charges are constant within a period in which they are supposed to vary per stage of the process.

We therefore have a horizontal line of type y = constant.

EXAMPLE.– The variable expenses are proportional to the activity. Here, we consider the value of the projected turnover; 600 of VC for 1,000 of T/O, that is a ratio of 60% of the turnover and a function of type y = 0.6 x with α = 0.6

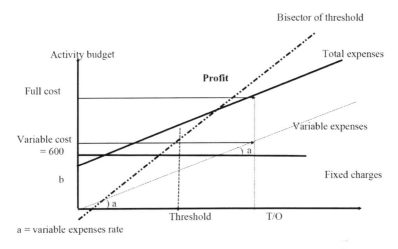

Figure 5.3. *The cost price is the sum of the two straight lines: (y = 0.6x) + (y = constant) according to y = ax + b*

By the equality between t variable cost margin and fixed charges, we know that:

– for a turnover (turnover) of 1,000, the variable cost margin (VCMR) = 600;

– for (TO) = 0, the variable cost margin, which is equal to the turnover minus the variable expenses = 0.

These two points (y = 600 and x = 1,000) and (y = 0 and x = 0) are sufficient to draw the line on VCMR. When it is equal to the fixed charges (y = constant = b), it cuts them. This is where the breakeven point is shown graphically.

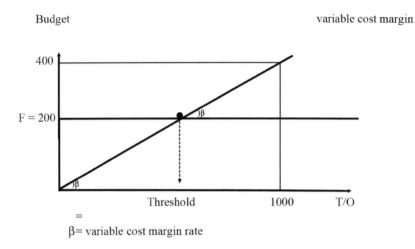

β = variable cost margin rate

Figure 5.4. *Graphic representation of the breakeven point*

5.3.2. *Indicators of profitability*

From this analysis, indicators can be calculated.

– *Safety margin*: SM = TO – threshold.

– *Security Index* (SI) = returns the SM to turnover SI = SM/TO. The higher the index, the larger the margin and the greater the profitability.

• *For example (1.000 − 500)/1.000 = 50%, which is very comfortable.*

– *Sampling index* IP = S/TO. This index makes it possible to compare several sales figures of several products, as here, the thresholds of profitability are presented in percentages.

• *In our example, it is 500/1,000 = 50%, which is considerable.*

5.3.3. Decision-making

Models of this type are estimated, but they can also illustrate the consequences of unfortunate decisions.

EXAMPLE.–

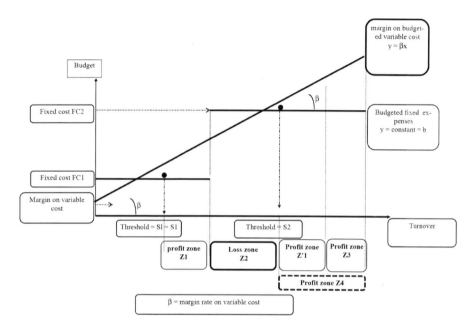

Figure 5.5. *Example of decision-making*

Given its production capacity, the company is located in a Z1 profit zone.

It wants to increase its profits and invest. Its fixed structural costs go from FC1 to FC2.

The company is moving from profit zone Z1 to the larger loss zone Z2.

It wanted to go from Z1 to Z3, to increase its profits. But it must avoid Z2 at all costs. At worst, it must ensure Z3 with the same profit Z'1 but this time prefiguring Z3.

The mistake usually made is that the company invests following a decision made based on criteria of financial profitability of investments, whereas it would have been necessary to invest according to criteria of yield, productivity and profitability of exploitation, specific to the activity.

If, for example, with three machines, the company manufactures and sells 3,000 products, and if it invests in two other machines, it is not because it can obtain them with favorable financial conditions that would prove that the financial profitability of this investment is better than another project, but because the development of its business is in the ratio 5/3 or will be done quickly. Achieving with five machines what it did with three led the company from a Z1 profit zone to a zone of severe loss, Z2.

The disproportions of cost growth and profitability are further accentuated if we imagine that the variable cost margin rate is also changing.

There are two solutions in case of a bad decision, the company:

– can go back, while there is still time, disinvest and at best it will still stagnate in Z1;

– can battle until arriving in Z4. From there, Z3 is in sight.

EXAMPLE.–

ALD is a center for assembling and selling electronic products. The human resources department consists of people on indefinite permanent contracts and students working on previously constructed products. ALD has focused on two product families, A and B, and its activity in hours for the period is in HM assembly hours and HC control as well:

Activities	Assembly	Control
Product A	450 HM	100 HC
Product B	150 HM	500 HC
Total	600 HM	600 HC

For the period excluding purchases of components invoiced according to consumption:

	Activities				
	Support	Principles			
Budget expenses	Management	Assembly	Control	Sales	Budget
Other management expenses	25%			75%	€400
Management expenses	1/15	4/5	1/15	1/15	€1,500
Depreciation allowance		€4,110	€80		€4,190
Provision expenses				100%	€240
Supplies	2/3			1/3	€8,400
Levies and taxes				100%	€820
Fitter Salaries		100%			€2,400
Vendor salaries				100%	€540
Student salaries			100%		€1,680
Manager salaries	100%				€1,680
33% of payroll taxes imputed in proportion to the salaries of the activities					€2,100
				Total indirect costs	**€23,950**

Component use	A	B
	€8,500	€12,300

	Quantity	Price	value
Sale of finished product families A and B	270 A	€100	€27,000
	230 B	€95	€21,850

To calculate current results by products

a) Set up the indirect charge allocation table and calculate the unit costs for cost allocations.

b) Determine the center's budget and results by product family.

c) Calculate the profitability of each product family A and B.

Cost drivers are the quantities associated with the activities.

Let us draw up the distribution table of the indirect costs and calculate their costs for the main activities if the management expenses are to be distributed by 1/3.

256   Financial Management

Budget expenses	Management	Assembly	Control	Sale	Budget
Other management expenses	€100			€300	= €400
Management expenses	€100	€1,200	€100	€100	= €1,500
Depreciation allowance		€4,110	€80		=€4,190
Provisioning				€240	= €240
Supplies	€5,600			€2,800	= €8,400
Levies and taxes				€820	=€820
Fitter salaries		€2,400			= €2,400
Seller salaries				€540	= €540
Student salaries			€1,680		= €1,680
Manager salaries	€1,680				= €1,680
Social charges 33%	€560	€800	€560	€180	= €2,100
Primary distribution	€8,040	€8,510	€2,420	€4,980	=€23,950
Secondary distribution	−€8,040	+€2,680	+€2,680	+€2,680	= €0
Total indirect expenses	0	€11,190	€5,100	€7,660	= €23,950
Vectors and other cost indicators		HM	HV	US	
Number of vectors and other cost indicators		600 HM	600 HC	500 US*	
Unit cost to be charged		€18,650	€8,500	€15,320	= €42

*US = units sold

Let us determine the center's budget and the results by product family:

Expenses	Products A	Products B	Budget
Material consumption	€8,500	€12,300	= €20,800
Imputed indirect assembly costs	€8,393	€2,798	= €11,190
Indirect overhead costs charged	€850	€4,250	= €5,100
Indirect expenses of imputed sales	€4,136	€3,524	=€7,660
ALD budget	**€21,879**	**€22,871**	**=€44,750**

Let us calculate the probability of each product family A and B:

	Product A	Product B	Budget
Sales figure	€27,000	€21,850	= €48,850
ALD budget	€21,879	€22,871	= €44,750
Management results	€5,121	−€1,021	=€4,100

ANALYSIS.– The result of ALD is profitable but only one of the two products is profitable. This may come from the distribution of indirect costs that do not correspond to the economic realities of the consumption of resources by the two products.

DIAGNOSIS.– It would be wise to consider a more detailed analysis of the expenses and to envisage their separation between those which are variable and those which are not.

PROGNOSIS.– In any case, if analysis remains constant, it is the product B that must be abandoned.

RECOMMENDATIONS.– ALD could abandon one of the two products. In this case, the number of students could vary according to the single activity and all capacities would be devoted to the only product remaining. The market is then able to absorb all the production retained.

A finer analysis has broken down the resources allocated to activities in fixed and variable costs.

To determine the result by product family, calculate the successive margins and the performance indicators.

The expenses of the *activities* of:

– management are fixed;

– assembly are mainly proportional to the activity except some that are fixed such as:

  - €2,100 in salaries, knowing that social charges remain proportional,

  - all depreciation allowances.

– sales are mainly proportional to the activity except some that are fixed such as:

  - wages and their social charges,

  - €100 management expenses.

– control is totally proportional to the activity.

Let us draw up the distribution table of fixed and variable indirect costs and calculate their costs for the main activities

Budget expenses	Management F	Assembly F	Assembly V	Control V	Sale V	Sale F
Other management expenses	€100				€300	
Management expenses	€100		€1,200	€100		€100
Depreciation charge		€4,110		80 €		
Provisioning					€240	
Supplies	€5,600				€2,800	
Levies and taxes					€820	
Fitter salaries		€2,100	€300			
Seller salaries						€540
Student salaries				€1,680		
Manager salaries	€1,680					
Social charges	€560	€700	€100	€560		€180
Total indirect expenses	€8,040	€6,910	€1,600	€2,420	€4,160	€820
Work units (WU) and cost drivers Number of WU and other indicators			HM	HC	US	
			600 HM	600 HV	500 US	
Unit cost to be charged			€2.67	€4.03	€8.32	

Let us calculate the margin in regard to variable cost of distribution

Expenses	Product A	Product B	Budget
Sales figures	€27,000	€21,850	€48,850
Indirect sales expenses imputed	€2,246	€1,914	€4,160
Margin on variable cost of distribution=	€24,754	€19,936	€44,690

DIAGNOSIS.– The commercial activity thus absorbs the expenses that it generates and the fixity of the wages and social charges because the margins are all positive.

Calculate the variable cost margin of each product

Expenses	Product A	Product B	Budget
Material consumption	€8,500	€12,300	€20,800
Imputed variable indirect loading costs	€1,200	€400	€1,600
Indirect verification expenses	€403	€2,017	€2,420
Total other variable expenses	**€10,103**	**€14,717**	**€24,820**

Expenses	Product A	Product B	Budget
Margin on variable cost of distribution	€24,754	€19,936	€44,690
Total other variable expenses	€10,103	€14,717	€24,820
Margin on variable cost of each product	**€14,650**	**€5,220**	**€19,870**

ANALYSIS.– The negative result regarding product A does not come from the manufacturing process or marketing. As a result, there is no reason for the choice to stop the manufacture of A or outsource it to improve the result.

Let us calculate the fixed costs and find the result

Margin on variable cost of each product	€19,870
Fixed charges	**€15,770**
Result of management accounting	**€4,100**

PROGNOSIS.– If the strategy is to abandon a range of products to focus on a single product, then it is the least profitable that must be designated, therefore B. However, as part of the strategies, to keep both ranges or to abandon one, one must first determine the breakeven points and the results.

Let us calculate the performance indicators: sales, variable cost margins, margin rates, profitability thresholds, dates of occurrence, safety index and the expected results in the cases, where ALD manufactures:

– two products [A+B]; and

– either [A] or [B].

For example, breakeven point turnover = margin on variable cost.

If we produce the products [A + B] indexed x			
the **T/Ox** turnover would be:			= **€48,850**
the margin on variable cost **μx** would be:			= **€19,870**
the margin rate **Tx** would be:	€19,870 / €48,850		= **40.7%**
the break-even point **Sx** would be:	€48,850	$\dfrac{X\ €15,770}{€19,870}$	= **€38,770**
the **Dx** date at which it would be reached would be:	$\dfrac{€38,770\ \ X\ 360d.}{€48,850}$		**286 days**
	€48,850 − €38,770		= **€10,080**
the result **Rx** would be:	€19,870 − €15,770		= **€4,100**

If only product A is produced			
the **T/Oa** turnover would be:	€27,000	$\dfrac{X\ 600\ HM}{450\ HM}$	= **€36,000**
the margin on variable cost **μa** would be:	€14,650	$\dfrac{X\ 36,000\ €}{27,000\ €}$	= **€19,534**
the margin rate **Ta** would be:	€19,534 / €36,000		= **54.3%**
the break-even point **Sa** would be:	€36,000	$\dfrac{X\ €15,770}{€19,534}$	= **€29,064**
the **Da** date at which it would be reached would be:	$\dfrac{€29,064\ \ X\ 360d.}{€36,000}$		**291 days**
the safety margin **Ia** of:	€36,000 − €29,064		= **€6,936**
the result **Ra** would be:	€19,534 − €15,770		= **€3,764**

If only product B is produced			
T/Ob turnover would be:	€21,850	$\dfrac{X\ 600\ HM}{150\ HM}$	= **€87,400**
the margin on variable cost **μb** would be:	€5,220	$\dfrac{X\ 87,400\ €}{21,850\ €}$	= **€20,879**
the **Tb** margin rate would be:	€20,879 / €87,400		= **23.9%**
the break-even point **Sb** would be:	€87,400	$\dfrac{X€15,770}{€20,879}$	= **€66,014**
the date Db at which it would be reached would be:	$\dfrac{€66,014\ \ X\ 360d.}{€87,400}$		**272 days**
the margin of safety Ib of:	€87,400 − €66,014		= **€21,386**
the result Rb would be:	*€20,879 − €15,770*		= ***€5,109***

Therefore, in view of the result, if we have to abandon a product it would be A and not B.

Let us represent profitability thresholds, the dates of appearance and the expected results

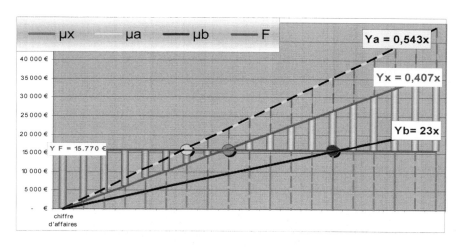

Figure 5.6. *Graphic representation of the breakeven point turnover. For a color version of this figure, see www.isteco.uk/levy/financial/zip*

RECOMMENDATION.– *Let us establish a table of multicriteria financial analysis by noting preferences 3 to mean the best and 1 to mean the worst.*

Strategic financial dashboard	Abandonment B	A and B	Abandonment A
Turnover	1	2	3
Margin	1	2	3
Profit margin	3	2	1
Breakeven point	3	2	1
Breakeven date	1	2	3
Safety margin	1	2	3
Result	1	2	3
Preference	11	14	17

– If it is the profitability that prevails, then it will be the criterion of the maximum result, and only option B will be retained: B = 5,109 €;

– if this is the risk, then the earliest date on which the breakeven point will be reached retains option A because it is obtained at the earliest point;

– etc.

Finally, the profitability–risk ratio is the most moderate because it keeps two ranges (between 11 and 17). This is especially the case when abandoning a product as we lose networks, suppliers, etc.

5.4. Operating leverage

A lever makes it possible to multiply an action.

If we consider in the models that the explanatory variables and the explained variables are connected, then the observed variation of an action explains the variation of the other. In fact, the structure of operating or financial costs is a bit more complex. Some are operational and some structural. An operational cost is variable according to the activity without this variation being automatically proportional.

A structural cost evolves, depending on the levels of the activity. It is relatively fixed over a period of time and for a given level of activity. One can therefore consider when studying a model that structural costs are fixed. There is then a significant impact of fixed costs on the profitability of the business, as there is a notable impact of financial expense on the profitability of the business. The first is called operating leverage, and the second is financial leverage.

While it may seem satisfying to determine the breakeven point, it is fundamental to ask whether the company has an interest in moving as far as possible from this threshold. Or more exactly, does a variation (Δ) of the activity lead to a Δ of profitability, and in what proportion?

The operating lever L_E measures the sensitivity of the current result Rc, compared to a Δ of the turnover. There will be a favorable L_E effect if profitability is multiplied upward and a disastrous leverage effect (mass effect) if the gearing is in the opposite direction.

With: turnover T/O, total cost TC, variable cost V, fixed cost F, variable cost margin M, current operating income (T/O − V − F) variable expense V/turnover, then:

Operating leverage $= LE = \dfrac{\Delta COI/COI}{\Delta TO/TO}$ and $COI = T/O - TC = TO - (V + F) = TO - V - F = M - F$.

Let for two periods 1 and 0 and a constant fixed cost, $BE1 = M1 - F$ and $BE0 = M0 - F$

$$= LE = \dfrac{(COI_1 - COI_0)/COI_0}{(TO_1 - TO_0)/TO_0} = \dfrac{(TO_1 - V_1 - F) - (TO_0 - V_0 - F)/TO_0 - V_0 - F}{(TO_1 - TO_0)/TO_0} = \dfrac{[(TO_1 - V_1) - (TO_0 - V_0)]TO_0}{(TO_0 - V_0 - F) - (TO_1 - TO_0)}$$

By dividing by (TO 1- TO 0), we obtain $\dfrac{\frac{TO_0[(TO_1-TO_0)-(V_1-V_0)]}{TO_1-TO_0}}{TO_0-V_0-F} = \dfrac{((TO_0(1-V)/\Delta TO)}{COI_0} =$

$\dfrac{((TO_0(\Delta V*TO_0)/\Delta TO)}{COI_0} = \dfrac{(TO_0-V_0)}{COI_0} = \dfrac{M_0}{COI_0} = \boxed{\dfrac{\text{Margin on variable cost}}{\text{operating profit 0}}}$

For example:

Data	Year 0	Year 1
T/O = 100%	800	1,000
V = 60% of T/O	480	600
→VCMR = 40% T/O	320	400
F = 25%	200	200
Re =	120	200

Year 0:

Le = VCMR/COI= 320/120 = 2.66

ANALYSIS.– This means that with the existing fixed cost structure, the adjusted earnings have increased by almost 2.7 times. There is a favorable operating leverage corresponding to maintaining the breakeven points:

$S0 = \dfrac{800 \times 200}{320} = 500$

$S1 = 1,000 \times 100/400 = 500 \times \dfrac{1,000 \times 100}{400}$

DIAGNOSIS.– This analysis is interesting for developing activities with high leverage, but with high potential. This lever comes from overabsorption of fixed costs. This productivity at the level of current operations allows for a high operating profitability.

PROGNOSIS.– If the fixed costs increase and are at an upper level, the leverage goes in the opposite direction with as much amplitude. Thus, potential profitability is linked to a potential risk of the same intensity.

RECOMMENDATION.– The search for profitability has led companies to minimize the variable and variable costs to the detriment of a significant increase in indirect fixed costs (IT, communication, etc.). This tends to prove that the choice between several investment projects is toward those who generate the least structural costs (fixed) and hence the need for offshoring for products to be imported in direct costs.

EXAMPLE.– The Star Top Business Unit manufactures components and its financing depends on its results. The unit wonders whether it should maintain production in-house or outsource it according to its breakeven point and margin of safety. The unit provides its current operating budget as shown below:

Sales figures	€3,400	
Total products	€3,400	
Purchase of materials		€360
Other variable charges		€340
Fixed staff costs		€646
Depreciation and amortization		€731
Other fixed charges		€153
Total expenses	€3,230	
Profit	€170	

ANALYSIS.– Let us calculate the breakeven point (B/E), safety margin (MS) and safety rate (TMS = MS/CA).

– *Breakeven point*

Turnover	€3,400
Purchase of materials	€1,360
Other variable expenses	€340
Margin on variable cost	**€1,700**

Turnover	€3,400
Total of fixed charges	€1,530
Margin on variable cost	€1,700
Breakeven point	**= €3,060**

Fixed staff costs	€646
Depreciation charge	€731
Other fixed charges	€153
Total of fixed charges	**€1,530**

– *Safety margin (SM)*

Turnover	€3,400
Breakeven point	€3,060
Safety margin SM	**= €340**

– *Security rate (SR = SM/TO)*

Security rate = 340/3,400 = 10.00%

DIAGNOSIS.– Let us look at the impact of a variation in activity of ± 20% by expressing the "R" result of Star Top based on "x" revenue.

As:

R = (Turnover TO) − (Cost price CB) = CA − (Variable expenses V) − (Fixed charges F) =

R = Margin on variable cost MOVC − F = (unit margin µ) × (Quantities sold) − F

µ = MSCV/CA = €1,700/€3,400 = 50%

F = €1,530

so, R = 0.50x − €1,530.

Growth		+20%	−20%
New turnover		€4,080	€2,720
New results R		€510	−€170
	Growth of R	**+200%**	**−200%**

PROGNOSIS.– If we are considering outsourcing production, it is important to check if the hypothetical results have changed, even in a small way.

– *The operating budget becomes*:

Turnover	
Total products	€3,400
Purchase of goods	
Other variable charges	
Fixed staff costs	
Depreciation charge	
Other fixed charges	€17
Total expenses	€3,230
Result	€170

– *Thus, its new margin on variable cost would be*:

Turnover	€3,400
Purchase of goods	€2,980
Other variable charges	€80
Margin on variable cost	€340

– *Its new breakeven point would be*:

Turnover	€3,400
Total of fixed charges	€170
Margin on variable cost	€340
Breakeven point	**€1,700**

– *Its new safety margin would be*:

Fixed staff costs	€119
Depreciation charge	€34
Other fixed charges	€17
Total of fixed charges	**€170**
Turnover	€3,400
Breakeven point	€1,700
Safety margin	**€1,700**

• *Security rate = 50.00%*

We see that, in the event of outsourcing of production, the threshold is lower, the safety margin increases and the security rate increases.

PROGNOSIS.– *Let us study the impact of the possible variations of activity ± 20% on the result "R" according to turnover "x".*

As:

R = TO − BOI = TO − V − F = VCMR − F = µ.q − F

µ = VCMR/TO = 340/3,400 = 10%

F = 170 €

Then, R = 0.10 x − €170.

Hypothesis of variation	+ 20%	−20%
New turnover	€4,080	€2,720
New results	€238	€102
Growth rate of R	**40%**	**−40%**

In the hypothetical situation of outsourcing, the risk of profitability is less strong in case of variation of the activity. The safety threshold is lower, so the safety margin is higher, and the 20% drop in activity would give a positive and non-negative result, as in the current situation, where there is too much clubbing effect because of the high fixed costs. At the level of performance is the flexibility that is no longer the same when you have too many fixed charges.

PROGNOSIS.– In order to set up risk indicators in the dashboards, is the operational lever LE = VCMR/R usable to predict the sensitivity of the result to the variation of the activity and express it simply as the reverse of the security rate (1/TS)? Let us calculate this indicator in the present case and in the hypothesis of subcontracting.

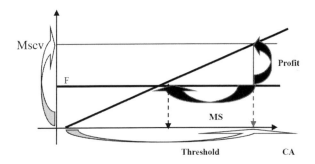

Figure 5.7. *Graphic representation of the security rate in the case of subcontracting*

According to the mathematical relationship of proportionality:

$$\frac{VCMR}{TO} = \frac{R/MS}{TO} \rightarrow \frac{SM}{B} = \frac{TO}{SM} \rightarrow L_E = \frac{1}{SM/TO} = \frac{1}{TSM}$$

T. indicator of B	Activities	
	Actual	hypothetical
Lever L_E	10	2
1/TSM	10	2

PROGNOSIS.– Let us show that these indicators also express the sensitivity of the result in relation to the growth of the activity, ($\Delta R/R$) compared to ($\Delta TO/TO$), and let us make the computation in the two hypotheses of preserving or externalizing:

As $R = VCMR - F = \mu.x - F$, then $\Delta R = \mu . \Delta Ca - 0$

The growth of the result compared to the growth of TO = Elasticity E= ($\Delta R/R$)/($\Delta TO/TO$) = Lever L_E

T. indicators of B.	Activities	
	Actual	Hypothetical
Actual TO	€3,400	€3,400
Result	€170	€170
ΔTO	€680	€680
ΔR	€340	€68
$\Delta R/R$	2	0.4
$\Delta TO/TO$	20%	20%
Elasticity (E)	**10**	**2**

This shows that the lever LE is much lower in the event of an outsourcing because it has a direct and variable influence on the maximum of fixed costs on which the lever was based.

PROGNOSIS.– Let us express for T, from B, the variation of the result ΔR and the result in case of externalization as a function of E, R and the growth of the turnover ΔTO.

$$\text{Elasticity } E = \frac{\Delta R/R}{\Delta CA/CA} => \frac{\Delta R}{R} = \frac{E \Delta CA}{CA} => \Delta R = = \frac{E*R*\Delta CA}{CA}$$

As the result according to the proposed new hypothesis $R_{expected} = R_P$ = (Actual result R) + ΔR.

then, $R_{expected} = R + \Delta R = R + (E \times R \times \Delta TO)/TO$.

Therefore, the expected result RP would be indicated by the relation of type: $Rp = R [1 + (E \times R \times \Delta TO)/TO]$.

PROGNOSIS.– Let us test this indicator of "expected result Rp", in the case of the current situation of production, and for the hypothesis that you suggest, and this for a greater variation of the activity of the order of −30%

T. indicators of B.	Activities	
	Actual	Hypothetical
R	€170	€170
Constant	1	1
Δ	10	2
ΔTO/TO	−30%	−30%
Rp	−€340	€68

The current result has greater volatility compared to the growth of the activity. The three indicators put in place in the management dashboard finally express the same phenomenon: the current operating risk. The TMS margin rate is a technical, operating leverage, which, linked to the financial leverage, will give the overall leverage of the company and E the economic elasticity and can be reduced or confronted in the indicators of different dashboards.

PROGNOSIS.– In the event of a likely strong increase in activity, will the breakeven point be achieved under the same conditions in both cases (current and outsourced)?

Months	T/O = x	
1	€2,800 k	
2	€2,850 k	
3	€2,650 k	
4	€2,850 k	
5	€3,100 k	
6	€3,500 k	
7	€4,300 k	
8	€2,650 k	
9	€2,950 k	
10	€3,200 k	
11	€2,750 k	
12	€2,400 k	
	€3,000 k	Average = $E(x)$
	€500 k	standard deviation = $\sigma(x)$

$$P\{x>\text{Threshold}\} = P\{\frac{[S-E(x)]}{\sigma(x)}\}.$$

REMINDER:–

TO − COI= R = VCMR − F = μ.x − F => E{R} = μ [E{qx} − F]
and Δ{R} = μ [Δ{x}]

		Product	Outsourcing
	Threshold = T	€3 k=	€2 k
	E(S)	€3,000	€3,000 k
	Δ(S)	€500 k	€500 k
	$\frac{[S - E(x)]}{\sigma(x)}$	−6.00	−6.00
	P{t>	−6.00	−6.00
	= 1 − P {<	−6.00	−6.00
Reading table or excel function		45.22%	99.53%
Probability of reaching this threshold		low	with certainty…

RECOMMENDATION.– What strategic recommendations can be proposed between keeping production and outsourcing it?

In case of strong changes in business conditions, the company seems to be interested in being flexible. However, during recession, it would be handicapped by high fixed costs that increase the risk of profitability and compromises its funding. However, in case of expansion, it obtains a leverage multiplier by the rigidity of its fixed costs. Therefore, everything depends on whether the company expects an expansion in the long term and it is then the profitability that prevails and the maintenance of an internal production or if it is recession that is looming and it is then the risk that must be minimized by outsourcing.

5.5. Return on equity

Profitability is calculated by correlating the annual net profit of the income statement and balance sheet to shareholders' equity.

This ratio is called return on equity. If the calculation gives a rate of 15%, it means that for €100 k of equity, the result amounts to €15 k.

ROE will be low in industrial activities such as large-scale industry, steel, nuclear or passenger and goods transport that require significant structural investment. Return on equity will be weak but recurrent.

ROE will be high for service sectors, digital engineering, etc. that require low investment, but which have an expectation of profitability from strong and quick investors called short term.

Longitudinally, the ROE makes it possible to follow its evolution over several years (if there has been no change in equity) or to compare several companies in the same sector. But what conclusions can be drawn? Not many if you do not deploy the elements that compose it.

Indeed, profitability combines three fundamentals of financial management: profitability × resource management × leverage.

$$ROE = \frac{net\ profit}{Equity} = \frac{Operating\ income}{Turnover\ HT} \times \frac{Turnover\ HT}{Active} \times \frac{net\ profit}{Operating\ income} \times \frac{Passive}{Equity}$$

$$ROE = \frac{Bn}{CP} = \frac{Ro}{TOHT} \times \frac{CAHT}{Active} \times \frac{Bn}{Ro} \times \frac{Passive}{CP}$$

$$ROE = \frac{Bn}{CP} = (Operating\ Margin \times Rotation\ of\ Economic\ Assets) \times (Cost\ of\ debt \times Levier)$$

$$ROE = \frac{Bn}{CP} = Economic\ profitability \times Effect\ of\ levier$$

5.5.1. *Economic profitability*

Economic profitability is the ratio of operating profit or current net of tax to economic assets.

"It consists of the product of operating or operating margin and the rate of turnover of the economic asset. This rate is not affected by the financial structure of the company. It is important for the financial diagnosis as it measures the profitability of the company".

Economic assets are calculated using fixed assets and cash flow requirements. This is also referred to as "invested capital".

5.5.2. *Leverage*

Leverage is one of economic profitability. If the internal rate of return on capital employed is higher than the debt ratios, then the increase in debt increases the return on equity by the favorable rate differential. However, in return, the debt increases the risk.

It consists of the cost of debt × leverage.

5.5.3. *Financial Leverage*

For operating leverage, one wonders to what extent one has an interest in exceeding the breakeven point and that an effort to increase the activity generates more proportional profitability. In the financial leverage effect (LF), we want to know whether a company has a financial interest in getting heavily into debt and under what conditions.

Of course, it is in any case compelled to find sources of financing outside its shareholders, but given the multiple sources of financing, under certain conditions, it may be overburdened to automatically improve the return on equity ROE, provided that the shareholders have an interest in letting the company go into debt to improve their profitability rather than providing capital but not without risk. Indeed, the multiplier of profitability can be reversed heavily (mass effect).

Financial leverage measures the sensitivity of earnings per share (equity) to a change in operating income.

LF = Variation of BPA/Variation of BE = ΔBPA/ΔBE.

Formulation

With:

OI = Operating income before financial expenses (F) and before tax (I)

CP = Current profit = OI net of financial charges but before tax = OI − F

P = Net profit = net of financial expenses and net of tax = OI − I

P = Shareholders' equity

D = Debt

K = Equity capital = P + D

i = Interest rate that calculates the financial expenses F

s = Corporate tax rate

F = D x i

Then:

e = Operating profitability = K × e

f = Financial profitability = B/P

and:

BC = BE − F = e × K − iD = e(P+D) − iD = e. P + e. D − i.D = e. P + D (e − i).

Then:

BC/P =   e. P/P − (D/P) (e − i) = e+ (e − i) D/P

Therefore:

e = Operating profitability = K × e

f = Financial profitability = B/P

and:

BC = BE − F = e × K − iD = e(P+D) − iD = e. P + e. D − i.D = e. P + D (e − i).

Therefore:

BC/P =   e. P/P − (D/P) (e − i) = e+ (e − i) D/P

With: Bnet = BC − I = BC (1 − s)

With: Bnet = BC − I = BC (1 − s)

B/P = [e + (e − i) E/P] − I =

B/P = $\dfrac{e+[(e-i)}{P[1-s]}$ = (e − i)/P

Financial profitability = Rf = B/P = [1 − s] [e + [(e − i) E/P]

Thus, the overall financial profitability of return on equity improves:

− if [1 − s] increases. For the first member to increase, it suffices that s, the rate of corporate tax, decreases. However, it went from 33.33% to 33%. This has the effect of improving the financial profitability of the beneficiary companies.

− if [e + (e − i) E] increases, so that the second member increases, e > (e − i) E/P.

So, (e − i) > 0 and the largest possible.

Then, the operating profitability "e" is higher than the cost of the debt "i", and the financial profitability of the equity "P" improves by leverage of financing "E".

EXAMPLE.− There are two companies, S1 and S2. The first has only own funds and the second uses indebtedness at the average rate of 10%.

	S1	S2
P = Own funds E = Endebtedness	1,000	500 + 500
K = Committed capital	1,000	1,000
BE = Operating profit	120	120
F = Financial burden at 10 %		50
Bc = Current profit	120	70
I = Income tax # 33 %	40	23,3
B = Net profit	80	46,7
Rf = Financial profitability B/P	8 %	9.34 %
e = Operating profitability BE/P	12 %	24 %

ANALYSIS.− Thus, S2 has better financial profitability, because it has allocated its financing in equity and abroad, and enjoys a favorable leverage effect.

If the companies show loss-making results, then the leverage effect works in the opposite direction and we obtain a club effect.

DIAGNOSIS.– Suppose the debt ratio goes to 15%, we would have S1 identical if it is not indebted and S2 becomes:

	S2
P	500
D	500
K	1,000
BE	120
F to 15%	75
BC	45
I #33%	15
B	30
Rf = B/P	3 %
e = BE/P	24 %

It can be seen that the operating rate of return is not modified but that the financial return on equity is only 3%, which is lower than that of S1 = 8%, while operating profitability remains at 24%.

PROGNOSIS.– One could conclude that the debt of a company can increase the overall profitability of capital or contain the decline in profitability. This conclusion is a bit hasty if we take into account the risk of debt-related interest rates, the company's ability to cover the debt burden and the requirements of shareholders who want a profitability that is all the higher as the overall risk of the company increases.

On this last point, we can say that the increase of the overall risk of the company is compensated by the improvement of the automatic profitability of its own funds.

RECOMMENDATION.– If a company borrows 50 to buy back its shares at the lowest price, then it eliminates them once the price has risen, reduces the denominator and thus mathematically increases the ROE. All companies that repurchase shares to increase their share price see the return on equity increase.

With uncontrollable stock markets, companies carry out these operations, especially at the time of the timely management of stock options.

6

Analysis by Ratios: IFRS

Diagnosis must be enriched by the determination of the relative values allowing us to locate the company in space and time.

6.1. Composition and evolution ratios

Ratio analysis links the restated balance sheet and income statement data for financial analysis, in order to derive relevant data for diagnosis and recommendations. Neither the French chart of accounts nor the IFRS have proposed it, and the analysts have linked characteristic data and indicated their meaning.

– A ratio is not a division in the mathematical sense, because:

- When we divide any given data by any other, we obtain a result from which we can only extract huge amounts of information. One must have an idea of what the ratio should mean, if we just give the figures found (the profitability ratio increased from 23.65% to 32.42%, so it increased by (32.42 − 23.65)/23.65, etc.) it is irrelevant, if no relevant diagnosis is made, no prognosis is drawn and no recommendation is proposed.

- For a ratio to increase:

Numerator	Denominator
Increases	Increases less than the numerator
Increases	Remains the same
Increases	Decreases
Remains the same	Decreases
Decreases	Decreases more than the numerator

There can be five reasons for a ratio to increase, with five different comments for the same result found. Therefore, a simple observation of the rate of growth or de-growth of a ratio offers no interest.

EXAMPLE.– If the ratio $\frac{\text{Wages}}{\text{Added Value}}$ increases, it may mean that:

- value added has decreased ☹ and staff costs have further decreased ☺;

- value added has increased ☺ and staff costs have further increased ☹;

- added value has increased ☺ and staff cost has remained constant ☺;

- but in terms of dynamics compared to other years, this ratio is on a favorable line ☺ or an unfavorable one ☹; and

- in static relation to the sector, this ratio is normally ☺.

– A ratio is not elucidated when it is reduced to a percentage.

Indeed, it does not state whether it is better to invest 100 to get 25 (25%) or to invest 20 to have only 5 (25%).

To reduce everything to a percentage is dangerous because obtaining a rate of return of 25% does not express that the company is undercapitalized, that it profits momentarily from a leverage effect, etc.

An increase of 30% (of a position that represents 10% of the total) is lower than a 20% increase (of a position that represents more than 15% of the total).

A percentage is the number of shares of a 100th of the total, but it does not give any indication of the size of this total.

– Before calculating a ratio, you must have an idea of the expected result.

It is useless to calculate a ratio, if no comment can improve the diagnosis significantly. If the analysis is not finalized, that is to say, what is sought is not clearly indicated at each step with the ratios that we want to implement to support the diagnosis, we will fail in our mission. This is why it is preferable at first to build a simple framework of analysis and to develop it as soon as anomalies arise.

– A static analysis, that is to say, from the documents of a year is probative.

We do not necessarily need the 5-year figures. In many cases, situations evolve over time to adapt to changes in markets, activities and technologies. We must judge the present, consider corrective actions in the short term and then propose a possible strategic change. An analysis of the past is always useful, but we do not need this history to give a detailed opinion. While the industry is an acceptable standard for judging company ratios, abnormal behavior is also detected outside the sectoral context.

– A dynamic, i.e. retrospective, analysis is essential as you learn from the company's past.

One needs a traceability of one's data and information; one's mistakes and one's successes. However, the analysis of the past does not replace that of the future and the internal contexts and external environments that have evolved.

– There are no good and bad ratios.

We have to get used to some ratios for which we have a particular sensitivity. If a problem of financing, profitability, efficiency, cash flow, etc. exists, then it must appear immediately and be confirmed following several calculations expressed in a homogeneous and consistent analysis.

The problem is that, strictly speaking, there is no standard in this area, but instead tendencies that are commonly accepted. The comparison of the quantities entered in the social accounts is necessarily done in a combinatorics of positions or homogeneous families of posts, between balance sheet levels and flows in the profit and loss account.

6.1.1. *Flow/Level*

To start a financial investigation using ratios, let us recall that:

– A flow variation[1] is a flow. For example, allocating rental lease flow to amortization and financial expense will increase the amortization flow and the financial charge flow in the income statement.

– A level variation is a flow. For example, the level of the initial stock (Balance at the end of the previous year N – 1 = Stock at the beginning of the year N) has varied up to the level of the final stock of the balance sheet. This variation is a flow recorded in the "inventory change" account or in the "stored production" account of the income statement.

– A difference in flow remains a flow. For example, in the profit and loss account, the flow of merchandise sales minus the flow of purchase cost of goods sold is a cash flow in the intermediate management balances: "commercial margin". In this way, all intermediate management balances are flows born from differences in homogeneous sets of flows.

---

1 The flows are all recorded in the income statement, except for the net profit and loss, which is also entered in the balance sheet liabilities.

– A difference in level remains a level. For example, the level of gross fixed assets less depreciation is a level of net fixed assets. Or again, the level of financing minus the level of non-current investments determines the level of the working capital fund, or finally the level of the working capital fund less the level of the working capital requirement gives the level of the cash flow, and not the cash flow. Cash flow will only be discussed in the context of funding.

The ratios result mainly from a combination of the following four sets from the summary accounting documents:

– two categories of levels, active and passive; and

– two categories of flows, charges and products.

These two-by-two sets give four possible combinations of levels and flows.

6.1.2. *Level/Level*

$$\text{Structure Ratio} = \frac{\text{L Level}}{\text{L Level}}$$

The networking is done around the three major functions or operations, namely funding, current investment and distribution (proud). Three groups of ratios are then determined. For example, there are those that report exclusively on:

– liabilities between them;

– assets between them; and

– combine these two major parts of the balance sheet.

6.1.2.1. *Financing structure*

$$\frac{L}{L} = \frac{\text{Own Funds}}{\text{Total liabilities}} = \text{Financial autonomy}$$

ANALYSIS.– There is no optimal debt standard and we cannot know whether the rate found is favorable or not. Its weakness can be noted if it is approximately 10% and prolong the investigation.

$$\frac{L}{L} = \frac{\text{Equity}}{\text{Non-current liabilities}} = \text{Term debt capacity}$$

ANALYSIS.– If there is no debt standard, then we can say that the company should not have a debt greater than its retired capital, otherwise the lenders will make it pay dearly the risk of non-repayment that it presents by too little guarantee. As long as own funds are greater than half of the non-current resources, the company still has a debt capacity with no risk premium.

$$\frac{L}{L} = \frac{\text{Reserves}}{\text{Own Funds}} = \text{Propensity to self-financing}$$

ANALYSIS.– This ratio expresses the level of precautionary reserves. Thanks to them, the company will be able, for example, to keep a dividend policy even if its results are sometimes lacking. It corroborates the principle of prudence.

$$\frac{L}{L} = \frac{\text{External debts}}{\text{Total Liabilities}} = \text{Level of risk related to lenders}$$

ANALYSIS.– This is a structural fragility ratio. It expresses the vulnerability of the company compared to other financiers who could quickly require a strategic change, a short-term vision of profits, in order to return to their fund even at the risk of the survival of the company.

$$\frac{L}{L} = \frac{\text{Operating Debts}}{\text{Current liabilities}} = \text{Level of current operating financing}$$

6.1.2.2. Structure of the investment

$$\frac{L}{L} = \frac{\text{Fixed or non-current assets}}{\text{Total Assets}} = \text{Level of growth investments}$$

ANALYSIS.– Taken in their entirety, the tangible, intangible and financial investments reported in the balance sheet show the growth rate (internal and external) that must be compared over several years and in relation to the sector, industry, country, etc.

This helps to determine the capital intensity of the company and its relationship between capital invested and work.

$$\frac{L}{L} = \frac{\text{Depreciation Amount}}{\text{Gross depreciable fixed assets}} = \text{Level of obsolescence of operating capital}$$

ANALYSIS.– If capital assets are recent, then the lower this ratio is, the higher the capacity for self-financing in the future. One must be aware that the recent provisions on depreciations of depreciable property modify the conclusions that one might be used to making[2].

---

2 See depreciation rules.

If this ratio increases, it may mean that the company is outsourcing.

$$\frac{L}{L} = \frac{\text{Amount of stocks}}{\text{Current Assets}} = \text{Level of a need for financing from current operations}$$

This is an important element of commercial stock.

ANALYSIS.– If this ratio is high, then it may indicate a slump that other ratios will confirm. However, if it is about raw materials, then one can be in the presence of speculative stocks favorable for financial management (raw materials, kerosene, etc.).

$$\frac{L}{L} = \frac{\text{Amount of operating receivables}}{\text{Current assets}} = \text{Level of a financing requirement arising from current operations}$$

This is an important element of commercial stock.

6.1.2.3. *Financing of current operations*

$$\frac{L}{L} = \frac{\text{Amount of current operating suppliers}}{\text{Amount of current operating receivables}} = \text{Level of needs or resources due to commercial outstanding}$$

Outstanding business is the result of the company's ability to delay supplier settlements (short-term debts) and shorten customer payments (short-term assets to finance).

ANALYSIS.– This ratio is an indicator of the financial tensions in terms of working capital requirements and dependence on economic and commercial partners.

(N)/N = (Current assets)/(Passive to CT or current) = General cash level

$$\frac{L}{L} = \frac{\text{Current Assets}}{\text{Short term or current liabilities}} = \text{General cash level}$$

It is arithmetically equivalent to the working capital ratio, but is analyzed differently.

ANALYSIS.– As the components are not similar, the diagnosis will not cover the same elements, nor will the analysis.

$$\frac{L}{L} = \frac{\text{Non-current liabilities and sinking funds}}{\text{Gross investment + WCR}} = \text{Cash equilibrium level}$$

ANALYSIS.– If this equilibrium ratio is <100%, then we can think that cash is structurally negative.

$$\frac{L}{L} = \frac{\text{Receivables and related accounts + available}}{\text{Short term or current liabilities}} = \text{Level of working capital requirement}$$

ANALYSIS.– This ratio is generally <1 because the operating debts must finance the credentials but also the stocks.

6.1.2.4. *Financing the investment*

$$\frac{L}{L} = \frac{\text{Amount of non-current liabilities}}{\text{Non-current assets}} = \text{Working capital level (overall net)}$$

ANALYSIS.– The higher the ratio, the more structurally comfortable the company is. However, this can reveal either an over-indebtedness, or a lack of investment, or that one is in the presence of a distribution company (WCR <0), or that it is a subsidiary without risk because the capital is guaranteed by a powerful parent company.

$$\frac{L}{L} = \frac{\text{Amount of own funds}}{\text{Non-current assets}} = \text{Level of own financing of internal and external growth}$$

ANALYSIS.– It is a ratio that indicates the absence of risk due to the requirements of external financers. Only shareholders have a say here.

$$\frac{L}{L} = \frac{\text{Amount of stocks}}{\text{PAR Amount}} = \text{Level of stocks not financed by current exploitation}$$

6.1.3. *Levels/Flows*

$$\frac{\text{Level}}{\text{Flow}} = \text{Delay ratios } \frac{L}{F}$$

Let us recall that a level = flow × delay.

Indeed, to reach a certain level, it depends on the flow (output) and flow time. Applied to current operations, this set of ratios specifies the average duration of specific settlements of the elements of the current operating cycle.

These reports mainly apply to the operating cycle and especially to the elements of the operating cash requirements OCR.

We note that only items of receivables and debts correspond to the amounts owed by customers[3] and suppliers on invoices; therefore, the amounts are inclusive of VAT (TTC)[4].

$$\frac{L}{F} = \frac{\text{Amount of current operating receivables}}{\text{Amount of daily revenue flow TTC}} = \text{Average time to receipt of operating receivables}$$

ANALYSIS.– The shorter the time, the lower the need for funds.

$$\frac{L}{F} = \frac{\text{Amount of current operating debts}}{\text{Daily purchase flow amount TTC}} = \text{Average settlement time of operating supplier debts}$$

ANALYSIS.– The longer this period takes, the lower the working capital requirement and the working capital fund.

$$\frac{L}{F} = \frac{\text{Amount of material and merchandise stocks}}{\text{Amount of daily purchases stream DF}} = \text{Average period of financing of the operating stocks}$$

ANALYSIS.– The shorter this period, the lower the need for working capital. All the optimal management of stocks as well as the methods and models for calculating the need for fair financing (kanban, tense flow, Wilson, etc.) can be explained by the desire to minimize as much as possible the cost of financing the stocks.

(N)/F = (Amount of stocks of finished products and work in process)/ (Daily sales flow amount TTC) = Average period of financing of product stocks

$$\frac{L}{F} = \frac{\text{Amount of stocks of finished products and work in progress}}{\text{Daily sales flow amount TTC}} = \text{Average period of financing of product stocks}$$

The fact of producing on an almost "make to order" basis, thus in drawn and undepressed flows, with shortened production times, is an explanation of the search for a decrease in stocks of finished products for sale.

These ratios are used to determine the working capital requirement in days of turnover excluding taxes.

---

[3] Dso (days sales outstanding) is the average payment time of the customers, expressed in days of turnover TTC.
[4] The time of payment providers in number of days. Dpo = item suppliers ttc × 360/Purchases TTC of the period. We must isolate the providers of capital and overhead.

ANALYSIS.– It should be understood that the times that have been calculated are average times expressed in days but are heterogeneous. Indeed, we have sales days including VAT, purchases without taxes and purchases including VAT. They cannot be added up by deriving a net average duration to finance without reducing them to the same denominator: days of turnover excluding tax.

6.1.4. *Flux/Flux*

(F)/F = Performance ratios: competitiveness, efficiency, productivity, profitability but no profitability ((F) /

$\frac{F}{F}$ = Performance ratios: competitiveness, efficacy, productivity, profitability but no efficiency ($\frac{F}{L}$)

$$\frac{F}{F} = \frac{{}_0^T \text{Variation of TO} = \Delta \text{TO} = (\text{TO}_1 - \text{TO}_0)}{\text{TO}_0} = \text{Competitiveness}$$

This ratio should be studied in terms of value (in common currency) and volume (constant currency) and on a market products grid or by strategic activity area.

$$\frac{F}{F} = \frac{\text{Variation in value added VA} = \Delta \text{VA} = (\text{VA}_1 - \text{VA}_0)}{\text{VA}_0} = \text{Apparent growth (in value)}$$

ANALYSIS.– Growth is only apparent because, as we shall see, it is sufficient to take into account components that cannot be controlled by the firm (exchange rate, inflation, price drift, etc.) but which affect the calculation of value added and changes the growth rate.

$$\frac{F}{F} = \frac{\text{Staff Wages}}{\text{VA}} = \text{Apparent productivity (in value) of the work}$$

ANALYSIS.– It must not be forgotten that while human capital is an essential part of the added value, it is essentially the source of its creation. Monitoring this productivity rate makes it possible to control any disproportion of the remuneration of capital in relation to work.

$$\frac{F}{F} = \frac{\text{Financial Burden}}{\text{EBITDA}} = \text{Cost of debt charge}$$

ANALYSIS.– This solvency risk indicator is one of the key ratios of the Banque de France Z score function. A high ratio accounts for up to 40% of a company's risk of financial failure.

$\dfrac{F}{F} = \dfrac{\text{Current profit before tax on profit}}{\text{TO}} = $ Profitability of current operations

With this tendency to make the company always more profitable, the current operations are asked to absorb the expenses of activity including the recurring financial charges.

DIAGNOSIS.– This ratio supersedes the current operating margin ratios.

6.1.5. *Flow/Level*

$\dfrac{F}{L} = \dfrac{\text{Flow}}{\text{Level}}$ / Profitability level in the broad sense

This type of ratio expresses a coefficient that can be interpreted in several ways:

– this can be a rotation coefficient. Indeed, this ratio is the inverse of the deadline ($\dfrac{L}{F}$). As a deadline is the time that a flow takes to reach a level, $\dfrac{F}{N} = \dfrac{1}{\text{delay}}$ is a rotation, as seen in the development of return on equity financial return ratios;

– It can also be a weighting, which explains part of the profitability.

$\dfrac{F}{L} = \dfrac{\text{Cost of purchase of goods and materials}}{\text{Average Stock Level}}$ Coefficient of rotation of average stock purchased

ANALYSIS.– In this type of ratio, the larger the N (denominator), the lower the ratio. The lower the average stock, the more it should be profitable for the company that does not immobilize the financing of its stocks for a long time, provided that there is no correlative decline in activity that would explain it.

$\dfrac{F}{L} = \dfrac{\text{Change in stocks } (\Delta S)}{\text{Average Stock Level}}$ Coefficient of rotation of average stocks

Or

$\dfrac{F}{L} = \dfrac{\text{Stored Production}}{\text{Average Stock Level of products}}$ Coefficient of turnover of stocks of finished products and stocks

ANALYSIS.– These ratios are symptomatic of a slowdown or acceleration of activity. Overstocking is either beneficial in the case of preparing a large order or in the case of speculative stock (materials), or bad in a downturn of activity.

$\dfrac{F}{L} = \dfrac{\text{Depreciation and amortization}}{\text{Level of operating investments}}$ Autonomous financing of organic growth

ANALYSIS.– The higher the rate of consumption of productive capital, the better the financing of internal growth. However, as a ratio does not anticipate the importance of the quantities it yields, the new way of taking into account the depreciation and the value of the depreciable property presents a risk of bias in the analysis, which is diluted.

$$\frac{F}{L} \frac{\text{Financial burden}}{\text{Loan Level}} \text{ Cost of borrowed capital}$$

DIAGNOSIS.– This is an important indicator for determining the share of the cost of external liabilities in the average cost of capital invested.

$$\frac{F}{L} \frac{\text{Dividends paid}}{\text{Level of Equity}} \text{ Cost of equity}$$

ANALYSIS.– The higher the ratio, the more costs the company incurs, but the more likely it is to find investors because it is also the precise calculation of the financial return on capital (ROE).

$$\frac{F}{L} = \frac{\text{Net Profit}}{\text{Equity}} \text{ Return on equity}$$

However, given the multiplicity of performance indicators that emanate from the income statement (management balances of the GAP or retired Banque de France, IFRS) and the different ways of calculating the capital invested in the company, this ratio can be declined in many ways.

6.1.6. *Combination*

The example of return on equity is significant.

Process of financial investigation.

ANALYSIS.– This concerns the annual or perennial calculation of the return on equity.

The ratios fall into several distinct categories and they must combine favorably for the company to perform well. Two attitudes are then possible: either we try to combine a maximum of data or we try to reconstruct the company's footprint; this is what the Banque de France does by sophisticated analysis; or we try by using a small number of indicators to develop a "flash" analysis model to diagnose the most important thing.

The ratio diagnosis can range from the most rudimentary to the most sophisticated. For illustration, we will present a "flash evaluation" from several ratios. Then, in contrast, we will present the analysis of the observatories of companies, which are central banks. That of the Banque de France by its methodology allows inter-company and sectoral comparisons in both France and abroad.

DIAGNOSIS.–

This shows the origin or composition of the ROE:

$$\text{Return on Equity} = \frac{F \text{ Net Profit}}{L \text{ Equity}} = \frac{F \text{ Net Profit}}{F \text{ Revenue}} \times \frac{F \text{ Revenue}}{L \text{ Assets}} \times \frac{F \text{ Net Result}}{F \text{ Current result}} \times \frac{L \text{ Liabilities}}{L \text{ Equity}}$$

$$R1 \quad \times \quad R2 \quad \times \quad R3 \quad \times \quad R4$$

Return on Equity = Profitability × Asset Income × Financial Cost × Leverage

Profitability increases by as much + as … and the margin is relatively high, then… …the company has a propensity to transform into business flow, the external financing it has… …and this phenomenon is amplified by the relative level of external resources in its own financing (leverage)…

DIAGNOSIS.– Combined with other ratios (e.g. BdF), it is possible to position oneself because this profitability is good.

RECOMMENDATION.– Given the age of the company, its sector, strengths and weaknesses as well as opportunities, threats etc., it should advocate a strategic plan over 4 years.

6.2. Database

The Central Balance Sheet CBS Office is a database. The information managed by the BdF is "a database of companies monitored individually over time".

Since 1994, the CBS has been based on the nomenclature of French activity NFA of the Insee, which codifies the activity of various companies according to their main Activity code exercised APE. The objective set for the Banque de France sample aims to:

– obtain all firms with more than 500 employees;

– achieve a sector coverage rate of approximately 50% for industrial companies with 20–500 employees, or a slightly lower rate if the number of companies is large enough; and

– collect information from companies with fewer than 20 employees to reach a coverage rate of approximately 10%.

The financial analysis that is presented is based on an architecture, where the financial analysis file describes the essential elements on which to base the strategic choices resulting from the management of a business:

– realized performances: evolution of activity, margins, profitability, etc.;

– cash flows generated by the business and those related to investment and financing decisions; and

– financial structure, which results from both performance and decisions taken.

These elements can be found in the following four parts of the file:

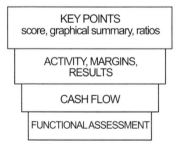

They offer a rough outline of financial diagnosis.

> **KEY POINTS**
> score, graphical summary, ratios

– The score function is a linear combination of ratios sensitive to the difficulties of the company. It results from a discriminating analysis between failing companies that have been subject to legal proceedings and non-defaulting companies. The score measures the company's exposure to the risk of default. The higher the score, the better the company's situation. The lower the score, the more risky the business situation.

– The graphical summary provides a quick visualization of the last 4 years of growth (turnover, value added, gross operating income, profit for the year), economic and financial profitability, distribution revenues between the various players (staff, lenders, State, associates, company), cash flows, financial balances (overall net working capital, working capital requirements, net cash), the evolution of indebtedness and financial expenses.

– The ratios put the company in perspective within its sector of activity. The ratios published in the file allow for an analysis of the operating structure, growth, yields, profitability, autonomy and financial structures.

> **ACTIVITY, MARGINS, RESULTS**

The income statement is in the form of interim management balances from the activity to the profits of the enterprise.

Activity is the primary source of income; over several years, its evolution reflects its commercial efficiency.

Margins and results measure the ability of the enterprise to generate income to remunerate the resources used, i.e. staff and borrowed capital, ensure the payment of taxes and cover the depreciation of assets as well as various risks.

6.2.1. *Activity ratios, profitability, balance, investment, debt, profitability of the Banque de France*

Numerous analyses have shown that there are warning signs of default, at least 3 years beforehand, and in this case, we must advocate an imperative recovery strategy.

The financial analysis from the Banque de France database is typical of a comparative analysis. It should not be used systematically for an internal analysis of a company without a possible comparison. This is why it is located between the French Accounting Plan functional analysis and the IFRS functional analysis for purposes of international comparison.

6.2.1.1. *High Risk of failure*

A small company may have the characteristic of being:

– Young: this is not, strictly speaking, a *start-up* because it is located in a niche already exploited and is without "force" against the threats of competition:

- a *start-up* is risky because it is located in an innovative niche (information and communication technologies, biotechnologies, bioethics, etc.)

- the young company has a high risk of failure because it bases the growth of its activity on few customers (20% of customers represent 80–90% of turnover) and few suppliers. It has not yet developed its business portfolio.

– Governed by few people who, contrary to *start-up*s, do not totally adhere to modern methods of management (digital company, network, etc.). A study has shown that successful start-ups in the United States were created and run by a very small team with solid financial (family or network) assets.

6.2.1.2. *Low risk of failure*

Successful companies are developing globally and do not base their future performance solely on the technical development of their productions but invest in research, innovation and so on. In fact, instead of hoping to draw illusory performances from their products, because sometimes the decline in the product life of the products is shortened, they incorporate a strategic reflection; monitor market-product grids; develop a communication and image policy; find alliances, partnerships and favorable outsourcing and so on. However, the fundamental balances of the balance sheet structures and the dynamics of the management remain references of risk.

The Banque de France in its "individual business analysis file" uses approximately 30 ratios. It determines the significant progress and informs the average ratio of the sector. It is thus a static and dynamic analysis as it integrates 4 years. The ratios do not only take the data from the balance sheet and the profit and loss account, but also consider data from the Appendix (R1).

6.2.1.3. *Current operating structure*

The Banque de France database presents an analysis of ratios grouped in a homogeneous way, and the aggregates presented are used at national and international levels. Nine ratios, R1 to R9, make it possible to probe the structure of the operation.

$- R1 \ \dfrac{\text{(Exploitation of operations (excluding land and buildings))}}{\text{Workforce}}$ = equipment rate of the work tool per employee

Operating fixed assets are calculated as follows:

Functional assessment	Gross			
	N − 3	N − 2	N − 1	N
Intangible assets excluding establishment expenses				
+ Tangible fixed assets				
+ Fixed assets in lease management				
= **OPERATING ASSETS** A				

ANALYSIS.– Operating assets are highly fluctuating according to the branch, the sector (primary, secondary, tertiary) or the methods of exploitation (done or to be done).

R1, nevertheless, gives the capital intensity of the enterprise and its degree of substitution of the capital and labor factor. The trend is the digital business and this ratio suffers.

$- R2 \ \dfrac{F \ \text{Export turnover}}{F \ \text{Total turnover}}$ = Export variation

ANALYSIS.– R2 gives the measure of the company's ability to be recognized outside its borders and to be competitive. With globalization, this ratio tends to increase very rapidly. It is an index of the level of intangible capital if the mark is recognized outside the borders.

$- R3 \ \dfrac{\text{Value added (CoB BdF)}}{\text{Total Production+operating grants received}}$ = Value added ratio

REMINDER.–

Central Balance Sheet B. of F
Merchandise sales – Purchase price of merchandise sold
= **Commercial Margin**
+ Sold production + stored production + Fixed production
= **Production of the exercise**
– Outsourcing of manufacturing
= **Own Production**
– Cost of material consumed
= **Industrial margin**
+ Commercial margin
+ Industrial margin
= **Gross Operating Margin**
- Purchases and external expenses (excluding outsourcing of manufacturing, rent, external staff)
+ Operating subsidy received (if = additional price)
= **Added Value B of F**

ANALYSIS.– R3 shows that there is no strong link between the company's performance and R3.

If R3 is low, it may show poor performance but may also mean that its management methods are specific (outsourcing, very commercial activity, etc.).

Thus, R3 can vary with equal production. It can also be influenced by exogenous data such as prices of goods and services.

This problem of price influence in dynamic ratio analysis is important.

$$- R4 \; \frac{\text{Commodity Inventory}}{\text{Commodity Purchasing}/360j} = \frac{\text{Commodity Inventory} \times 360}{\text{Commodity Purchasing}} = \text{Turnover Times for Merchandise Inventories}$$

DIAGNOSIS.– R4 is a ratio of working capital requirement in days of turnover. It is modifiable according to a search for the lightening of the financial burden that constitutes the need in working capital fund. This change is made by increasing the frequency of supplies and the speed of deliveries, as well as all the methods that we use in the optimal inventory management models.

$- R5 \; \dfrac{\text{Product Inventory} \times 360}{\text{Productions}}$ = Turnaround times for product stocks and outstanding production

DIAGNOSIS.– R5 is close to R4 except for production processes, the problems of quality of the service associated with the products, the differentiation of each product and the opening of the range with the costs engendered, which make it a more difficult element to reduce the need in funds.

$- R6 \; \dfrac{\text{Supply Stocks} \times 360}{\text{Supply Purchase}}$ = Turnover times for supply stocks

ANALYSIS.– R6 is close to R4 but retains some specificity. Supplies are completely related to production but not to customers, as is the case for goods. Thus, without supply, no production, but the over-stocking of production or the slowing down of manufacturing increases or decreases R6 accordingly. It is therefore not autonomous, while its place in the need for working capital is important.

$- R7 \; \dfrac{\text{Accounts receivable TTC} \times 360}{\text{Business Volume TTC}^*}$ = Customer settlement periods in days of sales including VAT

ANALYSIS.– This business volume is in R7 plus receivables on trade receivables (previously recorded as financial income) and reduced by settlement discounts granted (previously recorded as financial charges). R7 is one of the two elements of the commercial stock. The goal of the company is to minimize R7 without losing big customers. Depending on the size and specificity of the product, huge disparities may exist. Moreover, within a group, customers are sometimes also suppliers and the outstanding amount then takes unexpected proportions. R7 is, in any case, one of the main components of the working capital requirement that the company must seek to reduce to a minimum, because its financing is of course expensive.

$- R8 \; \dfrac{\text{Debts Suppliers TTC} \times 360}{\text{Purchases and adjusted external charges incl. VAT}}$ = Delay time in days of purchasing including VAT

ANALYSIS.– For this R8 ratio, external purchases and expenses are modified by:

- increasing interest on commercial debts, if recorded in financial expenses; and

- decreasing settlement discounts obtained, if recorded in financial products.

$- R9 \; \dfrac{\text{BFE} \times 360}{\text{Business Volume}^\dagger \text{ HT}}$ = BFE financial weight in days of turnover excluding tax

---

* Sales volume TTC = Turnover inclusive of VAT + Commission operations including VAT.
† The business volume (R7) is here understood as HT.

ANALYSIS.– R7 is the expression of the rotational delay $\frac{N}{F}$. Once R9 has been calculated, if questions weigh on the indications that it provides, the ratios R4 to R8 must then be supported.

6.2.1.4. *Growth*

$$- R10 \frac{F}{F} \frac{CA\ HT1 - CA\ HT0}{CA\ HT0} = \text{Growth rate of turnover excluding VAT}$$

ANALYSIS.– The growth of turnover makes it possible to appreciate the dynamism of the activity of the company. However, a company can increase its turnover and still run to bankruptcy, if it ignores its costs and sells at a loss. It can also increase its turnover on a smaller and smaller number of products and not develop its business portfolio; the "cash cow" products will quickly become dead weights. The risk of bankruptcy is greater as the company deals with a limited number of economic partners.

– R10 can also include all the volume of business handled by integrating the commissions collected.

$$- R11 \frac{F}{F} \frac{VA\ HT1 - VA\ HT0}{VA\ HT0} = \text{Growth rate of value added HT}$$

ANALYSIS.– R11 is an indicator of wealth creation. Without a significant added value, the company cannot exist for a long time and besides, the central balance sheet excluded those whose added value is negative from its analyses.

On a national level, the value added makes it possible to judge the contribution of the enterprise to the economy, as the sum of the added values is roughly represented by the gross national product. This added value depends on the adequacy between capital and labor factors. The CdB states that, once corrected for monetary erosion, this ratio constitutes an indicator of growth, and that is where the problem of the rate of change in value added arises. What the Bank of France suggests by structure is not a static analysis of the broad balance sheet structure, but a relationship between the operating performance and capital intensity.

$$-R12 \;\frac{N \text{ Operating investment excluding lease-back}^*}{F \quad VA \text{ CdB HT0}} = \text{Operating investment rate}$$

+ Intangible assets excluding establishment expenses
+ Tangible fixed assets
+ Fixed assets in lease management (lease-back) excluding lease-back*
= **OPERATING INVESTMENTS**

ANALYSIS.– R12 makes it possible to judge the maintenance and the development of the activities without being forcibly strategic investments. This ratio is a measure of the company's internal growth.

6.2.1.5. *Performance and productivity*

Capital–labor substitution must not escape the financial analyst. It can mean a redeployment to other activities, a drop in activity masked by research for productivity gains, etc.

The competence of the workforce is important. We can, in our conjuncture, hire pre-retirement staff for the benefit of young people with low wages and very low social charges (noria effect) but the problem transfers to the nation (societal cost), i.e. the cost of maintaining retired staff. This is one of the reasons why the retirement age has been increased.

Human resource productivity is a combination of capital intensity and the return on intellectual capital. Substitution of capital at work is not necessarily profitable in the long term. It should be noted that the quality of the workforce (skills management) is investment (digital machines, mobile computers, ergonomics of places, etc.), often escaping the analyst.

$$-R13 \;\frac{\text{Value Added CdB}}{\text{Average Workforce}} = \text{Human Resources Productivity}$$

DIAGNOSIS.– The efficiency of the production processes of goods and services can be approached by several indicators. R13 is one of them and is at the level of the apparent productivity of human resources.

We can explain this ratio in a combinatorial of other ratios such as:

$$\frac{\text{Value Added CdB}}{\text{IT Equipment}} \times \frac{\text{IT Equipment}}{\text{Average Workforce}}$$

---

* *The lease-back is a financial transaction that consists of a company selling assets it owns in its balance sheet to another company (financial) that relets them. Thus, the first company selling its headquarters, for example, collects the sale, which makes it a substantial inflow of funds. It continues to use the property for lease payments that it pays to the financial temperament.*

ANALYSIS.– These ratios measure the degree of digitization of the company, office investment, intranet and extranet, new information and communication technologies, etc.

– R14 $\quad \dfrac{F}{Q} = \dfrac{\text{Personnel Expense}}{\text{Average Staff}} =$ Apparent cost of human resources

– R15 $\quad \dfrac{F}{Q} = \dfrac{\text{Value Added BdF}}{\text{Operating capitalization*}} =$ Productivity of equipment

ANALYSIS.– R15 takes into account the existence of ongoing projects, its progress and deadlines for expected benefits.

6.2.1.6. *Profitability*

– R16 $\quad \dfrac{F}{F} = \dfrac{\text{Trade Margin}}{\text{Merchandise Sales}} =$ **Commercial Margin Rate**

ANALYSIS.– R16 is the ultimate profitability indicator, which mainly concerns commercial enterprises. This rate is "in the crosshairs" of the internal managers, management controller, pre-chair general manager and external, tax, bank, etc. Maintaining this margin rate is essential for many business owners who are initially excellent sales people. However, between the economic flows and their receipts, a shift is created, which can quickly lead to the cessation of payments. Many companies cease their activity or redeem themselves with their order books full of orders for several years.

R16 is similar for all companies in the same sector or branch but not at European level, of course. The comparison is therefore rather vis-à-vis the outside rather than internally and retrospectively.

– R17 $\quad \dfrac{F}{F} = \dfrac{\text{Market Margin}}{\text{Own Production*}} = \;\;=$ Margin rate on own production

Merchandise sales – Cost of purchase of merchandise sold
= **Commercial margin**
+ Sold production + Stored production + Immobilized production
= **Production of the exercise**
– Manufacturing outsourcing
= **Own Production†**

---

*Excluding land and buildings.
† Business volume = Turnover HT + commission transactions HT.

ANALYSIS.– R17 expresses the importance of the results of the production process.

– R18 $\dfrac{F}{F} = \dfrac{\text{Gross Operating Surplus}}{\text{Business volume*}} = $ Gross operating surplus rate

R18 must be high especially if the capital intensity of the company is significant and the depreciation is substantial.

ANALYSIS.– When R18 falls, profitability and self-financing also fall and the debt ratio will increase; therefore, the financial structure risks become unbalanced.

– R19 $\dfrac{F}{N} = \dfrac{\text{Business Volume}}{\text{Operating capital}} = $ Turnover rate of operating capital

– R20 $\dfrac{F}{N} = \dfrac{\text{Gross Operating Profit}}{\text{Operating Capital*}} = $ Gross rate of return on operating capital

ANALYSIS.– R20 depends on the profitability of the activity and the speed of rotation of the capital. Let R20 = R18 × R19.

– R21 $\dfrac{F}{N} = \dfrac{\text{Overall Net Income}}{\text{Equity+Financial Debt}} = $ Net rate of return on operating capital

ANALYSIS.– Global net income differs from gross global income by deducting capital consumption (net of write-backs and amortization). It determines a balance when the company has absorbed the depreciation of its assets. R21 measures net economic profitability. It is a ratio that explains the financial profitability, especially associated with the ratios of the cost of capital and the ratio of indebtedness R22.

– R22 $\dfrac{F}{N} = \dfrac{\text{Profit for the Year}}{\text{Equity called*}} = $ Financial rate of return on equity

+ Subscribed capital, called and paid
+ Premium issue, merger, etc.
+ Revaluation differences
+ Reserves, undistributed profits
+ Report again
= **Equity** *
+ Investment grants
+ Provision regulated
= **Own Funds**

* Operating capital = Operating investments + Operating capital requirements.

ANALYSIS.– Shareholders' equity varies exceptionally with changes in capital. R22 is therefore an indicator of financial profitability. This is a function of overall net profitability, the cost of borrowed capital, debt ratio and so on. R22 must be greater than the cost of borrowed capital so that the multiplier effect, the leverage effect, can play.

6.2.1.7. Financial autonomy

$$- \text{R23} \quad \frac{F}{F} = \frac{\text{Interest Expense}}{\text{Gross Global Result}} = \text{Interest weight}$$

ANALYSIS.– R23 is a reliable indicator of the risk of business failure. It is more symptomatic than the report of the interest charge on turnover.

$$- \text{R24} \quad \frac{N}{F} = \frac{\text{Bonds} \times 12}{\text{Internal Cash Flow}} = \text{Apparent repayment time}$$

ANALYSIS.– R24 expresses the number of months to repay loans by cash. This is very theoretical because a company does not systematically repay its loans because its activity in development requires resources. Moreover, operating cash is generally made for this type of operation. As a result, the retrospective and prospective follow-up of this ratio clarifies the financial coherence of the company.

$$- \text{R25} \quad \frac{F}{N} = \frac{\text{Internal cash flow}}{\text{Investments}} = \text{Internal hedging of investments}$$

ANALYSIS.– R25 is the very type of dynamic ratio because it only makes sense over several years. It expresses the coherence of the investments and their propensity to secrete a cash flow.

6.2.1.8. Financial structure

$$- \text{R26} \quad \frac{N}{N} = \frac{\text{Financial Debts*}}{\text{Equity Capital}} = \text{Debt ratio}$$

ANALYSIS.– R26 is an independent financial ratio. It also explains the cost of borrowed funds.

$$- \text{R27} \quad \frac{N}{N} = \frac{\text{Financial debt} - \text{Active cash flow}}{\text{Equity capital}} = \text{Debt ratio}$$

---

* Financial debts = Borrowings + Passive cash flow.

ANALYSIS.– We must detail the financial debt and highlight the share of:

- bank loans, current bank credits, receivables sold and those not yet due; and

- current bank credits that show the vulnerability of the company in its financing.

– R28 $\dfrac{N}{N} = \dfrac{\text{Current bank loans} + \text{receivables sold}}{\text{BFR}}$ Recurrent financing of working capital requirements

ANALYSIS.– R28 specifies the current financing of the working capital requirement. The relationship between cash and working capital requirements is based on working capital. However, the ratio of negative cash flow to working capital requirement indicates either an inadequacy with the working capital requirement or the real weakness of the working capital.

Therefore, from the simplest to the finest, and regardless of its degree of elaboration, the financial analyst must follow a common thread. Their analysis should never allow for the calculation of all-out ratios, in order to connect the entire company. This is not a survey that should provide a list of answers to a list of questions, because reality cannot fit completely into an accounting information system. It is an analysis, with which it induces as false equilibria, unanswered questions and degree of uncertainty of the future.

6.2.2. *Expeditious method of* credit managers

Some key ratios provide an overview of financial management. This quick financial analysis can be elaborated according to the following mnemonic steps (GPBAR):

Growth

Profitability

Balanced

And

Risk

6.2.2.1. *Growth*

Growth is expressed by Activity, Results, Means and Exploitation (ARME).

– Activity. The analysis of activity focuses on growth indicators such as turnover and value added. If possible, these indicators should be corrected and, in a volume analysis, the endogenous "productivity" component of the exogenous "prices" should be separated. The latter must itself determine the part which comes from desired, and therefore strategic, variation of prices from the one that originates from a drift of the market, and is thus not controllable.

Given these observations, value added can become a key indicator of business growth. It is the result of a good combination of capital and human resources.

The two indicators can be related as follows:

Value added/(turnover + subsidies)

This value added rate expresses the general productivity of the factors of production. However, it does not allow us to draw conclusions about the performance between companies because it differs according to the methods of exploitation. Over several years, this ratio is sensitive to changes in operating structures (external staff, outsourcing, price changes). As we have indicated, elements are to be reprocessed (leasing, subcontracting, taxes, levies, similar payments, etc.).

– Result. The intermediate balances of management, in their approach of the French Accounting Plan or reprocessed by the Banque de France, are differences of flows. For example:

- Gross operating margin rate $= \dfrac{\text{GOS}}{\text{Sales turnover excluding taxes}}$

- Gross profitability of operating capital $= \dfrac{\text{GOS}}{\text{Operating Capital}}$

– Means. This is understood by means of production, the fundamental factors of production or, in other words, capital and labor, to which we must add the effects of their combination or productivity.

- Human resources can be analyzed by:

    - reporting their total compensation to the full complement;

    - classifying the workforce into pilot, control and operational modules;

    - assessing the risks of social tension by the rate of change in the number of employees and the rate of increase in compensation; and

- judging information and decision making in the organization according to its ± pyramidal or alveolar structure in responsibility centers.

– Capital resources of the company. Business growth has followed an external growth pattern (mergers, acquisitions, shareholdings, contributions, etc.) rather than growth (investments in industrial equipment, etc.), which is why profitability was significantly higher in the second mode of growth than in the first.

In industrial investments, it is necessary to decide between expansion investments, investments to maintain production potential and strategic redeployment investments.

– Current: indicators such as the rate of: commercial margin: (sales − purchases)/purchases and mark-up = (sale − purchase)/(sale) evaluate the growth of commercial exploitation.

6.2.2.2. Profitability

Profitability is assessed by a criterion, the return on equity $\frac{Profit}{Equity}$, which is explained by four ratios that will be developed.

6.2.2.3. Equilibrium

Equilibrium is established at structural level and at the level of the means implemented. In terms of structure, we must judge:

– the hedging of invested capital (assets), by both long-term and short-term financial resources (liabilities); and

– the financial independence calculated by comparing the total own resources of the liabilities.

The ratio of own resources to the amount of indebtedness is important in determining leverage.

6.2.2.4. Risks

The risk coverage of:

– interest rates and exchange rates are provided by appropriate financial instruments; and

– default is measured by the Banque de France by a score that will be seen at the master level.

– Cash flow is covered by either:

  - working capital fund for working capital requirements; or

  - the sum of cash flows from operations, financing and investments. In case of overdrafts, all permits and cash loans are usable but expensive.

7

Analysis by Flux Tables: IFRS vs. US GAAP

Dynamic analysis, by cash flow and treasury flow, is used to judge the ability of the company to prevent potential failures.

The tables explaining the change in the balance sheet's cash flow can be classified into two main categories, namely the French Chart of Accounts financing table and the flow of treasuries:

1) the GAP cash flow statement explains the change in treasury ΔT by the difference between the change Δ in the strategic working capital (WC) and the Δ in the working capital requirement (WCR). This GAP financing table is the one that is always accepted for the individual accounts of companies in France. It is presented in two tables:

– the first (Table 1) divides the items that changed the working capital through:

- on the one hand, the increase in liabilities and the decline in assets;

- on the other hand, the increase in assets and the decrease in liabilities;

– the second (Table 2):

- indicates changes in working capital requirements;

- at the end, loops the change in the net cash position of the balance sheet, checking that it is at the same time equal to:

– the cash balance of the final balance sheet, less that of the initial balance sheet;

– the change in total net working capital – change in WCR.

2) The cash flow tables that explain the variation of the cash balance by its origins in major functions are current, investment and financing. Despite the evocation of the concept of functions, it is not quite the functional approach of the GAP.

7.1. Functional chart of the French Accounting Plan

7.1.1. *Table of changes in total net working capital WC*

Between the balance sheet items of the year A_N (of the calculation) and those of the year A_{N-1} (of reference), we observe variations in levels.

To obtain Table 1 expressing Δ global net working capital, it is necessary to analyze these variations by allocating them as either resources or uses. Thus, Table 1 consists of all elements of overall net working capital, but broken down depending on they were a resource or a working capital requirement in the year.

Changing from the level variation table to that of the GAP financing chart allows a financial reading of the documents, and no longer simply an accounting.

7.1.1.1. *Change in fixed or non-current assets*

A transfer of immobilization, at its transfer price (as it is a question of understanding the resource), is inscribed with resources and not in subtraction of needs.

For example, to determine the change in gross fixed assets:

+ net book value N−1
+ fixed assets acquired in N (employment)
− assets transferred in N (resources)
= net worth of an asset in N's balance sheet

And not the value of a net asset in the balance sheet of N = fixed assets of N − 1 + net changes in fixed assets in N.

This is fair accounting but does not explain the resources and uses that this account was behind.

We can also determine the gross value from the net value:

Δ net fixed assets
+ net book value of disposals (employment)
− depreciation charge N (resources)
= **depreciation charge N (resources)**

EXAMPLE.– The balance sheet never gives the raw values of $N-1$ but only the net values. Therefore, you have to find these raw values from the accounting documents.

Assets			Gross	Am. P	Net	$N-1$
Intangible		Administration fees				
		Research and development costs				
		Concessions, patents and similar rights	60	30	30	36
		Commercial fund including right to lease				
		Other intangible assets				
		Advances and down payments on immobilizations				
		= TOTAL	60	30	30	36
Property, plant and equipment		Land				
		Construction				
		Industrial installations, equipment and tools	260	60	200	100
		Other tangible fixed assets	94	26	68	44
		Assets in progress				
		Advances and deposits				
		= TOTAL	354	86	2.68	2.44

– From the profit and loss account of N, we note that depreciation charges for:

  - Concessions, patent and similar rights = 10

  - Installations, equipment and industrial tools = 20

  - Other tangible fixed assets = 12

– From the appendix, we note:

- Industrial installations, equipment and tools:

Acquisition value 50 and net book value = 20

- Other tangible fixed assets:

Acquisition value 20 and net book value = 9

Calculation of accumulated amortization on the balance sheet in N − 1

+ Depreciations on N's balance sheet
+ Writebacks of N (including those of assets sold in the year)
− Depreciation and amortization of N
= Depreciations on the balance sheet of N − 1

	Amort. N	Endowment N	Recovery N	Amort. N − 1
Concessions, patent and rights	30	10		20
Installations, equipment and tools	60	20	30	70
Other tangible fixed assets	26	12	11	25

Installations, equipment and tools worth 20 were acquired at 50, so they were depreciated for 50 − 20 = 30.

Gross fixed assets in the balance sheet N − 1 = Net n − 1 + Depreciation N − 1

	Net N − 1	Amort. N − 1	Gross N − 1
Concessions, patent and rights	36	20	56
Installations, equipment and tools	100	70	170
Other tangible fixed assets	44	25	69

Acquisitions of fixed assets N = Gross N − Gross N − 1 + ceded

	Gross N − 1	Ceded	Acquired	Gross N
Concessions, patent and rights	56		4	60
Installations, equipment and tools	170	50	140	2.60
Other tangible fixed assets	69	20	45	94
			189	

7.1.1.2. The variation of non-current resources

As a rule, a flow comes from either the activity (income statement) or a change in the level of a balance sheet account.

– *Change in balance sheet items*:

	Table 1 of the PCG cash flow statement	
Decrease in non-current resources	Administration fees	**Increase in non-current uses**
	Research and development costs	
	Concessions, patent and similar rights	
	Commercial fund including right to lease	
	Other intangible assets	
	Advances and down payments on intangible assets	
	Land	
	Constructions	
	Industrial installations, equipment and tools	
	Other tangible fixed assets	
	Assets in progress	
	Advances and down payments on tangible fixed assets	
	Investments (equity method)	
	Other participations	
	Receivables related to equity investments	
	Other fixed securities	
	Loans	
	Other financial assets	

Increase non-current resources	Share capital	**Decrease in non-current uses**
	Share premiums, mergers, contributions, etc.	
	Revaluation differences	
	Legal reserve	
	Statutory or contractual reservations	
	Regulated reserves (including + VLT and price fluctuation)	
	Other reserves	
	Investment grants	
	Regulated provisions	
	Participatory securities issued	
	Conditioned advances	
	Risk provisions	
	Provisions for expenses	
	Convertible bonds	
	Other bonds	
	Loans of credit institutions	
	Loans and other financial debts	

– *Sale or reduction of fixed assets*:

- For fixed assets:

– tangible fixed assets; we take into account the transfer price (transfer proceeds) corresponding to the actual resource received;

– financial items such as accrued and unmatured interest are not taken into account.

– *Increase in shareholders' equity, capital increase or contribution*:

- as the increase in sustainable resources is sought, capital increases by incorporation of reserves are not taken into account.

EXAMPLE.– Calculation of the change in equity from the balance sheet

	Liabilities of the Balance Sheet	Net N	Net N − 1
Equity	Share capital (of which paid in N = 650)	740	400
	Issue premiums, mergers, contributions, etc.		
	Revaluation differences (including equivalence difference)		
	Legal reserve		
	Statutory or contractual reservations	274	330
	Regulated reserves (including + VLT and price fluctuation)		
	Other reserves		
	Report again		
	YEAR PROFIT (profit or loss)	40	24

Assuming no dividend distribution was made in N,

Statutory or contractual reserves N	+ 330
The result of the exercise	+ 24
Statutory or contractual reservations N − 1	− 274
= Capital increase by incorporation of reserves	**= 80**

So

+ Share capital N (of which 650 paid)	+ 740
− Share capital N − 1	− 400
+ incorporation of reserves	− 80
− Unpaid capital	− 90
= Increase in equity	**= 170**

Only *the part named and paid* is to be taken into account, according to the same logic when we have an increase of capital in cash.

– *Increase in other shareholder's equity*

These are:

+ Investment grants		
+ Regulated provisions		
Increase in own funds (I)		

Investment grants are amounts previously received and are returned annually to the state through a set of paperwork.

The "investment grants" liability account is reduced (debited) by a share that is credited to the income statement as if the enterprise had made an additional turnover of this amount. To replenish the resource due to a subsidy increase:

+ Subsidy recorded in equity in year N	
− Subsidy recorded in equity in year N − 1	
+ Share of the grant transferred to the profit and loss account	
= Increase in the investment grant	

– *Increase in financial debts*

These exclude current bank overdrafts, credit balance of banks and bond repayment premium.

The principles to be respected for these increases in financial debts are the same as those stated for the treatment of financial debts put in non-current uses, so any short-term influence is to be avoided.

EXAMPLE.– *Calculation of the change in financial debts*:

		N	N-1
+ FINANCIAL DEBTS	Convertible bonds		
	Other bonds		
	Loans of credit institutions	380	400
	Borrowings and other financial debts *		
Conversion differences in financial liabilities over one year		4	3
Active translation differences in financial debts over one year		1	2

* Of which interest accrued and not due: N − 1 = 5 and N = 4.

Current bank loans: N − 1 = 52 and N = 25.

Part due in the year: N − 1 = 77.

The calculation of the repayment of financial debts is as follows:

	N	N-1
+ Loans from credit institutions	+ 380	+ 400
+ Translation differences on financial liabilities over 1 year	+ 4	+ 3
− Currency translation differences on financial debts over 1 year	− 1	− 2
− Accrued interest that is not due	− 4	− 5
− Bank overdrafts	− 25	− 52
= Restated financial debts	= 354	= 344

Distribution in the variation of the debts between the part, which returns:

To non-standard jobs:

Repayment of financial debts in jobs	N
+ N − 1 debts due in the year	+ 77
− Accrued interest that is not due	− 5
− Bank overdrafts	− 52
= Reimbursement of financial debts	= 20

To sustainable resources:

Increase in financial debts in resources	N
− restated financial debts N − 1	− 344
+ restated financial debts N	+354
+ Reimbursement of financial debts	+ 20
= Increase in financial debts	= 30

7.1.1.3. Table of jobs and resources

Any level variation is a flow. Therefore, in the flowchart, we record:

− in non-current jobs:

- the *increase* in *non-current assets*;

- the *decline* in *sustainable liability items*;
- and a flow of dividends paid;
– in sustainable resources:
- the *increase* in *sustainable liability items*;
- the *decrease* in *non-current assets*;
- and a *cash flow of self-financing*.

Table 1 of uses and resources for the year					
Uses	N	N – 1	Resources	N	N – 1
Dividend distribution for the year			Cash flow		
Acquisition of fixed assets:			Disposal or reduction of fixed assets:		
Intangible assets			Intangible assets		
Tangible assets			Tangible assets		
Financial fixed assets			Financial fixed assets		
Expenses to be spread over several years (a)					
Decrease in equity			Increase in equity		
Repayment of financial debts (b)			Capital increase or contribution		
			Increase in other equity		
			Increase in financial debts (b) (c)		
Total employment			Total resources		
Change in total net working capital (net resource)			**Change in net working capital global (net replacement)**		
a) gross amount transferred during the year b) except current bank credit and bank credit balance c) excluding bond redemption premium					

– Dividends distributed during a fiscal year

These are the dividends that were paid in year N and which of course come from the results of year N – 1. These were partly set aside and partly distributed as dividends. The analyst has an allocation table in the appendix but, failing that, he can reconstruct the dividends paid in this way. For all balance sheet accounts, the equation is:

$$\boxed{\text{Initial level} + \text{Increase}} = \boxed{\text{Decrease} + \text{Final level}}$$

In the balance sheet, we are dealing with levels of assets and liabilities. These levels are stocks as they represent an accumulation.

EXAMPLE.– Calculation of dividends

			Balance sheet liabilities	Net N	Net N−1
Own funds	Equity	Net situation	Share capital (1) (including paid)	120	100
			Issue premiums, merger, contribution, etc.		
			Revaluation differences (2) (including equivalence difference)		
			Legal reserve (3)	12	10
			Statutory or contractual reservations	80	70
			Regulated reserves (including + VLT and price fluctuation)		
			Other reserves (including live artists)		
			Report again		
			Result	34	46

It is assumed that the change in capital is due to the incorporation of reserves

Reserved N	− Reserved N − 1	+ (Outputs for) capital incorporations	= Δ Reserved
80	− 70	+ 120 − 100	= 30

Dividend distribution for the year = Result N − 1 − Δ Reserves = 46 − 30 = 16.

Reimbursement of financial debts

On the one hand, they are considered as excluding current bank overdrafts and credit balances of banks, and on the other hand, only the part relating to sustainable resources should be considered. Therefore, any influence in the short term is to be avoided.

EXAMPLE.– Calculation of repayment of financial debts

		N	N − 1
+ **Financial debts**	Convertible bonds		
	Other bonds		
	Loans of credit institutions	100	70
	Loans and other financial debts		

If a new loan of 44 has been contracted in N, then the repayment of the financial debts is: N − 1 loan − N + loan increase loan of N = 70 + 44 − 100 = *14*.

If there are short-term elements, their influence must be removed:

		N	N − 1
+ Financial debts	Convertible bonds		
	Other bonds		
	Loans of credit institutions		
	Borrowings and other financial debts*	380	400
Conversion differences in financial liabilities over one year		4	3
Active translation differences in financial debts over one year		0.6	2

* Of which interest is accrued and not due: N − 1 = 5.
Current banking contest: N − 1 = 52.
Part due in the year: N − 1 = 77.

The calculation of the repayment of financial debts is done simply as follows:

+ N − 1 short-term debt	77
− Interest that is accrued and not yet due	−5
− Bank overdrafts	− 52
= Repayment of financial debts	**= 20**

7.1.1.4. *Diagnosis of the table*

– Subscribed capital not named and not paid: this represents the part of the capital on which the company cannot count for its resources as it has not been paid. This item is therefore to be removed from the assets and its amount is to be subtracted from equity.

– Disposals of fixed assets: these are mainly in the non-current section. In addition, in the tables in the appendix, disposals of fixed assets are recorded at their entry value in the portfolio, in order to recover the selling prices per unit sold. This requires calculations that are not always easy for an internal analyst and that are practically impossible for a former analyst.

– Expenses to be spread over several years: these no longer exist in the balance sheets of 2006 but before then they were registered. So, for an analysis over several years, they must be taken for their gross amount while they appear in net balance sheet. These excessively high expenses are initially recorded as expenses in the income statement. Then, they are transferred to the assets of the balance sheet so that they can be amortized directly without going through a depreciation account. Therefore, we do not have the value of their depreciation on the balance sheet. To find the raw value, we have the following:

| + Net redistributable expenses |
| + Accumulated depreciation |
| = **Expenses to be apportioned gross of N** |

- The amortization table mentions those corresponding to the expenses to be spread over several years. It suffices to add them to the expenses to be spread over several net years of N to obtain the gross values. However, accumulated depreciation is to be added to the depreciation and allowance fund recorded in equity, as is done in the functional analysis.

- The trend of the disappearance of these expenses to be spread over several years currently makes them register as non-values, which eliminates them as.

– Change in equity. The balance sheet of N − 1 is presented after distribution of the results and the balance sheet N before. Therefore, the dividends were placed in a short-term debt account: "dividends to pay". Thus, it suffices to place these dividends in Table 1 in the *pro forma* capital and to exclude from Table 2 various debts. We note that it is necessary to avoid placing with the increase of the equity, that of the reserves. The sums placed in reserve result from the undistributed profit which is itself included in the self-financing capacity. Otherwise, all decreases in equity items are to be considered except:

- the reversal of investment grants because they are systematically recorded in the income statement as calculated expenses and are added to the self-financing capacity;

- reversals of regulated provisions, for similar reasons;

- losses because the result is not taken into account, as such.

Among the capital increases that should not affect the increase in sustainable resources, there are not only the incorporation of reserves and distributions of free shares but also the conversion of convertible bonds.

– Current account of creditors. If they are stuck, they stay with the financial debts, otherwise they are relegated to the off-course resources.

– Reductions in financial debts. In these financial debts, we include:

- bank overdrafts and bank credit balances. We must therefore remove them from Table 1 to keep only the sustainable resource and not the one that falls during the year.

- accrued and unmatured interest. These must therefore be removed from fixed assets or financial debts in order to include them in other receivables and other debts, thus, if necessary, in off-balance funds (Table 2).

EXAMPLE.–

Active	N – 1	N	Passive	N – 1	N
Gross financial assets	€2,000 k	€2,800 k	Loans	€6,400 k	€9,000 k
of which accrued interest	€100 k	€160 k	of which accrued interest	€480 k	€640 k
Miscellaneous receivables	€960 k	€200 k	Sundry debts	€2,200 k	€1,800 k

In N, the company increased its borrowings by 300 and sold a financial asset recorded for €6,000 k. According to the accounting principle:

Financial Asset N = Active end N –1 + Increase N – Decrease N

Therefore:

– In Table 1 of the financing table:

- the acquisitions of financial fixed assets amount to:

+ Fixed assets N (€2,800 k – €160 k = €2,640 k)

+ Decreases (€2,800 k – €2,000 k = €800 k)

– N – 1 fixed assets (€2,000 k – €100 k = €1,900 k)

= Increases (€2,640 k – €1,900 k + €800 k = **€1,540 k**).

Which corresponds to the table in the appendix:

	Gross value beginning N	Increase		Decrease		Gross value end N
		Transfer from post to post	Acquisitions	Transfer from post to post	Gross value beginning N	
Assets	€1,900 k		**€1,540 k**		€800 k	€2,640 k

- repayments of financial debts amount to:
  + End N debts (€9,000 k − €640 k = €8,360 k)
  − End N − 1 debts (€6,400 k − €480 k = €5,920 k
  + Increases (= €6,000 k)
  = Decreases (€5,920 k − €8,360 k + €6,000 k = €3,560 k).
− In Table 2 of the financing table:
  - the claims in Table 2 are:
    + Receivables N (€1,000 k + €160 k = €1,160 k)
    − N − 1 receivables (€960,000 + €100 k = € 1,060 k)
    = Variation of other receivables = €1,160 k − €1,060 k = €100 k).
  - the various debts of Table 2 are:
    + N debts (€1,800 k + €640 k = €2,440 k)
    − N − 1 debts (€2,200 k + €480 k = €2,680 k)
    = Variation of various debts = €2,440 k − €2,680 k = −€240 k).

− Exchange differences change financial debts according to whether they are on the assets or liabilities side. We must therefore cancel their influence, which remains in the short term.

EXAMPLE.−

Active	N	Passive	N
Operating receivables	€26,000 k	Loans	€74,000 k
		Loan conversion difference	€2,800 k
		Credit conversion difference	€600 k

In Table 2 of the cash flow table, the variations between N and N − 1:
  − the foreign currency translation differences show an increase in the receivables:

| + N receivables (€26,000 k) |
| − N passive conversion difference on asset item (€600 k) |
| = N − 1 claims = (€26,000 k − €600 k = €25,400 k) |

— the exchange differentials show a decrease in debt:

| + N loans (€74,000 k) |
| + Non-recurring liability N on liability item (€2,800) |
| = N − 1 loans = (€74,000 k + €2,800 k = €76,800 k) |

– Bonds. These must take into account only the issue price, and therefore, the influence of the share premium must not be affected. It should be noted that the financing table notes the repayment of financial debts: "excluding bond redemption premium".

Bond repayment premiums. These correspond to the final effect of the repayment of the bonds. As a result, they are currently considered non-securities and are to be removed from the assets. Correlatively, the amount of the loans concerned will be reduced accordingly.

EXAMPLE.– Premium loan calculation

A bond issue is issued at the beginning of N. It consists of 100,000 bonds of €2 k, amortizable over 10 years by constant annuities in fine. Repayment premiums follow the amortization of the loan.

Active	Gross N	Net N	Passive	N − 1	N
Loan repayment premiums	€9,000 k	€9,000 k	Bond issues		€180,000 k

Table 1 of the cash flow statement shows the net financial resources of the redemption premiums.

Reimbursement premiums:

Amortization of the premium for N = 10% of Bonus → € 9,000 k = 10% of the Premium → Premium = €10,000 k, or financial resources €200,000 k − €10,000 k = €190,000 k.

Decrease in borrowings at end N:

Loan N − 1 (€0 k) − Loan N (€180,000 k) + Increase in borrowings (€200,000 k) = € 20,000 k.

– Self-financing capacity. This is a monetary surplus consisting mainly of endowments. However, the chart of accounts requires that depreciation not appear in the liabilities with the capital and the result, but in subtraction of assets. Therefore, the fact that the chart of funding of the PCG remedies this financial oddity seems justified.

– Advances and down payments in N − 1 and fixed assets in progress of N − 1 have been taken into account in the acquisitions of fixed assets. We must therefore be careful not to include them again in the mobilizations acquired in N.

EXAMPLE.–

	Raw values N − 1	Raw values N
Construction	12,000	17,000
Material	8,000	10,000
Assets in progress	2,000*	
Advances and deposits	700**	200

* Completed construction in N for 4,000.

** For a good delivered in N for 3,000.

Disposal of material in N of material registered for 1,300.

The table of fixed assets is then the following:

	Gross value beginning N	Increases		Decreases		Gross value end N
		Transfer from post to post	Acquisitions	Transfer from post to post	Gross value beginning N	
Constructions	2,400	400	600 [1]			3,400
Material	1,600	140	520 [2]		260	2,000
In progress	400			400		
Advances and deposits	140		40	140		40
Acquisitions of tangible assets			1,160			

1)

| + Constructions N (2,400) |
| + Increases (1,000) |
| − Decreases (0) |
| = Constructions N − 1 (3,400) |

So,

+ Increases (1,000)
− In progress (400)
= **Acquisition of N constructions (600)**

2)

+ Material N − 1 (2,000)
+ Increases (1,600)
− Decreases (260)
− Advances and deposits (140)
= **Material N (520)**

The first part of the financing table:

− makes it possible to analyze the financing and investment strategies of the company by checking the main principles of structural balance of the balance sheet.

This table (1), which explains the change in net working capital, presents new resources and new investments by reclassifying them. However, any new investment, except those replacing the old ones, should generate a growing activity and therefore an additional need. It is therefore not unrealistic to verify that this equilibrium is dynamic insofar as the excess of non-current financing over sustainable resources makes it possible to finance the working capital requirement, thus essentially the operating cycle;

− shows that if the principles are not respected, the analyst cannot ignore that the balance sheet is balanced. He or she can predict that the adjustment is precarious, and with it the solvency risk which remains attached to the cash.

7.1.2. Table of changes in working capital requirement

Change in total net working capital requirement	Needs 1	N Degagement 2	Balance 2 − 1	N − 1 Balance
Variation "Current and not current"				
Variation in operating assets:				
Stocks and sums outstanding				
Advances and down payments				
Customer receivables and accounts receivable				
Variation in operating debts				
Advances and down payments received				
Trade payables and related accounts				
Total	X	X		
A. "Current" net variation			± X	± X
"Off-the-shelf" variations:				
Variation in other receivables (a) (b) (c)				
Variation of other payables (a)				
Totals	X	X		
B. Net variation "out of current"			± X	± X
Total A + B:				
Need for working capital			± X	± X
or				
Release of the working capital exercise			± X	± X
Cash flow				
Variation of availabilities				
Variation in current bank overdrafts and bank credit balances				
Total	X	X		
C. "Treasury" net variation			± X	± X
Change in total net working capital				
A + B + C:				
Net employment			−	+
Net resources			+	−

a) Including recognized costs of advances according to their allocation to the firm or not.

b) Including recognized revenue from advances according to their standard allocation or not.

c) Amounts with the sign (+) when the clearances outweigh the requirements and the sign (−) in the opposite case.

d) Including marketable securities if they are not transferable at any time and without risk of loss.

Saint Gobain example – working capital requirements:

"Inventories are valued at their lowest cost or net realizable value, which includes acquisition costs (net of vendor rebates), processing and other costs incurred in bringing the inventory to the place and condition it is found in. It is generally calculated using the weighted average cost method and, in some cases, the first-in-first-out method, and may include the unwinding of cash flow hedges related to cash and cash equivalents. Net realizable value is the sale price in the ordinary course of business, less the estimated costs of completion and those required to make the sale; the sub-activity is excluded from valuation of stocks.

Trade receivables, trade payables, other receivables and other debts are recorded at their net book value, which, taking into account payment terms generally less than three months, is close to fair value. Depreciations are established to cover the risks of non-recovery of all or part of the receivables".

7.1.2.1. *Financial treatment of BFRE positions*

Change in current operating assets in gross value
+ Stocks and sums outstanding
+ Advances and down payments
+ Trade receivables and related accounts net of tax
+ Discounted and unmatured effects
+ Prepaid expenses
+ Asset translation differences relating to current operating assets
− Foreign currency translation adjustments relating to current operating assets

Change in operating liabilities at gross value
+ Advances and down payments received
+ Trade payables and related accounts
+ Tax and employee income taxes net of tax and employee profit sharing
+ Foreign currency translation adjustments relating to current operating liabilities
− Asset translation differences relating to current operating liabilities

7.1.2.2. Financial processing of OWCR positions

Change in non-current assets in gross value
Variation of other receivables (a) (b)
+ Subscribed and unpaid capital
+ Marketable securities not immediately available
+ Accrued and unmatured interest on current receivables
+ Exchange differential differences relating to non-current assets
− Liabilities exchange differential relating to non-current assets

(a) Including recognized charges for advances

(b) Including recognized proceeds of

Change in non-current liabilities in gross value
Variation of other payables (a)
+ Profit tax debts
+ Accrued and unmatured interest on current liabilities
+ Deferred income on other current account receivables
+ Unblocked current accounts
+ Exchange differential related to current liabilities
− Asset exchange differential relating to the current liability

(a) Including recognized charges for advances

ANALYSIS.– This second table is a simple differential table, a state of Δ WCR positions without further analysis as in Table 1.

DIAGNOSIS.– Cash does not include the marketable securities it leaves in the WCR. This is the option of the OAE[1] and IFRS cash flow statements.

This position is not taken in the table of the Banque de France.

We often systematically dismiss the discounted and unmatured effects to put them back into cash, while the order of accountants has taken a contrary position.

---

1 Order of accounting experts.

7.1.3. Synoptic diagram of the links between two-year financial statements

Income account N
+ Sale of goods
− Cost of purchasing (Cost of Goods Sold)
= Commercial margin
+ Production sold, stored and immobilized
− Intermediate consumption
= Added value
+ Operating grant
− Levies, taxes and payments
− Staff costs
=GOS

Income account N (cont.)		Financing table N
± Share of operations made jointly	=	± Share of operations made in common
− Employee participation	=	− Employee participation
− Income tax	=	− Income tax
+ Other exploit products	=	+ Other exploit products
− Other operating expenses		− Other operating expenses. (1)
+ Financial products		+ Financial Products (1)
− Financial expenses		− Financial expenses (1)
+ Exceptional products		+ Exceptional products (1) (2)
− Extraordinary charges		− Extraordinary Charges (1) (3)
= Result of N		**= Self-financing capacity**

Balance sheet N − 1	Financing table N (cont.)	Balance sheet N
+ Equity	− Dividend distribution	+ Equity
+ Depreciation and amortization	**= Self-financing**	+ Depreciation and amortization
− Fixed assets (5)	+ Disposal of fixed assets	− Fixed assets (5)
	− Acquisition of fixed assets	
	− Charge to spread over several years	
	+ Increase in equity	
	− Decrease in equity (4)	
+ Increase in financial debts (6)	+ Increase in financial debts (6)	+ Increase in financial debts (6)
	− Reimbursement of financial debts (6)	
= Global net working capital N − 1	**= Δ Total net working capital**	**= Global net working capital N**

(5) In raw values
(6) Except bank overdraft

+ Operating assets (5)	Δ = Variation whatever the direction of the variation	+ Δ Operating assets (5)	+ Operating assets (5)
− Operating debts		− Δ Operating debts	− Exploitation debt
= WCR N − 1	(1) Excluding calculated charges: allocations − reversals	= Δ WCE N − 1	= WCE N
+ Other debtors (5)	(2) Except proceeds from the sale of fixed assets and the subsidy of investments transferred to the income statement	+ Δ Other debtors	+ Other debtors (5)
− Other payables		− Δ Other creditors	− Other payables
= Overall net WCR N − 1		= Δ WCR global net N	= Net WCR net end N
+ Availabilities	(3) Excluding net book value of transferred assets	+ Δ Availability	+ Availabilities
− Bank loans	(4) Except dividend distribution	− Δ Bank loans	− Curr. Bank loans
= Cash N − 1		= Δ Treasury N	= Fine Treasury N

+ FR net overall end N − 1		+ ΔFR global net N	+ FR net global end N
− net WCR net N − 1		− Δ WCR global Net	− WCR net overall end N
= Cash start N	±	= Δ Treasury N =	= Fine Treasury N

7.2. Financing table of the Banque de France

7.2.1. Functional balance

7.2.1.1. Employee resources

Functional assessment	Gross			
	N − 3	N − 2	N − 1	N
Employee resources				
Intangible assets excluding establishment expenses				
+ Tangible fixed assets				
+ Fixed assets under finance leases				
= **Fixed assets A**				

Equity interests and securities				
+ Other non-current assets *including group loans, groups and debtor partners*				
= **Other fixed assets B**				
Total stock				
+ Trade receivables and other operating receivables				
− Suppliers and other operating debts				
= **Required current fund C**				
Operating capital = [A + C]				
Invested capital = [A + B + C]				
Receivables − income tax debts				
+ Receivables − capital tax debts				
+ Claims − miscellaneous debts				
= **Required current fund D**				
Availability				
+ Marketable securities				
+ Cash advances to groups and associates				
= **Active cash E**				
Total jobs = [A + B + C + D + E]				

7.2.1.2. Resources released

Functional assessment	Gross			
	N − 3	N − 2	N − 1	N
Resources outputs				
Equity capital F				
− Depreciation, amortization and provisions for depreciation, risks and charges G				
Clean financing = [F + G]				
Bond issues				
+ Bank loans *(including indebtedness for lease management)*				
+ Other loans *(including borrowings from groups and associates)*				
= Loans H				
Current bank loans				
+ Unissued transferred receivables				
+ Cash advances received from groups and associates				
+ Negotiable debt securities issued outside the group				
= Liquidated cash I				
Financial debt = [H + I]				
Total resources = [F + G + H + I]				

Financial balance				
+ Non-current financing [F + G + H]				
− Immobilized assets [A + B]				
= Global net working capital				
− Working capital requirement [C + D]				
= Net cash (assets − liabilities) [E − I]				

7.2.2. Cash flow statement

Cash would supplant the result as a strategic variable of the company. It is not subject to caution and accounting interpretation as the results are and it provides a major indication on the ability of the company to mitigate the risk of failure, by collecting funds and recovering those incurred.

Beyond the monitoring of realizable and available values in the short term, the balance of cash flows in the financing table of the Central Balance Sheet Office of the Banque de France provides a strategic view of cash flow: financial flexibility, potentiality, "war treasure", etc.

The Banque de France's cash flow statement is a table that explains the change in balance sheet cash by the main functions. It is close to the cash flow tables of the order of the accounting experts and especially the international ones under IFRS norms.

It therefore differs from the GCP funding table, which still remains appended to the individual accounts of the companies.

As any change in levels (in the balance sheet) is a flow, the flowchart below explains the balance-of-cash variation of the balance sheet by calculating in each of the three functions, the sum of the variations of levels and the flows of collection and disbursement cash flow. This table of financing from the Banque de France is as follows:

CASH FLOW
(corrected flows of transfers from post to post)
Activity
+ Turnover excluding taxes and other operating income
± Change in trade receivables and other operating receivables
= Payments on operating products [A]
− Purchases and other operating expenses
± Variation in suppliers and other operating debts
= Decreases in operating expenses [B]
= Operating cash flow [A] − [B]
± Flow related to non-current operations
− Interest charges
− Income tax disbursed
− Flow allocated to employee participation
− Distribution paid
= Internal cash flow A

Investment

− Operating investment excluding capitalized production
− Acquisitions of investments and immobilized securities
± Change in other fixed assets excluding expenses to be allocated
+ Investment grants received
± Variation in debt on fixed assets
+ Receipts on disposals of fixed assets
= Flow related to investment   I

Funding

+ Increase or − reduction in equity	
± Variation in claims on called and unspent capital	
= Flow related to capital	[C]
+ New borrowings, including new lease commitments	
− Loan repayments	
= Variation of borrowings	[D]
± Change in current bank credits	
− Change in unmatured receivables	
± Change in cash advances received from groups and associates	
± Change in non-group negotiable debt securities	
= Passive cash variation	[E]
= Funding flow [C]+[D]+[E] = F	

Variation of Active Cash

± Variation of availabilities
± Variation in investment securities
± Variation in cash advances to groups and associates
= ACTIVE CASH VARIATION A − I + F

7.2.2.1. *Methods*

Cash flows are understood directly rather than indirectly.

7.2.2.1.1. Direct method

Receipts and disbursements are extracted directly from the income statement and reflect changes in the receivables and debt position of working capital requirements.

This method, which is more sophisticated and correct than others, offers the following advantages:

– provides richer and more relevant information on cashing and settlement flows;

– neutralizes the effect of inventory accounts. In fact, receipts ignore the valuation of changes in inventories and capitalized production, which do not give rise to any cash inflow.

As a result, there is a desire to release the internal cash flow from opportunistic accounting assessments. It is no coincidence that the IFRS cash flow statement recommends this direct method.

7.2.2.1.2. Indirect method

The indirect method provides a mathematically correct result, but it is the logic that suffers. Indeed, by the equality of the total income and expenses of the profit and loss account, we find the same value of the internal cash flow, making the algebraic sum of the positions left behind in the direct method.

EXAMPLE.–

Charges		Products
– Items recognized as an expense impacting cash flow included in the straightforward method = 800	Direct method	+ Items recognized as revenue with cash flow impact reflected in the direct method = 1,000
→ cash flow from operation = 200	Indirect method	
+ Items recognized as non-cash expenses included in the in-direct method (including net book income) = 400		– Items recognized as revenue that affect the cash flow included in the indirect method =200
Total expenses = 1,200		= Total products =1,200

7.2.2.2. Cash flow

The origins of the change in cash take precedence over the search for the major balance sheet balances.

– Activity generates operating and internal cash flows

The internal cash flow is composed of the operating cash flow and allocation.

Operating cash flow

This is determined by the difference in payments of operating income and expenses:

ACTIVITY

+ Turnover excluding taxes and other operating income *(flow)*
± Change in trade receivables and other operating receivables (variation in levels)
= PAYMENTS ON OPERATING PRODUCTS [a] *(flow)*
– *Purchases and other operating expenses (flow)*
± Variation in suppliers and other operating debts (variation in levels)
= DECREASES ON OPERATING EXPENSES [b] *(flow)*
= CASH FLOW OF OPERATING [a] – [b] (flow)

The influence of customer credit means that:

– any lengthening of the latter reduces the cash flow and increases the risk of default;

– any decrease in customer credit reduces cash flow.

Reciprocal supplier credit plays an equally important role in cash flow. To determine this operating cash flow, the impact of trade policies on cash flows is taken into account.

With regard to that:

– settlement discounts granted to customers are deducted from operating revenues;

– trade receivables are added to operating revenues.

On the contrary:

– settlement discounts obtained from suppliers are deducted from operating expenses;

– interest paid on commercial debts is added to operating expenses.

This is also the case in the IFRS cash flow statement.

This operating cash flow shows the difference between income and cash. Indeed, the company can:

– sell at a loss and get paid cash (so good cash but bad result);

– sell with significant settlement deadlines (bad cash but good result);

– suffer the insolvency of certain customers (good operating cash flow and good results but punctual insolvency).

When the business is growing, it increases its accounts receivable, so the gap between the increase in revenue and receipts increases. Therefore, the following two solutions are available:

– Increase supplier delays but with the risks that this entails in a period of growth when it needs them to stock up;

– Reduce inventories, increasing the change in inventories and reducing operating income accordingly. However, the operating cash flow will not be modified by this operation. We see a scissors effect.

In any case, any change in the working capital requirement not justified by a change in activity is a warning sign for a short-term operating cash flow problem.

Internal cash flow

Once these are paid, it must in principle remain an endogenous cash surplus: the positive internal cash flow.

+ OPERATING CASH FLOW
± Flow related to off-current operations × (flow)
– *Interest charges (flow)*
– Income tax disbursed (flow)
– Flow allocated to employee participation (flow)
– Distribution put in payment (flow)
= **INTERNAL CASH FLOW**　　　　　A

* In non-current transactions, recurring cash flows are placed, such as:

– financial products;

– results of operations carried out jointly;

– exceptional income and expenses on management operations.

This operating cash flow should be used primarily for allocation transactions. It must therefore mitigate the major risks relating to the non-payment of its creditors: predecessor bodies, the State, employees' participation and shareholders through the payment of dividends.

It is understood that a low or even negative internal cash flow is a warning signal of the risk of failure.

This internal cash flow:

– is composed mainly of operating cash flow;

– is premonitory of the risks of default because whether it remains negative or not, the company does not run out of enough cash for its current needs;

– indicates that previous investments have not secreted enough cash. Thus, for the calculation of the return on investments, this internal cash flow must be updated to calculate its profitability.

Cash flow linked to the investment

This second part adds all the cash flows from tangible, intangible and financial investments, including when they generate the cash inflow and outflow.

– Operating investment excluding fixed production (variation of levels)
– Acquisitions of participations and immobilized securities (variation of levels)
± Change in other fixed assets × non-distributable expenses (variation in levels)
+ Investment grants received (flows)
± *Change in debt on fixed assets (variation in levels)*
+ Receipts on disposals of fixed assets (flux)
= FLOW RELATED TO INVESTMENT   I

It should be noted that, in order to ensure inter-company comparability:

– investment grants received and recorded as liabilities are deducted from the decommitted flows for investments;

– the expenses to be spread over several years and the capitalized production are excluded from the cash flow related to the investment. In fact, the Central Balance Sheet Office of the Banque de France considers that these transfers of charges to assets are neutralized. Expenses have been included in the cash flow from the business;

– the value of assets acquired under finance leases is added to fixed assets and an equivalent amount will be added to loans (always to compare companies in their own right).

Internal cash flow cannot fund all investments alone. In general, internal cash flow finances the renewal investments that maintain the productive potential without modifying the profit and loss account.

However, if the company has to finance growth investments, then the internal cash flow is insufficient. Therefore, if the cash flow from the investment is negative, it is not alarming, provided the internal cash flow is positive and substantial.

Cash flow related to financing

This third part consists of flows related to own financing, long-term borrowings and cash overdrafts.

FUNDING

+ Increase or − reduction of equity (Δ of levels)	
± Variation of claims on called and unpaid capital (of levels)	
= FLOW RELATED TO CAPITAL (Flux)	[c]
+ NEW BORROWINGS including new finance lease commitments (Δ levels)	
− LOAN REPAYMENTS (Δ levels)	
= VARIATION OF BORROWING (Δ levels)	[d]
± Change in current bank credits (Δ levels)	
− Change in receivables sold without maturity (Δ of levels)	
± change in cash advances received from groups and associates (Δ of levels)	
± change in non-group negotiable debt securities (Δ levels)	
= PASSIVE CASH VARIATION (Δ of levels)	[e]
= FUNDING FLOW (Flow)	**[c]+[d]+[e] = F**

Here, we can see the pooled funds approach because in the flow related to financing, the table re-groups all sources of financing regardless of their term. However, long-term investments must be financed in a non-current manner, such as long-term borrowings or equity.

The change in capital excludes:

– dividends paid included in the internal cash flow;

– the financial expense because it is included in the distribution operations but includes the amount of the notional loan corresponding to the consideration of fixed assets acquired through a finance lease transaction.

This flow related to financing enlightens the analyst about the financing choices of the company. We have seen that the internal cash flow should have made it possible to cover all or part of the renewal investments. However, the search for sources of financing and the trade-offs between own and foreign financing in the long or short term are revealed.

If the internal cash flow has been positive, the financial burden following the use of the loan can be ensured by the profitability of the investments. But otherwise, the company distributes its cash more than it produces. The risk of failure is very high.

Cash change in assets

This consists of the change in accounts, "banks and related accounts", "fund" and "marketable securities". Marketable securities are considered cash and not included as needed in operating working capital (as in the GAAP or IFRS table). This variation shows a change in the cash position of the asset. In fact:

VARIATION OF ACTIVE CASH

± Variation of availabilities	
± Variation in investment securities	
± Variation in cash advances to groups and associates	
= ACTIVE CASH VARIATION	$A - I + F$

This cash flow statement makes it possible to assess the overall logic of the company in terms of its choices regarding risks:

– inconsistency between growth strategy and financing policies;

– inability to reduce the risk of default by securing cash flow consistent with each function;

– Abandonment of the accounting vision and its opportunistic attitudes for a traceability of unworkable treasuries.

7.2.2.3. *Diagnosis of the Banque de France flow table*

Investment activity includes both investments and divestments. It concerns several types of investments:

– investments of renewal: it is preferable that they be financed by operating cash;

– investments that are part of the financing function and the remainder of operating cash;

– investment of growth: they come under the financing function and the operating cash balance;

– that are strategic: they are solely the resources of the fund-raising activity.

Current operating revenues do not take into account:

– the change in product inventories;

– immobilized production;

– transfers of charges to be distributed and

– discounts granted.

Current operating expenses do not take into account:

– the change in inventories of materials, goods, etc.;

– discounts obtained;

– provisions for depreciation of items of current assets and

– lease-financing rents (leasing) because the lease finance is reprocessed in general in:

- reducing the rent paid;

- adding to the flows of the financing activity the part corresponding to the amortization of the property taken out of financing lease;

- adding to the cash flows of the internal activity the portion corresponding to financial expenses;

- adding in the first year of the contract the value of the property leased to finance the fixed assets;

- reciprocally adding to the liabilities the loan that would have been contracted by the company if it had financed by debt this property that it would have of course acquired in full ownership.

In the cash flows of the investment activity, *investment grants* are deducted because they are not considered as a source of financing but as a reduction of the corresponding investments.

Similarly, *dividends* are not considered as a deduction of cash flows from the financing activity but as a current activity.

Discounted and unmatured bills are restated as usual.

Marketable securities are recorded with cash, irrespective of their degree of immediate liquidity.

This cash flow statement does not clearly show the cash flows generated by the company and the owners' share, while the cash flow statement of the Association of Chartered Accountants is clearer in this regard. Indeed, it shows the share of shareholders in the financing of growth as we find in the financing activity, the capital contributors and their dividends.

7.3. Cash flow statement of the French Association of Chartered Accountants

The cash flow statement of the French Association of Chartered Accountants explains the change in cash on the balance sheet, not as recommended by the PCG, by the confrontation between working capital (strategy) and working capital requirement (policy) but by finding the cash flow within each of the functions that generated them: activity, financing and investment. So:

+ Net cash flow generated by the activity
+ Net cash flow generated by investment operations
+ Net cash flow generated by financing operations
= Δ of balance sheet cash = balance sheet closure − opening balance sheet

7.3.1. *Net cash flows from operations*

The flowchart of the order of accountants since 1997 (as those recommended by the Central Balance Sheet Office of the Banque de France or IFRS) explains the change in the balance sheet cash by those of major functions. These two tables have as an axial indicator the gross operating surplus, that of the CGP cash flow, but the cash flow statement of the Association of Chartered Accountants uses in its option 1 the gross profit margin, self-financing.

7.3.1.1. Cash flow, option 1

(OPTION 1)	N – 1	N
CASH FLOW RELATED TO ACTIVITY		
+ Net result for the year		
± Elimination of non-cash and non-operating income and expenses		
+ *Net additions to amortization and provisions EXCEPT provisions on current assets*		
+ *Book value of assets sold*		
– *Proceeds from disposal of divested assets*		
– *Share of investment subsidies transferred to the income statement*		
– *Increase in establishment costs*		
– *Transfer of expenses to the expense account to be distributed*		
= Cash flow^2		
– Δ working capital requirement related to activity in net assets		
– *Inventories (and advances and installments paid)*		
– *Operating receivables (customers, deductible VAT, prepaid expenses, etc.)*		
– *Other receivables related to the activity (various receivables concerning neither investment nor financing flows)*		
+ *Operating debts (suppliers, advances and down payments received, current tax and operating debts, accruals, etc.)*		
+ Other debts related to the business (various debts concerning neither investment nor financing flows)		
= Net cash flow generated by the activity [A]		

---

2 *Gross cash flow*. Measure indicator for profitability. The free cash flow is more interesting because it takes into account the variation of the BFR. The MBA is cash flow immediately available.

7.3.1.2. GOS and EOC, option 2

(OPTION 2)	N – 1	N
CASH FLOW RELATED TO ACTIVITY		
+ Operating profit		
± Elimination of income and expenses without impact on cash flow:		
+ *Depreciation, amortization and provisions net of reversals*		
− *Transfer of expenses to the account of expenses to be distributed*		
− *Other non-cashable revenues*		
+ *Other non-cashable operating expenses*		
+ Other non-cashable operating expenses		
− Δ working capital requirement and not extended to **activity in net assets**		
− *Stocks*		
− *Operating receivables*		
− *Other receivables related to the activity*		
+ *Operating debts*		
+ *Other debts related to the activity*		
= Cash flow from operations or operating cash surplus ETE		
± Other receipts or disbursements related to the activity		
+ *Financial products*		
− *Financial expenses*		
+ *Exceptional revenues* **EXCLUDING** *proceeds from asset disposals*		
− *Extraordinary expenses*		
− *Income tax*		
− *Employee participation*		
− *Increase in establishment fees*		
− *Δ working capital requirement linked to the activity but **not to the operation***		
= Net cash flow from activity		

7.3.2. *Net cash flows from investments*

Cash flow from investing includes the cash flows required:

– to acquire or sell:

  - fixed assets, some of which may have been produced by the company, such as capitalized development costs;

  - other financial fixed assets such as deposits and guarantees, securities excluded from cash such as fixed assets and equity securities;

  - a share of the capital of other companies through acquisitions and disposals;

– or make loans or advances to third parties or obtain their repayment.

The net cash flow generated by investment and divestment operations is obtained by difference between cash inflows and disbursements after changes in receivables and fixed asset debts.

– Acquisitions of tangible, intangible and financial assets		
+ Disposals or reduction of tangible, intangible assets and financial assets (net)		
± Change in receivables and debts on fixed assets		
= Net cash flow from investing activities [B]		

7.3.3. *Net cash flows related to financing*

The cash flows generated by financing transactions consist of:

– capital increases, new loans, investment grants and

– disbursements due to dividend distributions, loan repayments.

The net cash flow from financing transactions is calculated by differentiating between cash inflows and disbursement flows.

– Dividends paid		
± changes in subscribed capital not named, as well as named and not paid		
± Variation of financial debts		
+ Investment grants received		
= Net cash flow from financing operations [C]		

7.3.4. Change in balance sheet cash position

± Variation of treasuries	= [A+B+C]	
± Opening cash	[D]	
= Closing cash	= [À+B+C+D]	

7.3.5. Diagnosis of the financing table of the French Association of Chartered Accountants

The logic of the cash flow statement calculations is similar to that of the GAP cash flow table. Note however:

– *Provisions on current assets* (inventories and trade receivables). These are not deducted as other depreciations and provisions from the asset. The OAE considers that these provisions do not correspond to receipts but to short-term *debts that are disbursable. We do not add them to the net result* (option 1).

– *Variation in current assets*. This is *calculated in net values*. Advances and installments paid or received are taken into account.

– *The ± value of disposals of fixed assets*. These are restated because they correspond to *investment cash*.

– *Tax on profits*. This is registered with *cash flow activity*. We reclassify the portion of the significant tax on the capital gains of disposals of fixed assets. It is then added back to the net result (option 1) but subtracted from *the net investment cash flow [B]*.

– *Expected impacts not yet due*. Unlike GAPs, they are not reintegrated into accounts receivable but *deducted from cash*.

– *Income from financial investments* is recorded with the *net cash flow generated by*:

- *activity* [A];

- *investment transactions* [B] if they are considered as a flow entering an investment *profitability calculation*.

– *The finance lease* is not in principle entered in the balance sheet (Banque de France, PCG), but the OAE accepts it for the consolidated accounts (cash flow statement in IFRS). So:

- *at the signing* of the contract, *no flow* is recorded;

- in the net cash *flow generated by activity* [A], *the portion of the rent* corresponding to *financial expenses* is entered in *the notional loan*;

- in the net cash flow *generated by activity [A] (MBA)*, *the depreciation charge* corresponding to the *value of the property* acquired under finance lease is entered;

- in net cash flow *generated by financing operations [C]*, *the portion of the rent* corresponding to the *repayment of the principal amount of the loan* is entered;

- in net cash flow *generated by activity [A]*, *a deferred tax* expressing *the difference* between *the restated result* and that *before these restatements.*

– *Investment grants received.* They must be entered with net cash flow generated by *financing* operations *[C].*

– *The cash components selected by the association are*:

- *On the asset side*:

– funds,

– banks and current accounts,

– current bank loans, term accounts and accrued and unmatured interest (provided they have less than one quarter of existence before the balance sheet date and a maturity of less than 3 months in *the net cash flow related to financing transactions [C]),*

– investment securities that are risk-free and convertible into immediate cash immediately, securities of UCITS Mutual Funds or SICAV Mutual Funds, FCP Mutual Funds or bonds less than 3 months prior to maturity (otherwise to be invested in *the net cash flow related to investment transactions [B]).*

– *On the liabilities side*:

- credit balances of banks except revolving overdrafts,

- accrued interest not yet due on these credits,

– For the calculation of the operating result, *the amortization and provisions* have been removed but the reversals of amortization and provisions have been added:

+ Gross operating surplus (EBITDA)
+ Other operating income EXCEPT proceeds from disposals of disposed assets
− Other operating expenses excluding the book value of the assets sold
+ Transfer of charges
− Net amortization of recoveries
= Operating result

Because these net recoveries have not resulted in cash movements in the year, they must be reinstated. They retain their sign as we do not start from the GOS but from the operating result to find the GOS.

− The SFM (*self-financing margin*) had already been recognized when, in the late 20th century, the official journal gave it as a translation of the cash flow. We can slightly dismiss them as well as find similarities with the self-financing capacity.

7.4. Free cash flow table spanning several years

> "*Companies are currently facing liquidity-destruction problems, difficulties refinancing and adapting bank covenants to the new situation, created both by a decline in activity and by the new law, modernization of the economy, which requires a gradual reduction in payment terms, and despite positive cash flows, some companies are seeing their cash flow deteriorate!*"[3]

The current activity of the company not only generates cash, but also consumes some of this cash through the necessary maintenance of fixed assets and the financing of positive variations of the BFR.

It is essential to control the residual balance between production and consumption of cash. This balance is free cash flow. Listed in the CAC 40 listed documents is the chart called free cash flow. The many flowcharts are static and therefore not designed for analysis spanning several years. Thus, a flowchart established for the year N is published in the middle of the year N + 1, so one can only rely on accounting figures for 6 months and 6 months later. They would appear more as the observation of the past than as a piloting tool with a possibility to include the forecasts. It is difficult, therefore, to draw any edifying predictions.

---

[3] http://www.clairactu.fr/2009/04/18/plus-que-jamais-la-preservation-du-free-cash-flow-est-prioritaire/

EXAMPLE.– Danone 2016 Key figures

(in millions of euros except data per share in euros)	2014	2015	Δ
Net sales	10,000	11,392	4,6%
Free cash flow excluding exceptional items (c)	286	576	101%
Current operating income (c)	1,180	1,381	9,3%
Current operating margin (c)	11.3%	12.1%	+53 pb
Net current result – Group share (c)	683	831	9,7%
Diluted net income per share (c)	1.16	1.37	6,8%

a) On a comparable basis

b) In historical data.

c) See definition in Financial Indicators Not Defined by IFRS.

"Free cash flow amounted to €545 million in the first half of the year, impacted by €30 million in expenses related to the savings and adaptation plan for organizations in Europe. Free cash flow excluding exceptional items amounted to 576 million euros (5.1% of sales), a sharp increase of + 101% compared to the first half of 2014, driven by growth in revenues, sales and margin. This increase also reflects the sequence of industrial investments for the year, with lower investments in the first half (378 million euros, or 3.3% of sales) and expected in the second half of the year".

Cash flow from operations at free cash flow and free cash flow excluding exceptional items

	Period ended December 31st	Period ended June 30th	
(in millions of euros)	2014	2014	2015
Cash from operations	2,189	641	905
Industrial investments	(984)	(457)	(378)
Disposals and achievements of industrial assets	67	20	15
Acquisition fees with takeover (a)	6	3	3
Free cash flow	1,278	207	545
Cash flow relating to the savings plan and Adjustment in Europe (b)	123	79	30
Free cash flow excluding exceptional items	1,401	286	576

a) Represents the acquisition cost effectively acquired during the period.

b) Net of tax amount.

7.4.1. *The method*

The table of Free Cash flow spanning several years consists of the following four distinct mnemonic parts: E, F, G and H.

E: the first part, called exploitation balances, is composed of four elements:

GOS = **G**ross operating surplus
EOO = **E**xcess on operations
EOC = **E**xcess of operating or operating cash
E = Economic balance = available cash after financing of internal growth

F: the second financial part has two balances:

B = Bank balance
F = Financial balance

G: the third part expresses a general management balance such as:

G = E + F

H: the fourth part in which we impute everything that has not been taken into consideration in the previous three parts, in order to complete the table on the balance sheet cash flow.

This table focuses on the following three concepts: growth, profitability and strategy.

The preferred indicator of growth here is the added value.

It is not a question of financial profitability, but of economic, industrial and productive profitability. This Free Cash flow table uses the gross operating surplus as an axial variable. It allows us to calculate the operating cash flow using the following relation already seen: Operating cash surplus = EOC = GOS − Δ BFE.

This variation in the working capital requirement is not considered homogeneous because it contains:

– an element of the internal environment, inventory management;

– two elements from the external environment, the commercial outstanding. This latter component is judged to be strongly correlated with the risk of business failure.

As EOC = GOS − Δ BFE, if we remove the effect of the Δ of stock, then we get a new indicator Excess on ESO operations such as:

EOO = GOS − Δ stocks

Thus, the operating cash flow becomes: EOC = EOO − Δ of the outstanding commercial.

7.4.1.1. Strategy

Treasury:

It is the EOC that will finance the industrial and commercial investments of the year. These are just renewal investments as reported by the Banque de France in its cash flow statement. For growth or strategic investments, only the operating cash flow cannot suffice, and it is necessary to resort to more stable resources (capital, loans).

What is available after internal financing of growth

Free cash flow after financing for organic growth (E) represents cash flow after sustaining investments. The value of this € is an indicator of the company's policy. It is thus calculated as follows:

Free cash flow E = EOC − Renewal or maintenance investments.

Three possibilities appear to the analyst:

− If free cash flow is unduly negative, it could express:

- a poor return on previous investments, unable to generate sufficient profitability;

- a good profitability but an important over investment;

- recent investments for a start-up company;

- The company destroys its cash, increases its debt and cannot afford to pay its shareholders;

- Current investments and positive changes in the WCR exceed net income and depreciation. This situation can be further aggravated, of course, when the net result is negative.

− If free cash flow is slightly negative, we concede that the company has used external capital to finance growth.

– If free cash flow is slightly positive, the situation looks correct because:

- the company has a surplus of cash to reduce its debt and pay its shareholders;

- growth seems balanced in the long run;

- EBITDA roughly finances the need for operating financing and sustaining investments.

Financial activities

This part cannot be deduced from the previous one. It establishes in two parts the distribution resulting from the legal obligations of the company:

– the former mainly concerns financial lending institutions, it includes changes in the level of indebtedness and the corresponding financial flow to give bank balance B;

– the second remunerates on the one hand the debt toward the State by the taxes and on the other hand the human resources by the participation of the employees. The latter adds to the previous one and closes on the financial or external balance F.

Two possibilities appear to the analyst:

– if F is very positive, this expresses an over-indebtedness;

– if F is slightly negative, the policy followed is more in line with the global equilibrium because the re-debt rate to finance growth beyond what could be done with the balance E is not important.

Equilibrium

The equilibrium indicator of the financial management G is calculated by adding the flows E+F.

Because E should be slightly positive and F slightly negative, G should be close to 0 at equilibrium. So, schematically:

$$\boxed{[E \leq 0] + [0 \geq F] \; G \to 0}$$

7.4.1.2. *Links between significant quantities*

In this last part, the other variations of levels and the flows are placed to be sure to fall back on the variation of cash balance sheet.

350 Financial Management

```
┌─────────┐ ┌──────────────┐
│         │ │ Staff costs  │
│         │ ├──────────────┤ ┌──────────────────┐
│  Value  │ │   Surplus    │ │   Δ need for     │
│  added  │ │    gross     │ │ operational funds│
│   VA    │ │     of       │ ├──────────────────┤ ┌──────────────┐
│         │ │   treasury   │ │ Excess of        │ │              │
│         │ │    GOS       │ │ operating cash   │ │   Assets     │
│         │ │              │ ├──────────────────┤ ├──────────────┤
│         │ │              │ │ Excess cash from │ │              │
│         │ │              │ │   operating      │ │ Free cash flow│
└─────────┘ └──────────────┘ └──────────────────┘ └──────────────┘

┌─────────┐    ┌──────────────┐                    ┌──────────────┐
│ Growth  │    │   Economic   │                    │  Investment  │
│         │    │ profitability│                    │    Flows     │
└─────────┘    └──────────────┘                    └──────────────┘
```

7.4.1.3. *The framework*

	N – 2	N – 1	N
+ Production sold and immobilized			
− Intermediate consumption			
− Change in stocks and stored production			
= Added value			
− Apparent growth			
− Inflation and other price drifts			
− Real growth			
− Personnel costs			
= Gross operating surplus (GOS)			
+ Changes in production inventories (net)			
= Excess on operations (EOO)			
+ Changes in customer amounts outstanding (net)			
− Variations in trade payables (net)			
= Operating cash surplus (OCS)			
− Operating investments			
= Free cash flow (E)			

± Variation of financial debts			
– *Borrowing and leasing*			
– *Bank overdrafts*			
– *Discounted and unmatured effects*			
– *Financial expenses and leasing*			
= Bank balance B			
– Participation			
– Corporation tax			
– Dividend distributions			
= Financial balance F			

= Management balance G = (E) +(F)			

+ *Investment grants*			
+ *Proceeds from disposals*			
– *Acquisition of other fixed assets*			
+ *Increase in equity*			
± *Other extraordinary income and expenses*			
= Change in balance sheet closing balance sheet – opening			

7.4.1.4. Example

This table of financial flows spanning several years is used by the Renault Group[4] (in € m):

	2004 PCG	2004 IFRS	2005
+ Turnover	*40,715*	*40,292*	
+ Production	*40,715*	*40,292*	
− Intermediate consumption	*30,381*	*29,768*	
− Intermediate consumption	*10,334*	*10,524*	*+2%*
− Staff costs including participation	*5,426*	*5,437*	
= Gross operating surplus [A]	*4.908*	*5,087*	*+4%*
GOS/CA (%)	*12.05%*	*12.63%*	*+5%*
GOS /VA (%)	*47.49%*	*48.34%*	
+ Changes in inventories (net)	*116*	*116*	
+ Changes in customer amounts outstanding (net)	*−161*	*−161*	
− Variations in trade payables (net)	*53*	*53*	
= Variation of the BFE * [A']	*5,006*	*5,095*	
± Other variations (net)	*−51*	*−145*	
= Total change in the BFR [B]	*−149*	*−243*	
= ETE*	*5,057*	*5,330*	*+5%*
− Operating investments	*3,483*	*3,923*	
= Dafic * (cash available after internal financing of the growth)	*1,574*	*1,407*	*−11%*
− Corporation tax	*466*	*466*	
= Free cash flow ** Dafic net	*1,108*	*941*	*−15%*
− Financial investments	*127*	*127*	
+ Proceeds from disposals	*503*	*641*	
− Net financial expenses	*−226*	*−221*	
+ Increase in equity	*18*	*18*	
± Exceptional items	*−182*	*190*	
− Distributions	*418*	*418*	
= Value of net indebtedness	***−1,450***	***−1,466***	
Including variation in indebtedness	*−865*	*−477*	*−45%*

* Lines added to find the original balances.

** New management balance.

---

4 Revue Échange, September 2006, p. 50 and following.

This modified free cash flow table is more of a cash-based search.

The balance G or equilibrium is not mentioned, but the positive free cash flow shows that the organic growth is positive and is used to finance other investments, pay dividends, etc. The financial situation is therefore entirely correct.

Free cash flow is cash available to shareholders. Thus, in a strategic analysis, we can match the growth of the company with free cash flow:

		Growth	
		Important	Low
Free cash flow	High	**Stars**	**Milk cows**
	Low	**Dilemma**	**Dead weight**

It will be noted that:

– This free cash flow varies from 15 between its presentation in PCG and IFRS. Already, this calculation is not official, if in addition it fluctuates in accordance with norms, its relevance risks being reduced strongly for the analysts.

– Beyond free cash flow, the lower part of the table of financial flows spanning several years concerns the different types of staff to affect the cash flow variation. This is often the case in cash flow tables.

The Renault Group has also published the IFRS cash flow statement since 2005 for the consolidated group instead of the OEC cash flow statement.

7.5. Summary of the restatements of financing and flow tables

7.5.1. Table

Elements	Restatements of the main balance sheet items and income statement			
	GAP	Free cash Flow	B. de France	OEC
Current assets	Raw			Net of provisions
CC. not associate binds to dividends ↗ or capital	BFHE		Active treasury or liabilities (financing)	Either in financial transactions or in cash

Deferred expenses (CAR)	Non-current uses Table 1	Other fixed values	Neutralized neither in investment nor in CAR	
Bank overdrafts	Δ cash	Δ financial debts	Liability cash	Cash or financing
Dividends	Non-current uses Table 1	Sold F	Activity	Funding
Expected impacts not yet due	BFE and passive cash		Liability cash	No reprocessing
Income tax	Flux financial		correct the current	Flux financial
Tax on the results	CAF	Sold F	Internal cash	Activity or investment
Accrued interest on credit balances. of Bq	BFHE		With bank loans, BFE	Activity
Interests and loans	CAF	Sold F	Internal cash	Activity or financing
Leasing Funding	Retirement (option)			Retired (option)
Immobilized production	CAF and immobilizations	GOS and immobilizations	Neutralized	Activity and investment
Stocked production	In the CAF	Production	No	Exploitation results
Stocks	Δ BFR		No	ΔBFR
Operating Grants	CAF	GOS	TO	Exploitation result
Investment Grants	+ Sustainable Resources	– Tangible investments		Funding flow
Charge Transfer	CAF	Current balance	In operating income	In operating income except expenses to be allocated
Investment securities	BFHE or treasury		Treasury	

7.5.2. *Risk diagnosis*

- Do current operations generate positive cash flow?
- How is the cash generated by the activity used?
- Do activity-related flows help financial investments?
- How is the growth of the company financed?
- How will the cash flow situation of the company evolve?

7.5.2.1. *Heritage analysis*

The financial patrimonial approach was that of the creditors. It aims to ensure that the company does not risk illiquidity. It is appreciated here by the analysis of the treasury. For this, the financial analyst looks for the ability of the company to cover its debts by its liquid assets. This somewhat brutal approach is an approach in terms of a guarantee of insolvency and valuation of assets at their only market value. Fair value in the case of IFRS goes further.

7.5.2.2. *Permanent working capital fund*

Thus, any realizable asset or debt payable in a maximum year (budget period) is relegated to the bottom of the balance sheet. According to this principle, a company (non-financial or its equivalent, large-scale distribution) must in any case finance with its resources, in the long term, its long-term jobs. Otherwise, it would spend its time running after new funding each short time.

These resources, more than 1 year old, which must exceed the number of uses over 1 year, define permanent working capital or working capital funds. It is no longer the main functions, financing and investment that prevail as in the functional approach, but the maturity of balance sheet items.

EXAMPLE.– The annuity payable of a loan is to be relegated in the short term even if, at the reflection, the company manages a level of global indebtedness and automatically any maturity is not refunded but considered as re-borrowed again.

We therefore present the great equilibriums as follows:

+ Total assets
− Financial and operating debts (external liability)
= **Equity**

and

+ Equity
+ Long-term financial debts
− Long-term jobs
= **Permanent working capital fund**

or

+ Current assets
− Current liabilities
= **Permanent working capital fund**

This approach to permanent working capital by short-term elements shows the pre-eminence of liquidity and the risks associated with it. However, the difficulty of separating the "short term" assumed to be less than 1 year from the "long term" assumed to be more than 1 year is real.

7.5.2.3. Permanent working capital requirement

Short-term assets:

Current assets include:

– *Cash and Bank*. The balances of their accounts and the available necessary for the current operations. We note that restricted cash is included in current assets only to the extent that the duration of such restrictions is limited to the duration of an equivalent position, as the liabilities in the short term.

– *Securities* that the company does not intend to keep; they can therefore be realized at any time as the securities investment.

– *Customers and other receivables* that the company plans to cash only the following year. However, one can also include for the financial analysis all the accounts receivables, in the assets in the short term, under the condition of mentioning the fraction, which is realizable with more than 1 year.

– *Stocks* in their entirety, but on the condition that they have been valued taking into account the difference between the actual current and the normal current and that the valueless elements have been removed.

– *Advances and down payments* received for the purchase of short-term assets.

– *Prepaid expenses* that the company expects to have in the year following the closing date of the balance sheet.

Short-term liabilities:

Current liabilities include:

– *debts payable at the request of creditors;*

– *bank loans and other short-term resources*. A loan repayable according to a schedule established in agreement with the lender may be classified according to this schedule, even if the lender retains the right to demand the immediate repayment of his loan;

– *long-term debts* (loans) for the portion maturing in less than 1 year;

– *suppliers* and accrued expenses;

– *tax debts* payable;

– *dividends* payable;

– *differed revenue and down payments* from customers;

– *provisions for risks and expenses*.

7.5.2.4. Diagnosis of the heritage approach

– *Reprocessing*:

- the *balance sheet* must be presented in *net values and after distribution of the result*;

- *disposal of assets with no market value*. For example, we can mention:

– *establishment costs*;

– *research and development costs*;

– *translation differences* if they are not covered by provisions for foreign exchange losses on the liabilities side;

– *expenses to be spread* over several years;

– *redemption premiums* for bond issues.

- Reallocation to the assets of:

– *marketable securities*, which are considered as available cash;

– *discounted and unmatured effects* undergo the same treatment as in functional analysis;

– *unpaid subscribed capital* that is to be used with the items within 1 year; in the event of a cash flow problem, this capital can be paid promptly;

– *short-term tool stock items* are to be placed with fixed assets to the extent that minimum stock is in value, constant in the undertaken.

- Reallocation to liabilities of:

   – *translation adjustments*, which are reallocated to equity;

   – *dividends to pay*, which are extracted from the result pending allocation to reallocate them to short-term debts;

   – *provisions for risks and expenses*: if they have a reserve portion, it is reallocated to permanent capital;

   – *current account of associates*: if they are blocked, they are reallocated to permanent capital, otherwise they are relegated to short-term liabilities;

- *Unrealized tax debts* are to be dismissed. This is the case for investment grants, regulated provisions, reserves for contingencies and charges for which the part of the tax payable within 12 months is to be reinstated in the short term.

We do not dismiss the lease because it does not give rise to disbursement. Lease rent normally decreases cash flow each year when disbursed.

COMMENTS.–

– If the working capital fund is positive, then the risk of default by insolvency is low.

– However, the extreme fluctuation of the company's cash flow during the year and the seasonal nature of the activity can significantly distort the interpretation of the risk.

– If liquidity is the ability of the company to meet its immediate needs, this assumes that the company is able to meet its commitments by liquidating its assets, either one by one or all at a time and, in this case, the market value of each of them is no longer that indicated in the analysis.

– Resource and employment positions within 1 year therefore have different liquidation times.

– Having a positive working capital in the balance sheet on December 31 N, published after the shareholders' meeting in June N + 1, the date of the analysis of the corporate documents does not surely eliminate the risk of cessation of payment only in the functional approach.

– There is no cash flow statement explaining cash flow through working capital – working capital requirements.

In the pooled funds approach, the concept of working capital disappears. It is admitted that the company finances its assets with all the possible credits, in the short term or in the long term, according to market opportunities. Therefore, the fundamental structure of assets and liabilities no longer has much meaning to explain cash flow, as for example in a personal wealth.

7.6. Statement of cash flow analysis: US GAAP

In this section, the statement of cash flows will be presented and analyzed according to US GAAP.

7.6.1. *Features of cash flow statement*

The income statement provides a measure of the firm's profit over a given time period. However, it does not indicate the amount of cash the firm has generated. There are two reasons that net income does not correspond to cash earned. First, there are non-cash entries on the income statement, such as depreciation and amortization. Second, certain uses of cash, such as the purchase of a building or expenditures on inventory, are not reported on the income statement. The firm's statement of cash flows uses the information from the income statement and balance sheet to determine how much cash the firm has generated, and how that cash has been allocated, during a set period. As we will see, from the perspective of an investor attempting to value the firm, the statement of cash flows provides what may be the most important information of the four financial statements.

The statement of cash flows is divided into three sections, namely operating activities, investment activities and financing activities. The first section, operating activity, starts with net income from the income statement. It then adjusts this number by adding back all non-cash entries related to the firm's operating activities. The next section, investment activity, lists the cash used for investment. The third section, financing activity, shows the flow of cash between the firm and its investors. A template of a cash flow statement is shown in Table 7.1.

In this section, we take a close look at each component of the statement of cash flows.

	Year....	Year....
Operating activities		
Net income		
Depreciation and amortization		
Other non-cash items		
Cash effect of changes in		
Accounts receivable		
Accounts payable		
Inventory		
Cash from operating activities		
Investment activities		
Capital expenditures		
Acquisitions and other investing activity		
Cash from investment activities		
Financing activities		
Dividends paid		
Sale (or purchase) of stock		
Increase in borrowing		
Cash from financing activities		
Change in cash and cash equivalents		

Table 7.1. *Cash flow statement template*

Operating activity

The first section of the cash flow statement adjusts net income by all non-cash items related to operating activity. For instance, depreciation is deducted when computing net income, but it is not an actual cash outflow. Thus, we add it back to net income when determining the amount of cash the firm has generated. Similarly, we add back any other non-cash expenses (e.g. deferred taxes or expenses related to stock-based compensation).

Next, we adjust for changes to net working capital that arise from changes to accounts receivable, accounts payable or inventory. When a firm sells a product, it records the revenue as income even though it may not receive the cash from that sale immediately. Instead, it may grant the customer credit and let the customer pay in the future. The customer's obligation adds to the firm's accounts receivable. We use the following guidelines to adjust for changes in working capital:

1) *Accounts receivable*: When a sale is recorded as part of net income, but the cash has not yet been received from the customer, we must adjust the cash flows by deducting the increases in accounts receivable. This increase represents additional lending by the firm to its customers, and it reduces the cash available to the firm.

2) *Accounts payable*: Conversely, we add increases in accounts payable. Accounts payable represents borrowing by the firm from its suppliers. This borrowing increases the cash available to the firm.

3) *Inventory*: Finally, we deduct increases to inventory. Increases to inventory are not recorded as an expense and do not contribute to net income (the cost of the goods is only included in the net income when the goods are actually sold). However, the cost of increasing inventory is a cash expense for the firm and must be deducted.

Investment activity

The next section of the statement of cash flows shows the cash required for investment activities. Purchases of new property, plant and equipment are referred to as capital expenditures. We recall that capital expenditures do not appear immediately as expenses on the income statement. Instead, firms recognize these expenditures over time as depreciation expenses. To determine the firm's cash flow, we already added back depreciation because it is not an actual cash outflow. Now, we subtract the actual capital expenditure that the firm made. Similarly, we also deduct other assets purchased or long-term investments made by the firm, such as acquisitions or purchases of marketable securities.

Financing activity

The last section of the statement of cash flows shows the cash flows from financing activities.

Dividends paid to shareholders are a cash outflow. The difference between a firm's net income and the amount it spends on dividends is referred to as the firm's retained earnings for that year:

Retained earnings = Net income − Dividends

Also listed under financing activity is any cash the company received from the sale of its own stock, or cash spent buying (repurchasing) its own stock. Global did not issue or repurchase stock during this period. The last items to include in this section result from changes to the firm's short-term and long-term borrowing. Global raised money by issuing debt, so the increases in borrowing represent cash inflows.

The final line of the statement of cash flows combines the cash flows from these three activities to calculate the overall change in the firm's cash balance over the period of the statement. Although the firm's cash balance has increased, its negative operating cash flows and relatively high expenditures on investment activities might give investors some reasons for concern. If that pattern continues, the firm will need to raise capital, by continuing to borrow or issuing equity, to remain in business.

7.6.2. *Cash flow statement diagnosis*

From the balance sheet identity, we know that the value of a firm's assets is equal to the value of its liabilities plus the value of its equity. Similarly, the cash flow from the firm's assets must equal the sum of the cash flow to creditors and the cash flow to stockholders (or owners):

Cash flow from assets = Cash flow to creditors + Cash flow to stockholders.

This is the cash flow identity. It says that the cash flow from the firm's assets is equal to the cash flow paid to suppliers of capital to the firm. What it reflects is the fact that a firm generates cash through its various activities and that cash is either used to pay creditors or paid out to the owners of the firm. We discuss the various factors that make up these cash flows next.

Cash flow from assets

Cash flow from assets involves three components, namely operating cash flow, capital spending and change in net working capital. Operating cash flow refers to the cash flow that results from the firm's day-to-day activities of producing and selling. Expenses associated with the firm's financing of its assets are not included because they are not operating expenses. Some portion of the firm's cash flow is reinvested in the firm. Capital spending refers to the net spending on fixed assets (purchases of fixed assets less sales of fixed assets). Finally, change in net working capital is measured as the net change in current assets relative to current liabilities for the period being examined and represents the amount spent on net working capital. The three components of cash flow are examined in more detail next.

Operating cash flow

To calculate operating cash flow (OCF), we want to calculate revenues minus costs, but we do not want to include depreciation because it is not a cash outflow, and we do not want to include interest because it is a financing expense.

Operating cash flow is an important number because it tells us, on a very basic level, whether a firm's cash inflows from its business operations are sufficient to cover its everyday cash outflows. For this reason, a negative operating cash flow is often a sign of trouble.

In accounting practice, operating cash flow is often defined as net income plus depreciation.

The accounting definition of operating cash flow differs from ours in one important way: Interest is deducted when net income is computed. This definition of cash flow thus considers interest paid to be an operating expense. Our definition treats it properly as a financing expense. If there were no interest expense, the two definitions would be the same.

Capital spending

Net capital spending is just money spent on fixed assets less money received from the sale of fixed assets.

The net capital refers to purchases of fixed assets net of any sales of fixed assets. The capital spending is called CAPEX, which is an acronym for capital expenditures. It usually means the same thing.

Change in net working capital

In addition to investing in fixed assets, a firm will also invest in current assets. As the firm changes its investment in current assets, its current liabilities will usually change as well. To determine the change in net working capital, the easiest approach is just to take the difference between the beginning and ending net working capital (NWC) figures.

The total cash flow from assets is given by operating cash flow less the amounts invested in fixed assets and net working capital.

According to the cash flow identity, cash flow from assets equals the sum of the firm's cash flow to creditors and its cash flow to stockholders. Cash flow from assets sometimes goes by a different name, free cash flow. It refers to cash that the firm is free to distribute to creditors and stockholders because it is not needed for working capital or fixed asset investments.

Cash flow to creditors and stockholders

The cash flows to creditors and stockholders represent the net payments to creditors and owners during the year. Their calculation is similar to that of cash flow from assets. Cash flow to creditors is interest paid less net new borrowing; cash flow to stockholders is dividends paid less net new equity raised.

7.7. Statement of stockholders' equity

The most important elements of a firm's financial statements are the balance sheet, income statement and the statement of cash flows, which we have already discussed. In this section, we discuss the statement of stockholders' equity.

The statement of stockholders' equity (the statement of shareholders' equity) is a summary of the changes in the equity accounts, including information on stock options exercised, repurchases of shares and treasury shares. The basic structure is to include a reconciliation of the balance in each component of equity from the beginning of the fiscal year with the end of the fiscal year, detailing changes attributed to net income, dividends, purchases or sales of treasury stock. In addition, there is a reconciliation of any gains or losses that affect stockholders' equity but which do not flow through the income statement, such as foreign currency translation adjustments and unrealized gains on investments.

The statement of stockholders' equity breaks down the stockholders' equity computed on the balance sheet into the amount that came from issuing shares (par value plus paid-in capital) versus retained earnings. Because the book value of stockholders' equity is not a useful assessment of value for financial purposes, financial managers use the statement of stockholders' equity infrequently. We can, however, determine the change in stockholder's equity using information from the firm's other financial statements as follows:

$$\begin{aligned}\text{Change in stockholders' equity} &= \text{Retained earnings} + \text{Net sales of stock} \\ &= \text{Net income} - \text{Dividends} + \text{Sales of stock} \\ &\quad - \text{Repurchases of stock.}\end{aligned}$$

Since Berle and Means's study in 1932, the conflict between insiders and minority shareholders has been an object of research for scholars and a challenge for regulators. The separation of ownership and control results in information asymmetry, thus potentially leading to two types of agency problems – (1) agency problem between managers and outside investors (principal–agent) and (2) agency problem between controlling shareholders and minority shareholders (principal–principal) [JEN 76]. In general, agency theory predicts that ownership and control divergence negatively affect corporate value. The control divergence, as well as their informational advantage, motivates managers or controlling shareholders to expropriate corporate resources through their private control rights. Information asymmetries exist in all sectors, yet the problems arising for financial intermediaries may be aggravated by the complexity of the bank business [BEN 16].

Conclusion

The presentation of financial statements is the major difference between US GAAP and IFRS. However, they each have many similarities and they converge to the same business goal. In fact, under both US GAAP and IFRS, the major financial statements are: balance sheet, income statement (P&L statement), statement of retained earnings, cash flows statement, statement of shareholders' equity. According to US GAAP, the changes in shareholders' equity is allowed to be presented in the notes to the financial statements, while IFRS requires a separate statement for the changes in shareholders' equity. Moreover, both sets of standards require that the financial statements be prepared on the accrual basis of accounting with similar concepts. However, the specific guidance provided by each set of standards includes some differences, but all the companies around the world have the same business goal, practically, the different sets of accounting standards converge to the same purpose. We recall that, at the conceptual level, IFRS is considered more of a principle-based accounting standard. However, US GAAP is considered more rule-based. Hence, by being more principle-based, IFRS represent and capture the economic implication of transactions better than US GAAP.

According to an EY report of 2013, convergence in several important areas – namely, revenue, leasing and financial instruments – continued to be a high priority on the agendas of both the US Financial Accounting Standards Board (FASB) and the International Accounting Standards Board (IASB) in 2013. However, even after those projects are complete, differences will continue to exist between US GAAP as promulgated by the FASB and IFRS as promulgated by the IASB.

Glossary

Glossary of economic and financial concepts

The precise and standardized definition of concepts is one of the fundamental elements which distinguishes accounting management from financial management. The PCG has defined some of these: management balances, self-financing capacity, etc., and one of the references in this area is the Banque de France, which has had to specify, for its analysis, the extensively-used concepts which inspired IFRS, who do not define anything in this field.

Capital

Capital employed

= assets

+ WCR

+ WCRE

+ Availability

or

+ Equity financing including amortized finance leasing

+ Groups and associates

+ Indebtedness including leasing

Capital invested

= Fixed assets

+ WCR

+ Marketable securities

Economic capital

    = Property, plant and equipment

    + Working capital requirement (WCRE)

Financial capital

    = Capital committed

    + Group and partners in various debts

Operating capital

    = Production equipment

    + WCR

Charge to maintain productive potential

    = Depreciation, amortization and provisions

    + Amortization of rental lease

    − Reversals of operating provisions

Credit

Current bank credit

    = Discovered in current account

    + Mobilization of receivables

    + Expected discrepancies

    + Factoring

    + Cash loans

Inter-company credit

    = Accounts receivable

    + Expected discrepancies

    + Advances and payments made on orders in progress

    − Accounts payable

    − Advances and deposits received on orders in progress

Exploitation debt

= Suppliers and related accounts

+ Advances and payments received on orders in progress

+ Tax and social security liabilities excluding income tax

+ Returnable packaging

+ Deferred income

+ Discounts to be granted

+ Allowance for paid leave

Financing

Non-current financing

= Own funding

+ Financial debts of groups and associates

+ Loans

Self-financing

= Capital and bonuses

+ Self-financing reserves

Fixed assets

= Property, plant and equipment, financial and intangible assets

− Expenses of depreciable establishment and development

+ Tangible fixed assets held under finance leases

+ Expenses to spread over several financial years

+ Asset translation differences

− Translation adjustment for liabilities

Gross economic result

= Added value

− Human resources expenses

Human resource expenses

= Wages and salaries

+ Social charges

+ Provision for holidays

+ Outside staff

+ Employee participation

+ Personal benefits (stock options, golden retirement, etc.)

Indebtedness

= Loan

+ Current bank loans

+ Equity securities

+ Packaged advances

+ Expected discrepancies

+ Groups and associates

Investments

Physical investments

= Tangible and intangible operating assets

− Transfer of fixed assets in progress

Productive investments

= Tangible operating assets

+ Fixed assets leased

Loans

= Loans from credit institutions, including unamortized leases

+ Participatory loan

+ Bonds

+ Loans from the State, FDES, participatory fund, etc.

Net cash

= Total net working capital

− Fund needs

or

= Availability

− Current bank loans

Net jobs

= Productive investment

+ Acquisition of investments and changes in fixed assets

− Disposals and investment grants received

+ BFE Variation

+ BFHE Variation

+ Available variation

Operating receivables

= Clients and accounts receivable

+ Expected discrepancies

+ Advances and payments made on orders in progress

+ Personnel and related accounts

+ States (excluding income taxes) and social organizations

+ Packages to be returned

+ Discounts to obtain

+ Prepaid expenses

+ Operating grants receivable

Overall networking capital (NWC)

= Non-current financing

− Fixed assets

Overall production

- = Production
- \+ Sales of goods
- \+ Operating subsidies

Productive equipment

- = Tangible operating assets
- \+ Fixed assets leased

Purchases

- = Purchases of goods and materials
- \+ Subcontracting

Reserves of self-financing

- = Reserves
- \+ Result
- \+ Investment subsidies
- \+ Depreciation, including lease
- \+ Provisions for impairment
- \+ Regulated provisions
- \+ Provisions for liabilities and expenses (excluding holidays with pay)

Resources

Non-current resources

- = Own resources
- − Bank overdrafts
- − Undeliverable discounting effects

Own resources

- = Equity
- − Uncalled capital

+ Provisions for liabilities and expenses

− Provisions for paid leave

+ Amortization of tangible and intangible assets

+ Provisions for impairment of assets

+ Foreign currency translation adjustment

Result of the exercise

= Net cash flow

+ Investment subsidies transferred to the income statement

− Depreciation, amortization and provisions

+ Write backs of depreciation and provisions

Self-Financing Capacity (SFC)

Banque de France Method

Gross cash flow

= Overall gross surplus

− Interest on indebtedness with leasing rents

− Interests on groups and associates

− Income taxes

Net cash flow (NCF)

= Gross cash flow

− Expenses to maintain production potential

Gross cash flow

− Net provision for impairment

− Depreciation and amortization

− Depreciation and amortization of depreciation expenses, if any

− Depreciation and amortization of bond premiums

Faster additive method

= Net income

+ Depreciation, amortization and provisions

− Write back of depreciation and provisions

− Share of investment grants transferred to profit or loss

+ Net book value of assets sold

− Proceeds from sale of assets sold

Self-financing

= Self-financing capacity

− Dividends distributed

Subtractive method

= Gross operating surplus (GOS)

+ Other management products

− Other management expenses

+ Share of common operations

+ Financial products

− Finance expense

+ Exceptional products

− Extraordinary expenses

+ Proceeds from sale of assets

− Carrying amount of assets sold

+ Reversal of depreciation and provisions

− Allocation to provisions

+ Transfer of operating expenses

− Employee participation

− Income tax

Surplus

Gross operating surplus (restated CdB)

= Restated added value (CdB)

− Human resources expenses

Overall gross surplus

= Total added value (GVA)

− Human resources expenses

or

= GOS

+ Non-current products

− Non-current expenses

Overall cash surplus

= EBG

− Change in WCR

Net operating surplus (NSE)

= GOS (CdB)

− Cost of maintaining productive capital

+ Transfer of operating expenses

Value

Banque de France added value

= Overall production

− Procurement and supply expenses

− Purchase of external services

− Dues, taxes and assimilated payments

+ Financial leasing

+ External staff costs

Global added value

= Value added Banque de France

+ Non-current products

− Non-current expenses

Working capital

Non-current Working Capital Requirements (NWCR)

= Miscellaneous claims including the State

+ Groups and associates

− Debts on fixed assets

− Miscellaneous debts of which State

Working Capital Requirements (WCR)

= Working capital requirements of exploitation (WCRE)

+ Non-current (BFHE)

Working Capital Requirements (or FR resources) of Exploitation (WCRE)

= Stocks

+ Operating receivables

− Exploitation debt

Bibliography

[ARO 10] AROURI M., LÉVY A., NGUYEN KHUONG D., "ROE and value creation under IASIFRS: evidence of discordance from French firms", *European Financial and Accounting Journal*, vol. 3, no. 4, pp. 84–112, 2010.

[BEN 16] BEN BOUHENI F., AMMI C., LÉVY A., *Banking Governance, Performance and Risk-Taking: Conventional Banks vs Islamic Banks*, ISTE Ltd, London and John Wiley & Sons, New York, 2016.

[BER 32] BERLE A., MEANS C., *The Modern Corporation and Private Property*, Macmillan, New York, 1932.

[BER 14] BERK J., DEMARZO P., *Corporate Finance*, Third Edition, Pearson, 2014.

[DEL 17] DELOITTE, International Accounting Standards Board (IASB). Available at: https://www.iasplus.com/en/resources/ifrsf/iasb-ifrs-ic/iasb, 2017.

[EY 13] EY (ERNST AND YOUNG), US GAAP versus IFRS: The basics, November 2013.

[FAS 17] FASB, About the FASB, available at: http://www.fasb.org/jsp/FASB/Page/SectionPage&cid=1176154526495, 2017.

[FOC 18a] http://www.focusifrs.com.

[FOC 18b] http://www.focuspcg.com.

[JEN 76] JENSEN M.C., MECKLIN W.H., "Theory of the firm: Managerial behavior, agency costs and ownership structure", *Journal of Financial Economics*, vol. 3, pp. 305–360, 1976.

[LÉV 16] LÉVY A., AKEB H., "Efficience des marchés et finance comportementale, analyse de convergences théorique par étude d'un modèle de suivi des Trakers DJ, CAC et Nikkei de 2000 à 2014", *Revue Recherche en Sciences de gestion*, June 2016.

[LÉV 10] LÉVY A., BENSIMHON L., "The origin of stock-market crashes: proposal for a mimetic model using behavioural assumptions and an analysis of legal mimicry", *International Journal of Business*, Summer, vol. 15, no. 3, pp. 289–306, 2010.

[LÉV 15] LÉVY A., REZGUI H., "Professional and neo-institutional dynamics in the Islamic accounting standards-setting process", in BOJE D. (ed.), *Organizational Change and Global Standardization*, Routledge, New York, 2015.

[ROS 14] ROSS A.S., WESTERFIELD R.W., JORDAN B.D., *Fundamentals of Corporate Finance*, tenth edition, MacGraw-Hill Irwin, 2014.

[SEC 34] SECURITIES EXCHANGE ACT, American legal accounting data, 1934.

Index

A, B, C

added value, 186–188, 196, 200, 207, 278, 285, 293, 295, 326, 347, 350
annuities, 10, 19–23, 102, 320
bonds, 37, 40, 46, 48, 72, 83, 93, 136–139, 143, 166, 210, 299, 310, 312, 315–317, 320, 344
breakeven point, 95, 249, 250, 252, 259–266, 269, 272
budget, 98, 100, 105, 235–239, 247, 250, 255, 256, 258, 259, 264, 266, 355
business data, 57
capitalization, 2, 4, 9, 19, 48, 51, 95, 102, 103, 114, 171–173, 177, 216, 223
Central Balance Sheet CBS Office, 289
commercial margin, 180, 183, 184, 186, 279, 293, 297, 302, 326
current
 exploitation, 183, 283
 result, 58, 180, 182, 190, 192, 201, 205, 206, 229, 232, 235, 255, 262, 269, 288, 346

D, E, F

decision
 -making, 253
 tree, 123

diagnosis of the heritage approach, 357
discounting, 2, 4, 17, 38, 100, 102, 104, 105
efficiency, 50, 57, 179, 216, 219, 236, 279, 285, 290, 296
exploitation, 73, 79, 86, 88, 97, 131, 145, 146, 188, 190, 193, 197, 254, 292, 301, 302, 327, 347, 354
FCA indicators, 200
financial
 analysis, 57, 60, 61, 63, 64, 68, 69, 88, 89, 131, 133, 134, 141, 160, 183, 189, 192, 193, 195, 261, 277, 289, 291, 300, 356, 375
 debts, 64, 86, 89, 93, 136, 143, 144, 157, 199, 299, 310, 312–320, 326, 342, 351, 354, 355
 diagnosis, 271, 290
financing
 and flow tables, 353
 structure, 164, 280
flux, 78, 285, 305, 335, 336, 354
French accounting plan, 75–77, 81, 82, 86, 90, 92, 94, 131, 136, 141, 143, 184, 246, 291, 301, 306
full cost model, 228

G, L, M

global net revolving fund, 142
gross operating surplus, 58, 64, 181, 188–190, 196, 204, 298, 339, 345, 347, 350, 352
liability, 70, 71, 73, 74, 82, 83, 85, 89, 92, 94, 131, 166, 169, 194, 312, 314, 320, 325, 354, 355
liquidity, 6, 7, 47, 50, 52, 65, 74, 104, 105, 131, 150, 154, 161, 162, 170, 174–176, 193, 220, 339, 345, 356, 358
management indicators, 179, 193
margins, 59, 61, 141, 158, 195, 216, 219, 246–248, 257–259, 289, 290
market value, 35, 38, 48, 67, 69, 74, 82, 160, 161, 163, 170–172, 174, 176, 177, 207, 214, 216, 217, 355, 357, 358

N, O, P

non-current resources, 87, 143, 281, 309, 310
operating
  leverage, 262, 263, 269, 272
  structure, 290, 292, 301
productivity, 63, 104, 237, 238, 246, 254, 263, 285, 296, 297, 301

R, S, T, U

return on equity, 41, 136, 206, 217, 222, 245, 270–272, 274, 275, 286, 287, 288 298, 302
risk
  diagnosis, 354
  of failure, 70, 134, 147, 291, 335, 337
sustainable resources, 135, 310, 313–315, 317, 322, 354
table of jobs and resources, 313
treasury flow, 305
tree of cost calculation models, 227
uncertainty, 44, 46, 125, 141, 300
unearned income, 19

Other titles from

in

Innovation, Entrepreneurship and Management

2018

CORLOSQUET-HABART Marine, JANSSEN Jacques
Big Data for Insurance Companies
(Big Data, Artificial Intelligence and Data Analysis Set – Volume 1)

CROS Françoise
Innovation and Society
(Smart Innovation Set – Volume 15)

DOMINGUEZ Noémie
SME Internationalization Strategies: Innovation to Conquer New Markets

ERMINE Jean-Louis
Knowledge Management: The Creative Loop
(Innovation and Technology Set – Volume 5)

SACHETTI Philippe, ZUPPINGER Thibaud
New Technologies and Branding
(Innovation and Technology Set – Volume 4)

2017

AÏT-EL-HADJ Smaïl
The Ongoing Technological System
(Smart Innovation Set – Volume 11)

BAUDRY Marc, DUMONT Béatrice
Patents: Prompting or Restricting Innovation?
(Smart Innovation Set – Volume 12)

BÉRARD Céline, TEYSSIER Christine
Risk Management: Lever for SME Development and Stakeholder Value Creation

CHALENÇON Ludivine
Location Strategies and Value Creation of International Mergers and Acquisitions

CHAUVEL Danièle, BORZILLO Stefano
The Innovative Company: An Ill-defined Object
(Innovation Between Risk and Reward Set – Volume 1)

CORSI Patrick
Going Past Limits To Growth

D'ANDRIA Aude, GABARRET Inés
Building 21st Century Entrepreneurship
(Innovation and Technology Set – Volume 2)

DAIDJ Nabyla
Cooperation, Coopetition and Innovation
(Innovation and Technology Set – Volume 3)

FERNEZ-WALCH Sandrine
The Multiple Facets of Innovation Project Management
(Innovation between Risk and Reward Set – Volume 4)

FOREST Joëlle
Creative Rationality and Innovation
(Smart Innovation Set – Volume 14)

GUILHON Bernard
Innovation and Production Ecosystems
(Innovation between Risk and Reward Set – Volume 2)

HAMMOUDI Abdelhakim, DAIDJ Nabyla
Game Theory Approach to Managerial Strategies and Value Creation
(Diverse and Global Perspectives on Value Creation Set – Volume 3)

LALLEMENT Rémi
Intellectual Property and Innovation Protection: New Practices and New Policy Issues
(Innovation between Risk and Reward Set – Volume 3)

LAPERCHE Blandine
Enterprise Knowledge Capital
(Smart Innovation Set – Volume 13)

LEBERT Didier, EL YOUNSI Hafida
International Specialization Dynamics
(Smart Innovation Set – Volume 9)

MAESSCHALCK Marc
Reflexive Governance for Research and Innovative Knowledge
(Responsible Research and Innovation Set – Volume 6)

MASSOTTE Pierre
Ethics in Social Networking and Business 1: Theory, Practice and Current Recommendations
Ethics in Social Networking and Business 2: The Future and Changing Paradigms

MASSOTTE Pierre, CORSI Patrick
Smart Decisions in Complex Systems

MEDINA Mercedes, HERRERO Mónica, URGELLÉS Alicia
Current and Emerging Issues in the Audiovisual Industry
(Diverse and Global Perspectives on Value Creation Set – Volume 1)

MICHAUD Thomas
Innovation, Between Science and Science Fiction
(Smart Innovation Set – Volume 10)

PELLÉ Sophie
Business, Innovation and Responsibility
(Responsible Research and Innovation Set – Volume 7)

SAVIGNAC Emmanuelle
The Gamification of Work: The Use of Games in the Workplace

SUGAHARA Satoshi, DAIDJ Nabyla, USHIO Sumitaka
Value Creation in Management Accounting and Strategic Management: An Integrated Approach
(Diverse and Global Perspectives on Value Creation Set –Volume 2)

UZUNIDIS Dimitri, SAULAIS Pierre
Innovation Engines: Entrepreneurs and Enterprises in a Turbulent World
(Innovation in Engineering and Technology Set – Volume 1)

2016

BARBAROUX Pierre, ATTOUR Amel, SCHENK Eric
Knowledge Management and Innovation
(Smart Innovation Set – Volume 6)

BEN BOUHENI Faten, AMMI Chantal, LEVY Aldo
Banking Governance, Performance And Risk-Taking: Conventional Banks Vs Islamic Banks

BOUTILLIER Sophie, CARRE Denis, LEVRATTO Nadine
Entrepreneurial Ecosystems (Smart Innovation Set – Volume 2)

BOUTILLIER Sophie, UZUNIDIS Dimitri
The Entrepreneur (Smart Innovation Set – Volume 8)

BOUVARD Patricia, SUZANNE Hervé
Collective Intelligence Development in Business

GALLAUD Delphine, LAPERCHE Blandine
Circular Economy, Industrial Ecology and Short Supply Chains
(Smart Innovation Set – Volume 4)

GUERRIER Claudine
Security and Privacy in the Digital Era
(Innovation and Technology Set – Volume 1)

MEGHOUAR Hicham
Corporate Takeover Targets

MONINO Jean-Louis, SEDKAOUI Soraya
Big Data, Open Data and Data Development
(Smart Innovation Set – Volume 3)

MOREL Laure, LE ROUX Serge
Fab Labs: Innovative User
(Smart Innovation Set – Volume 5)

PICARD Fabienne, TANGUY Corinne
Innovations and Techno-ecological Transition
(Smart Innovation Set – Volume 7)

2015

CASADELLA Vanessa, LIU Zeting, DIMITRI Uzunidis
Innovation Capabilities and Economic Development in Open Economies
(Smart Innovation Set – Volume 1)

CORSI Patrick, MORIN Dominique
Sequencing Apple's DNA

CORSI Patrick, NEAU Erwan
Innovation Capability Maturity Model

FAIVRE-TAVIGNOT Bénédicte
Social Business and Base of the Pyramid

GODÉ Cécile
Team Coordination in Extreme Environments

MAILLARD Pierre
Competitive Quality and Innovation

MASSOTTE Pierre, CORSI Patrick
Operationalizing Sustainability

Massotte Pierre, Corsi Patrick
Sustainability Calling

2014

Dubé Jean, Legros Diègo
Spatial Econometrics Using Microdata

Lesca Humbert, Lesca Nicolas
Strategic Decisions and Weak Signals

2013

Habart-Corlosquet Marine, Janssen Jacques, Manca Raimondo
VaR Methodology for Non-Gaussian Finance

2012

Dal Pont Jean-Pierre
Process Engineering and Industrial Management

Maillard Pierre
Competitive Quality Strategies

Pomerol Jean-Charles
Decision-Making and Action

Szylar Christian
UCITS Handbook

2011

Lesca Nicolas
Environmental Scanning and Sustainable Development

Lesca Nicolas, Lesca Humbert
Weak Signals for Strategic Intelligence: Anticipation Tool for Managers

Mercier-Laurent Eunika
Innovation Ecosystems

2010

SZYLAR Christian
Risk Management under UCITS III/IV

2009

COHEN Corine
Business Intelligence

ZANINETTI Jean-Marc
Sustainable Development in the USA

2008

CORSI Patrick, DULIEU Mike
The Marketing of Technology Intensive Products and Services

DZEVER Sam, JAUSSAUD Jacques, ANDREOSSO Bernadette
Evolving Corporate Structures and Cultures in Asia: Impact of Globalization

2007

AMMI Chantal
Global Consumer Behavior

2006

BOUGHZALA Imed, ERMINE Jean-Louis
Trends in Enterprise Knowledge Management

CORSI Patrick *et al.*
Innovation Engineering: the Power of Intangible Networks

Printed and bound by CPI Group (UK) Ltd, Croydon, CR0 4YY